extra
bold

a feminist
inclusive
anti-racist
nonbinary
field guide
for graphic
designers

ELLEN LUPTON
FARAH KAFEI
JENNIFER TOBIAS
JOSH A. HALSTEAD
KALEENA SALES
LESLIE XIA
VALENTINA VERGARA

Princeton Architectural Press
New York

contents

MAY THIS CRISIS
DISMANTLE
ALL OF OUR
FAULTY
ASSUMPTIONS
AND FORCE US INTO
NEW TERRAIN

DR AISHA AHMAD

POSTER BY ELAINE LOPEZ   TYPEFACE | PIROUETTE | BY SHIVANI PARASNIS

about this book

The idea for this book germinated in March 2018, when Farah Kafei and Valentina Vergara organized an exhibition about women designers at Pratt Institute in Brooklyn. Kafei and Vergara, who were graduating seniors, were frustrated that their education at Pratt had focused on White male role models, despite the fact that Pratt is ethnically and racially diverse and that the majority of the school's design students are women.

On the night of their exhibition opening, Kafei and Vergara organized a panel discussion inviting several designers to talk about their experiences in the industry. The auditorium was packed with people who had come from around the city and beyond. In the Q&A session, designers stood up and spoke about their hopes and worries as women, immigrants, and transgender creatives starting their careers. They wanted tools for building a sustainable and inclusive design practice.

Inspired by the energy in that room, Ellen Lupton approached Kafei and Vergara about collaborating on a book. *Extra Bold* took root that night, and it grew and grew. Over time, a team of authors came together. Jennifer Tobias, an artist and scholar, created dozens of illustrations for the book and wrote about topics ranging from office politics to the lives of marginalized designers. Leslie Xia, an art director in New York City and a graduate of MICA (Maryland Institute College of Art), brought their expertise as a queer, gender-nonconforming designer of color. Kaleena Sales, a professor at Tennessee State University, wrote about teaching Black designers, and she explored theoretical concepts surrounding structural racism and equity in design. Josh A. Halstead, a designer, educator, and disability advocate, contributed essays about design and accessibility. Kafei and Vergara interviewed designers, shared their insights as young women entering the profession, and provided ongoing critiques of the book's structure, voice, and visual style. Lupton used her publishing experience to produce the book and to seek interviews, essays, projects, timelines, typefaces, and other material from dozens of contributors.

What's inside this book? *Extra Bold* is a mix of theory, history, and useful tips. Part textbook and part comic book, zine, manifesto, survival guide, and self-help manual, *Extra Bold* is filled with voices and stories that don't show up in other career books or design overviews. Both pragmatic and critical, *Extra Bold* explores power structures and how to navigate them. Essays link theories about feminism, racism, disability, and binary thinking to real people and practices. Type specimens, biographies, and interviews showcase the ideas of people marginalized by sexism, racism, ableism, and other systems of exclusion.

What started out as a feminist book became much broader. *Extra Bold* is designed for everyone, including readers who are cis, trans, intersex, genderqueer, gender neutral, or nonbinary, and for people with disabilities, diverse racial and ethnic backgrounds, and varying levels of economic and social privilege. *Extra Bold* is written primarily from the point of view of designers who are working in the US and who conducted some or all of their design studies in this country. The ideas discussed in this book will be relevant in varying degrees to creative people working, learning, and becoming designers in other parts of the world.

People begin their careers with different life histories. Those experiences affect what we know, how we work, and what gifts—and biases—we bring to our work. While teachers and managers hold explicit power, imbalances also exist among peers or "equals." Seeing oneself reflected in history confers power. Being expected to succeed confers power. Tools, information, and spaces that fit our minds and bodies—all of these confer power. Each individual can leverage their own power to amplify other voices and disrupt patterns of inequity.

Together, we thank our teachers, mentors, students, editors, friends, ancestors, and family members for bringing us to this place. We owe thanks to the generations of writers, designers, activists, and thinkers whose ideas we celebrate here. Producing this book required enormous learning from each one of us. Not only did we study theories and histories that were new to us, but we worked collectively and placed trust in one another. We thank you, our readers, for giving this book your time and attention. We hope you will enjoy it, use it, and make it your own.

authors

ELLEN LUPTON
FARAH KAFEI
JENNIFER TOBIAS
JOSH A. HALSTEAD
KALEENA SALES
LESLIE XIA
VALENTINA VERGARA

contributors (images, essays, interviews)

ADOLPHE QUETELET
AI HASEGAWA
AIMI HAMRAIE
AKSHITA CHANDRA
ALEJANDRO BATRES
ALFRED H. BARR JR.
AMY LEE WALTON
ANASTASIA COLLINS
ANDY CAMPBELL
ANGEL DE CORA
ANN SMITH FRANKLIN
ASH HIGHFILL
BARBARA KRUGER
BEN WARNER
BOBBY GHOSHAL
BOBBY TANNAM
BRIAN JOHNSON
CARLY AYRES
CHRISTINE SUN KIM
CLAUDE CAHUN
DAMYR MOORE
DECONG MA
ELAINE LOPEZ
ELIZABETH GUFFEY
EMILY WATLINGTON
ERNST NEUFERT
FIRMIN DIDOT
FRANCESCO GRIFFO

FREERANGE FUTURE
GARY ROBINSON
HANK WILLIS THOMAS
HANNAH SOYER
HATEM IMAM
HEATHER ABBOTT
IRENE PEREYRA
JARED ERONDU
JENNIFER WHITE-JOHNSON
JEROME HARRIS
JIMINIE HA
JOHN BERRY
JUNOT DÍAZ
KAYLA WORKMAN
KIM GOODWIN
KRISTY TILLMAN
MARCEL MOORE
MARY MATHIS
MAURICE CHERRY
MAYA MOUMNE
MOREL DOUCET
NAT PYPER
NATASHA JEN
N'DEYE DIAKHATE
NEIL MARCUS
NJOKI GITAHI
PAULA SCHER
POLYMODE

RAVYN MCCOLLINS
ROBERT WECHSLER
ROGER PEET
RUTH ELLIS
SABRINA HALL
SARA TORRES
SARAHGRAPHIX
SEAN-KIERRE LYONS
SHAINA GARFIELD
SHANNON FINNEGAN
SHIRA INBAR
SHIVANI PARASNIS
SILAS MUNRO
SKY CUBACUB
SOJOURNER TRUTH
STEPHANIE BORGOVAN
STEVEN HELLER
SUGANDHA GUPTA
TANVI SHARMA
THOMAS CARPENTIER
TOM OLIN
TRÉ SEALS
WALT WHITMAN
WILLIAM WELLS BROWN
YOLANDE BONHOMME

Creating a more just world requires struggle and debate. Over time, securing rights for some people has ended up excluding others. Graphic designers produce representations of society, and they help create access to information and ideas. But who gets to be represented, and who gets access? Eurocentric principles of modern design were conceived as egalitarian tools of social progress, yet they served to suppress differences among people across the globe. Indeed, alternative viewpoints and methodologies flourish outside the norms of Western design theory. Inclusive design is created by people with varied identities, backgrounds, and abilities.

feminism

TEXT BY ELLEN LUPTON

Feminism seeks equality among people of different genders. Historically, feminists have fought for social and economic rights for themselves and others. Any person can be a feminist—male or female; queer or straight; cisgender, transgender, or gender-nonconforming.

Social structures have suppressed groups based on gender identity and sexual orientation. These structures are reinforced by laws, education, media, employment practices, religious beliefs, beauty standards, local customs, child-rearing practices, and countless everyday interactions. Feminists seek to forge new patterns and practices by challenging social hierarchies.

Just as people of any gender identity or sexual orientation can be feminists, so too can any person reject feminism. Many critics of reproductive rights, abortion rights, and gay rights, for example, have been women. Around the world, people of all genders exist who believe strongly in a biological or religious basis for subordinating women and punishing individuals who don't conform to normative gender roles.

The meaning of feminism has always been contested. White women dominated the movement in the nineteenth century. White feminists excluded women of color, arguing that racial equality and gender equality are separate battles. African American women rejected this point of view. Born in Baltimore, Frances Ellen Watkins Harper (1825–1911) was a prominent poet and antislavery activist who belonged to Baltimore's vibrant community of educated free Black people. Her first book of poetry was published in 1849. Her 1866 speech "We Are All Bound Up Together" laid the groundwork for what we call "intersectionality" today. Harper said, "You white women speak here of rights. I speak of wrongs.…Let me go tomorrow morning and take my seat in one of your street cars…and the conductor will put up his hand and stop the car rather than let me ride." Harper, whose views were considered strident and offensive by many White feminists, continued to speak widely about her views.

In 1920, White feminists secured the right to vote in the US; this right was not protected for people of color until the Voting Rights Act of 1965, a law demanded by activists during the Civil Rights era. A second wave of feminism emerged in the US during this period. Once again, White women garnered extensive media coverage for their efforts to redefine women's social and economic roles. They argued that women's roles should not be limited to keeping house and raising children; they should have education and employment opportunities equal to those of men.

African American feminists, including Kimberlé Crenshaw, Audre Lorde, and bell hooks, have pointed out that such demands for equal opportunity reflected the middle-class privilege of White intellectuals. Poor and working-class women have always worked outside of the home, often in jobs that White women didn't want. Being a stay-at-home mom is not a choice everyone can make. hooks calls for a broad-based feminist movement that recognizes people from a range of racial and economic background. She writes, "All white women in this nation know that whiteness is a privileged category. The fact that white females may choose to repress or deny this knowledge does not mean they are ignorant: it means that they are in denial." White women hold advantages simply by being born into a society whose businesses, institutions, and mass media are dominated by White people.

According to hooks, women from all backgrounds can be feminists—and men can be feminists, too. Men can advocate for equality. They can share power and denounce gender violence. They can also seek their own liberation from oppressive standards of masculinity. Men can craft their own identities and reject stereotypical norms that reward aggression, violence, and physical strength.

What do these conflicts mean for designers? Many people feel intimidated to even begin engaging with feminism, given its contentious and problematic history. It often feels easier to avoid these problems than to address them. Comments like "I don't see race" or "I don't see gender" are statements that deny reality and avoid acknowledging one's own place in relation to the structures of power.

Let's start by defining feminism as a practice. Sara Ahmed, in her book *Living a Feminist Life*, explains that becoming a feminist involves recognizing inequality, sharing power, acknowledging privilege, and exposing bias. She says, "Living a feminist life does not mean adopting a set of ideals or norms of conduct, although it might mean asking ethical questions about how to live better in an unjust and unequal world." Feminism is a practice—a way of thinking and acting. Design is a practice, too. Creating a feminist design practice involves examining one's own bias and privilege, seeking to represent varied ways of being, and making space for underrepresented voices.

SOURCES Meredith McGill, "Frances Ellen Watkins Harper and the Circuits of Abolitionist Poetry," in *Early African American Print Culture*, eds. Lara Langer Cohen and Jordan Alexander Stein (Philadelphia: University of Pennsylvania Press, 2012), 53–74. bell hooks, *Feminism Is for Everybody: Passionate Politics* (New York: Routledge, 2015); Sara Ahmed, *Living a Feminist Life* (Durham, NC: Duke University Press, 2017).

Sexism doesn't happen to Black and White women the same way.

KIMBERLÉ CRENSHAW

systemic racism

TEXT BY KALEENA SALES

Recently, I overheard an assessment of a presentation that described the minority presenter as "not ready for prime time." That comment pierced through the usual noise of critique and affected me in a way that felt personal. I had no affiliation with the presenter but did share a similar identity and background. The person passing judgment felt that the presenter lacked refinement and did a poor job conveying important details. This assessment was partially fair—the presentation in question was far from flawless. So, why did the words *not ready for prime time* bother me so much? Because I suspected that the presenter's identity made them a target for harsher criticism. Other presenters made similar mistakes, but the feedback they received was squarely about the work, free from assumptions about their personal intelligence or potential.

This type of racially biased behavior is a microaggression that Blacks and other minorities face every day across America. Systemic discrimination affects how teachers treat students, how judges and juries determine innocence or guilt, how banks determine loans, how cops assess danger, and more. Systemic racism also affects our understanding of art, design, and culture. To understand systemic issues means no longer viewing racist behaviors as isolated events and instead acknowledging the connections and historical underpinnings that contribute to the problem.

My five-year-old son has an interactive map of the world that gives information about continents and countries. Most of the information concerns things like population density, land mass, and other technical matters. The exception is Europe. When this continent is selected, the recorded voice on the map exclaims, "Europe was the main location of several historical periods that made a huge impact on the world, like the Renaissance and the Industrial Revolution." The narrative that Europe is the hub of intellectual success appears so frequently that we often don't challenge the parallel narrative suggesting that other parts of the world lack cultural impact. Furthermore, it assumes a standard measure of success determined by colonial dominance around the world. This dominance erases other contributions over and over. An African proverb states, "Until the lion tells his side of the story, the tale of the hunt will always glorify the hunter."

As a design educator of mainly Black students, I think about the implications of historical narratives on my students' assessment of their worth and place in this industry. Much of what has informed graphic design education comes from the Western world, with a heavy emphasis on movements like the Bauhaus, Constructivism, and the International Typographic Style. This narrowed lens ignores design contributions from many parts of the world and perpetuates a narrative that good design must be derived from these origins. At what point are design educators responsible for challenging this narrative? We should do more to highlight design contributions from underrepresented cultural and social groups. The goal is not to deny Western contributions but to broaden the scope of what we discuss in the classroom. The habitual exclusion of Black and non-Western design practices is a part of a larger system of discrimination that positions White people as the standard, pushing others to the fringes. That's why many people are unaware of the contributions of minority designers—even those with long, prominent careers.

I first learned about African Adinkra symbols from Ms. Nina Lovelace, my art history professor at Tennessee State University, the HBCU (Historically Black College and University) where I attended undergrad and where I currently teach. Ms. Lovelace, a small-framed, soft-spoken Black woman, was a talented artist and incredibly intelligent person. Her art history course focused almost exclusively on African art. She reminded us that she was mostly self-taught about African history and often apologized for any mispronounced names or places. She taught us about the beautifully designed West African Adinkra symbols and about their complex significance to the Akan people of Ghana. While I don't remember the details of each symbol, those lectures taught me the more important lesson that Africans are intelligent, spiritual people whose art holds meaning and purpose. The othering

of non-European art creates barriers for those who don't conform to the strictures of the dominant culture.

If there was ever an antithesis to modern design movements such as the International Typographic Style, with its clean lines and desire for logic over emotion, it might be the boldly energetic artwork from the 1960s Chicago-based art collective AfriCOBRA (African Commune of Bad Relevant Artists). Founded by five artists seeking to establish a visual language based on positive Black culture, AfriCOBRA created a framework governing style and subject matter. The group's existence was an insurgency against the racist, exclusionary art world. Singular narratives carry the lie that we all share the same values or gauge success through the same lens. This feeds the belief that artists from certain backgrounds shouldn't be taken seriously if they resist cultural norms.

Challenging racism is easy when it overtly hits you in the face. Systemic racism is harder to fight because it hides in our day-to-day experiences, camouflaged by age-old practices and routine behaviors. That's the problem with systems. They are so pervasive and deeply embedded in society that we must aggressively shake ourselves free from their hold.

ADINKRA SYMBOLS Designed by the Akan people from Côte d'Ivoire and Ghana during the early 1800s. Many Adinkra symbols use radial or reflective symmetry and express deeply symbolic proverbs related to life, death, wisdom, and human behavior.

SOURCES Parts of this essay are adapted from Kaleena Sales, AIGA Design Educators Community, "Beyond the Bauhaus: How a Chicago-Based Art Collective Defined Their Own Aesthetic," Jan 14, 2020 →educators.aiga.org/beyond-the-bauhaus-how-a-chicago-based-art-collective-defined-their-own-aesthetic/; and "Beyond the Bauhaus: West African Adinkra Symbols," Nov 6, 2019 →educators.aiga.org/beyond-the-bauhaus-west-african-adinkra-symbols/.

anti-racism

TEXT BY KALEENA SALES

Black and Indigenous People of Color (BIPOC) share a history of violent oppression at the hand of early American colonizers. The acronym *BIPOC* has been used in recent years to distinguish these two groups from other, more privileged people of color, and to ensure that their underrecognized voices are heard. With that said, it's important to recognize the different experiences of Black and Indigenous groups in order to do the necessary work of anti-racism. In this essay, I discuss racism as it relates to the experiences of Black people in the US, and the residual effects of slavery in this country.

As a Black designer and educator teaching mostly Black students at Tennessee State University, I investigate the ways in which I can use my skills as a designer to advance Black issues and highlight injustices. Meanwhile, I work with my students as they each discover their own voice. In a class titled Arts and Social Practice, I challenge students to find ways to bring awareness to social issues that matter to them. Almost always, they choose topics concerning racial discrimination, police brutality, and bias. As minorities in a country permeated with racism, it's easy to feel compelled to use our voices to fight against systems of oppression. In doing some of that work, we even learn the ways in which we, as Black people, have been manipulated to believe widespread ideas and myths about racial inferiority.

In his book *How to Be an Antiracist*, Ibram X. Kendi explains that "one either allows racial inequities to persevere, as a racist, or confronts racial inequities, as an antiracist." If this generation is to hope for a better, more just future, individuals must work to heal the wounds of the past. To be anti-racist is to actively work against racism in all the different ways it presents itself in our lives. This process requires constant assessment and a willingness to set aside one's ego in favor of enlightenment and a pathway to a more just society.

Joining the fight In times of civil unrest, Black people and their allies have joined together—organizing, marching, and advocating on behalf of victims of police brutality, fighting against discrimination, and pleading for an end to racism. While these movements have made a significant impact on advancing important issues, too many people of privilege aren't engaged in the necessary work it takes to combat systemic racism. For racism to flourish, it must constantly feed on the indifference of people in power. Allies must acknowledge their inherited power and privilege and then be willing to do the work to disrupt the systems that have granted those advantages. This work can be difficult because it sometimes requires an exchange of power in favor of balance. This might mean listening instead of talking, or relinquishing space to make room for underrepresented voices. To change racist practices requires intentional analysis and action.

Decentering whiteness One of the pillars of a White supremacist society is that it denotes Whiteness as the status quo and subsequently treats other ethnic groups as substandard. In an interview with the *Guardian* in 1992, author Toni Morrison stated, "In this country American means white. Everybody else has to hyphenate." This type of White-centering happens so often that it often goes unnoticed and unchallenged. One example of this is when agencies tout "cultural fit" as a basis for hiring and firing. This practice makes outliers of those who don't share the personality and interests of the dominant culture (typically White and male) and sounds eerily similar to the "good old boy" network that excludes those deemed as other.

Avoiding tokenism As more attention is brought to issues of diversity and inclusion, many companies and organizations are scrambling to find ways to increase representation from minority groups. If not handled carefully, this focus on optics can easily take over, leaving some minority hires feeling ignored and manipulated. To avoid this type of racist behavior, managers and colleagues need to give proper consideration to the ideas of Black talent and to support diversity initiatives with time and resources.

Addressing biases We're all influenced by our experiences, by the information we choose to consume, by our upbringing, and by historical accounts fraught with inaccuracies and omissions that support White supremacist ideologies. American textbooks overemphasize the triumphs of White Americans and provide only a small, curated sampling of Black or minority accomplishments. All of these things, combined with skewed representations of Black people on TV and film and the segregation of communities according to race and wealth, make it possible for many people to hold biases based on incomplete or inaccurate ideas. Sometimes our biases seem innocent or even fun. Assuming that a Black woman will have a "sassy" personality or a Latino woman will add "flavor" to the work environment are examples of racial bias. While this type of bias stings, some race-based assumptions have dangerous consequences (e.g., assuming a young Black boy wearing a hoodie is up to no good). In order to expose the baggage we all bring along with us, we must work to assess our thoughts and rid our minds of unfair or harmful presumptions.

SOURCE Ibram X. Kendi, *How to Be an Antiracist* (New York: One World, 2019).

intersectionality

TEXT BY JENNIFER TOBIAS

In 1976, five Black women sued General Motors for discrimination after losing their jobs during a company-wide layoff. Employees who had worked at the firm for a certain amount of time kept their jobs, while people hired more recently were fired. Because no Black women had been hired in the earlier history of the company, every single one of them lost her job. According to the judges in the case, the Black women could not prove discrimination either on the basis of sex (because White women weren't fired) or on the basis of race (because Black men weren't fired either). Legal scholar Kimberlé Crenshaw studied this troubling US legal case and developed the theory of intersectionality, arguing that individuals experience multiple forms of oppression at the same time.

Crenshaw showed that discrimination cases tend to presume women to be White, while race discrimination cases presume that Black people are men. In each instance, this presumption excludes Black women, who experience discrimination differently than their White or male counterparts.

In another illuminating story, Crenshaw describes her experience as a law student at Harvard. A male friend became one of the first Black members of an exclusive private men's club. He invited her and another colleague for drinks at the club; together, they were excited about visiting this bastion of power and prestige as Black people. But at the entrance, they were told that women had to enter through the back door. Although Crenshaw felt humiliated, she chose not to speak out because she didn't want to lessen the experience of her fellow Black students. Nor did she want to "make a scene" that might be amplified by the race of her party of friends.

Crenshaw recounts a third story, told by law professor Patricia Cain. The professor asked each student to identify three factors important to their identity. The women of color all mentioned first their race and then their gender; the White women didn't mention their race at all. Their seemingly invisible Whiteness did not represent a source of adversity for them—and thus didn't merit mentioning—whereas the women of color faced more discrimination based on their race than their gender.

An image of a traffic accident can help us understand the concept of intersectionality. Crenshaw writes, "If an accident happens in an intersection, it can be caused by cars traveling from any number of directions and, sometimes, from all of them. Similarly, if a Black woman is harmed because she is in the intersection, her injury could result from sex discrimination or race discrimination."

Crenshaw's article focuses on the intersection of gender and race. Today, the concept encompasses multiple modes of identity and privilege. Imagine many streets intersecting: gender, race, class, religion, ability, age, and so on. Each street has multiple lanes, because many identities are possible within each category. Indeed, this fictional intersection could have an enormous number of streets divided

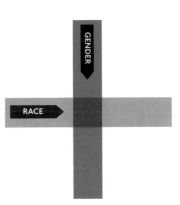

single-axis view of discrimination

intersectional view of discriminaton

into countless lanes. A cisgender woman could be Black, queer, and middle-class; she could also be a Muslim designer with a learning difference. Identities aren't fixed. At any given moment, we might experience some identities more strongly than others.

Some parts of identity are based in biology, while other emerge because of society. Over time, we make choices about who we are and how we want others to see us. Class, gender, race, disability, and religion are socially constructed categories. They are reinforced by laws, institutions, and designed environments as well as by individual actions and attitudes. In a college classroom or a creative agency, a designer

may be perceived differently because of their native language, nationality, age, immigration status, or family duties as well as their race or gender. Movements such as feminism and Civil Rights activism have helped transform social attitudes.

Over the course of a lifetime, a person may change lanes in one or more avenues of their identity. A person could come out as queer or gender-nonconforming, or embrace their identity as mixed race, or alter their economic status. Understanding one's own identity (including Whiteness or maleness) is a step toward understanding intersectionality.

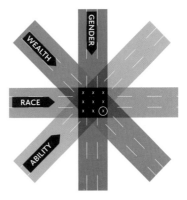

SOURCE Kimberlé Crenshaw, "Demarginalizing the Intersection of Race and Sex: A Black Feminist Critique of Antidiscrimination Doctrine, Feminist Theory and Antiracist Politics," *University of Chicago Legal Forum*, special issue: "Feminism in the Law: Theory, Practice and Criticism," 1989: 139–68.

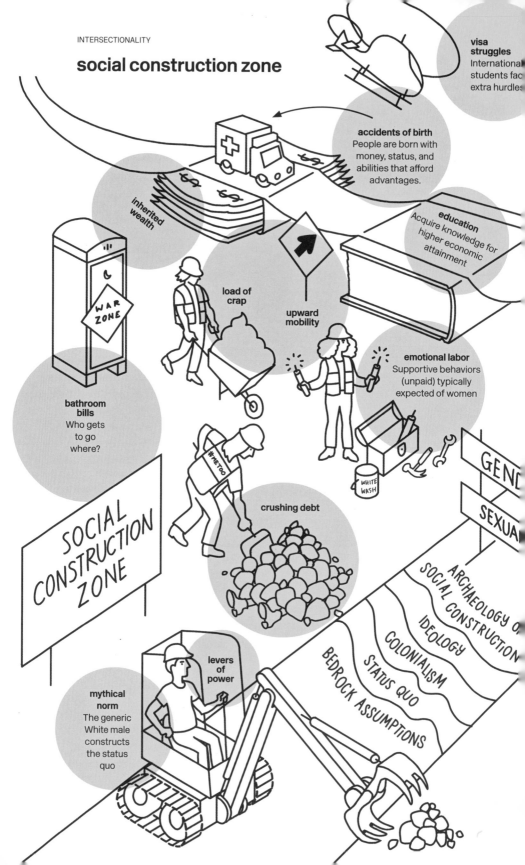

IMMIGRATION

ageism
Out to pasture

invisible disability

social support
Mentors, nds, chosen family

RACISM

ABLEISM

SEXISM

gender fluid

SANDWICH GENERATION

sandwich generation
Caring for children and elders

POVERTY

WEALTH

wage gap
Lower wages associated with gender or racial identity

racial profiling
Police targeting a person based on race, ethnicity, religion, or national origin

frayed safety net

ableism
Discrimination that favors people without disabilities

RACE

school-to-prison pipeline
Underfunded schools feed the prison industry

ILLUSTRATION BY JENNIFER TOBIAS
LETTERING BY AKSHITA CHANDRA

key terms
from the
intersection

#metoo Social media hashtag introduced by activist and sexual harassment survivor Tarana Burke in 2006. Sharing this hashtag signals solidarity with survivors.

ableism False assumption of a universal, superior standard for cognitive or physical difference

accidents of birth Circumstances of family or heritage that contribute to socioeconomic success or difficulty, glossed over by concepts such as meritocracy

ageism Discrimination based upon a person's age; may apply to any time of life but usually indicates bias favoring youth

bathroom bills Laws mandating segregation of toilets according to socially determined definitions of gender

colonialism Imposition of power by one group over another, traditionally involving nation-states claiming territory

crushing debt Burdensome borrowing caused in part by low wage growth in relation to cost of living, general wealth inequality, civic defunding, predatory credit systems, and high tuition costs

education dividend Studies show that higher education tends to result in higher lifetime earnings.

gender fluid Not identifying with a fixed masculine or feminine identity

immigration One-way movement between nation-states, involving navigation of complex laws and social obstacles

inherited wealth Accumulation of assets across generations

invisible disability Inconspicuous cognitive or physical difference affecting daily life

mythical norm False assumption of a White, male standard, as identified by Black feminist Audre Lorde

racial profiling Conscious or internalized discriminatory law enforcement based on race, gender, or ethnicity

safety net Metaphor for essential, tax-based services such as health care, public safety, shelter, and education

sandwich generation Adults responsible for taking care of their elderly parents as well as their own children; this work often falls on daughters.

school-to-prison pipeline Education practices leading directly or indirectly to incarceration, such as police presence in schools and "zero tolerance" policies

social support Material and psychological structures engendering human welfare

status quo Latin term describing established social or institutional conditions

upward mobility Positive change in socio-economic status based on a mix of social circumstances and individual actions

wage gap Unequal pay based on race, gender, ethnicity, or a job's perceived value

whitewashing Metaphor for covering up injustice—especially racial—through information suppression or spin

equality vs. equity

TEXT BY KALEENA SALES

It is cruel jest to say to a bootless man that he ought to lift himself by his own bootstraps. —MARTIN LUTHER KING JR.

Many of my graphic design students depend on the computer lab at Tennessee State University to access the equipment needed for their design courses. In a class of fifteen, it's common for me to have just one or two students who have both a laptop and design software. With this lack of access to basic educational supplies, it's no surprise that by the time of graduation, despite talent and intelligence, few of these students will have mastered the technical skills needed for a polished portfolio. When the COVID-19 pandemic forced an abrupt end to in-person instruction, I began receiving frantic e-mails from students concerned with how they would be able to complete their assignments. On top of the inequities that already existed, the pandemic pushed these students (mostly Black, first-generation college students) further behind peers who don't face such economic hardships.

Some people may assume that higher education serves as an equalizer, helping to level the playing field in favor of equality. Alas, the unfortunate truth is that the effects of an underprivileged background can travel with you throughout life, sometimes dictating which jobs to take or whether a creative career is even lucrative enough to pursue. In my case, coming from a family with no generational wealth meant taking out massive student loans to pay for tuition and living expenses while pursing advanced degrees from respected programs. In the years since, I've been shamed for having so much student loan debt by well-meaning people, who've gone as far as to advise me that I should have attended less-expensive schools or chosen a career with higher salaries. On the surface, this advice is reasonable and financially sound, but underneath is the ugly truth that systems have been designed in ways that make it difficult for people without wealth to advance, while rewarding those already at the top.

For generations, the concept of equality has been weaponized for political and social gain. In 1896, the US Supreme Court ruled in favor of "separate but equal." This ruling helped to legitimize racial segregation by granting Black people access to their own public accommodations, isolated from those offered to White people. In direct opposition to this policy, the 1954 case *Brown v. Board of Education* overturned racial segregation in public schools, helping to dismantle the assertion that simply labeling something as "equal" ensures equality. While many people viewed the success of *Brown v. Board of Education* as ushering in a new era as the Civil Rights movement was ramping up, the seeds of confusion had already been sewn about the meaning of "equality."

If we go back even further to the years immediately following the end of slavery in the US, we know that although Black people were theoretically granted their freedom, they were denied equal footing with White citizens. White supremacist beliefs allowed slavery to happen and persisted in Jim Crow laws and other government policies that restricted political and economic power for Blacks. Throughout history, the presumption of equality has been used to support White supremacist ideology, which claims that there must be something inherently deficient about Black people if they cannot succeed under the conditions of a free society. This is one of the reasons why programs like affirmative action (which grants favorable status to minority candidates in education and the workplace) and need-based scholarships receive such strong criticism, with opponents failing to see the generational impact of disenfranchisement and discrimination.

Having empathy and understanding surrounding issues of disenfranchisement impacts the measures one is willing to take to correct the racial imbalance in the design industry. When "equity" replaces "equality" as the goal, solutions are based on the specific needs of individuals and groups rather than the idea of treating everyone the same. This might mean that agencies reevaluate the fairness of unpaid internships and create opportunities that allow underprivileged students to participate. Agencies looking to be more equitable in their hiring practices might consider recruiting beyond existing networks to ensure more diverse represen-

tation. Those wanting more Black people in leadership roles will ensure proper training and support to back those initiatives. Organizations wanting more diverse membership might find ways to compensate key talent for their time and contributions, while creating membership payment structures that offer need-based assistance. Martin Luther King Jr. said, "I have almost reached the regrettable conclusion that the Negro's great stumbling block in his stride toward freedom is…the White moderate, who is more devoted to 'order' than to justice; who prefers a negative peace which is the absence of tension to a positive peace which is the presence of justice; who constantly says: 'I agree with you in the goal you seek, but I cannot agree with your methods of direct actions.'"

It can be difficult to believe that seemingly benign policies and practices have racist underpinnings, but the more that we dissect the systems we live within, the clearer it becomes how indifference fuels injustice. We must remember that pursuing a goal of equality alone doesn't account for the ways in which economic challenges and disadvantages contribute to success or failure. Equality is merely a baseline requirement for justice in a free society. Achieving equity requires equipping each individual to succeed. For example, a first-generation college student should have access to quality equipment and software, which may mean providing additional resources to those who have less wealth.

ILLUSTRATION BY JENNIFER TOBIAS

voice | kristy tillman

CONVERSATION WITH BOBBY GHOSHAL AND JARED ERONDU

Kristy Tillman is a designer and change advocate. She studied design at Florida A&M University and Kansas City Art Institute, and she has worked at IDEO and Slack as well as launching independent social change initiatives. She spoke with Bobby Ghoshal and Jared Erondu about diversity and the tech industry.

What about design is clear to you but not so clear to other people?
In our professional discourse, we don't really talk about the power dynamics and politics of design. Who's making things for whom? What are the processes we use to make things? I don't think that designers are well equipped, through our current education and our current discourse professionally, to handle the power of what we do. Designers are creating culture. We're creating the interface by which people engage with their futures. We don't have conversations that frame it like that, and I'm not sure as practitioners we are preparing ourselves to hold that level of power. I'd like to see a more intersectional discourse about the power of design. Instead of saying, "Hey, we're designers. We're powerful. We can make things," let's acknowledge that we're creating a future. How do we involve folks in that? How do our identities play a role in that? Who is making the future, and who are we making it for?

Do you think the designers talk over people's heads a lot?
Yeah, I do think a lot of design takes a very paternalistic approach. And just in practice, we assume that we know more than the people we're making for. We assume that we're the smartest people and the only people to do this kind of work. I feel we can benefit from more participatory processes, and we can learn a lot from people who don't wear the label "designer."

Why do people in our industry think we know everything?
I went to a traditional four-year, Bauhaus-Swiss typography type of design pro-gram [Kansas City Art Institute], and during that time, it was never said to me that I should be working with people on an equal level. It wasn't until I went to work

at IDEO that that idea popped in my head because of the way we did design research there and interviewed the participants. The idea that you participate with folks who aren't designers in the process is kind of revolutionary. Design education has a lot to do with it. Even before design became an academic pursuit, you worked under someone who taught you design, so there was always a power dynamic. I don't think we've ever gotten out from underneath that. Even the design research that I've done at IDEO could have been done better. There was still a power dynamic at play. Our profession just hasn't investigated this problem. It's time to ask that question because what you have right now is a small group of folks making things for a lot of different people. As a profession, how do we make things for people who are unlike us?

We make artifacts that people interface with every day, whether it's software, whether it's shoes, whether it's your car. We're making tools for other people to make things. And that has all kinds of implications for how people think. Say you're creating a keyboard for someone, a music production tool. The person that's going to come and use that is limited to the balance that you've created. And so, in that regard, software, shoes, eyeglasses—all have an inherent power dynamic, from the creator down to the people that use them.

Societal progress is determined not just by how well we designers design but how well organizations and companies design. Is that fair to say?
Yes, definitely. Institutions and organizations that employ designers or people who make things for other people all have to contend with that power dynamic. Diversity and design is a bigger conversation than "We need more Black designers" or "We need more Latinx designers." Instead, we

need to ask, "How do we engage people with all different points of view in this making process?" The making space needs to reflect the folks who are going to have to use these tools or these processes or this experience. Asking "Do we have enough Black designers at Google or at Slack?" is a shallow take on the topic. Instead, we should ask, "How do we make sure that we're making experiences and products that are useful for everyone?"

How do you define diversity?
To me, it's really about the intersectional interrogation of design problems. Will this thing work for this type of person or that type of person? Will it work in this particular instance or that particular instance? Will it work in this edge case or that edge case? This is not about meeting a diversity quota. We need to hold ourselves accountable to making things that reflect the user base we're designing for. If you're creating something for someone who has a particular disability, why would you not have someone who has contended with that disability on that team? The paternalistic approach is the idea that our design experience—in which we've never contended with that disability—gives us the knowledge to make things for that person.

Slack makes software for millions of people. We have an accessibility team here that has input into product design. In my own educational experience, the question of designing for different users never came up. We had color theory. We had CSS. We had Typography 1 through 18. We never asked, "Who are we making these things for? How do we get their perspective reflected in the process?"

SOURCE Interview adapted and excerpted from *High Resolution: A Video-Series on Design*, "#20: Slack Head of Comms Design, Kristy Tillman, on breaking through molds and improving diversity," Jun 25, 2017 →youtube.com/watch?v=VoFJKClkdV0.

teaching black designers

TEXT BY KALEENA SALES

As a Black professor of graphic design at Tennessee State University, an HBCU (Historically Black Colleges and Universities) in Nashville, Tennessee, I intimately understand the many challenges my students face as they prepare to enter a largely White design field, governed by Eurocentric design standards. In this essay, I offer insight into the cultural aesthetic differences and racial biases that impact many young Black designers.

Many of my students come from low-income, predominantly Black neighborhoods in cities like Memphis, Atlanta, and Chicago. Redlining, the practice of denying loans, insurance, and other services to marginalized neighborhoods, has shut off Black people from their White neighbors, sometimes living just blocks away. These Black urban areas often have visual textures and colors that aren't found in higher-income communities. For the people who live in these areas, views of urban roads, public transportation, graffiti, and more mix with the fresh paint and new construction of revitalization efforts. The vibrant complexities of the urban landscape create visual impressions in the mind, eventually serving as a mental library of stored images to use or reference when necessary.

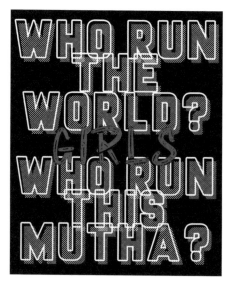

TEACHING AND LEARNING Over the course of my teaching, I've noticed the ways in which my students draw inspiration from urban Black culture. I work with my students to build the spirit and expressiveness of the work while refining their skills and craft. Poster by Kayla Workman; text from Beyoncé, "Run the World (Girls)"; course taught by Kaleena Sales, Tennessee State University.

TYPEFACE | TRADE GOTHIC DISPLAY | BY LYNNE YUN

TYPEFACE | HALYARD DISPLAY MEDIUM | BY JOSHUA DARDEN

Aesthetics In addition to environmental influences, it can't be underestimated how influential hip hop culture is to the design sensibilities of its fans. Hip Hop represents more than just the music. The rhythms and energy are seen in the visual stylings as well. In the 1990s, design firm Pen & Pixel pushed the elements of urban street culture to the extremes by creating in-your-face, blinged-out, heavily Photoshopped, layered designs for rap labels Cash Money Records and No Limit Records. Their influence can still be seen today in many urban brands. The routine intake of certain images, colors, or textures from our cultural environments significantly affects our perception of what's normal, even what's beautiful. In my students, I often see these influences translate to expressive, bold designs that combine textures and layers with vibrant color choices. This sometimes means there's a lack of interest in the flat colors and grid-based compositions offered by the International Typographic Style and other Eurocentric movements.

Furthermore, consider how experiences with wealth and poverty seep into our design aesthetic. If someone grows up poor, in a family that struggles to make ends meet, that person might view wealth in a fantastical, idealistic way. If asked to design a logo for a financial institution, they might opt for a representation of money that matches those idealistic feelings, such as…gold, extravagant, glitzy, big!

Conversely, if a person grows up well-off, where having lots of money is normal, then their design might be quieter and more corporate. The latter is more universally accepted as "good" design in most classrooms and design spaces. When thinking of how often a student is asked to design something and make it look "expensive," or "cool" or "trendy," it becomes clear how the cultural interpretation of those words will affect the fonts, colors, and symbols used to express those concepts.

Biases Of the many young Black designers I've taught, the ones who have been granted the most opportunities in this industry come to understand that all too often, their portfolios must communicate an appreciation for European design and must only showcase Black and urban design in specific brand choices. What's most troubling is that Black people have been assimilating to White culture for so long that we sometimes fail to recognize it as a problem. In fact, the process of getting closer to Whiteness in our design can be met with feelings of accomplishment, as graphic designers are typically taught against having a culture-specific aesthetic and learn instead to service a mainstream audience governed by Eurocentric principles.

Years ago, as I was searching for jobs after grad school, I interviewed for an art director job at a large minority ad agency in New York. This agency handled the African

American consumer market for several Fortune 500 clients. When I discussed the potential offer with an industry mentor (a White, male creative director at a successful, mainstream agency), he advised that I not take the position at the minority agency, as it would stigmatize me as only being able to do "that" sort of work. I took his advice. To work in this industry and be taken seriously meant that while my intersectionality of being a Black, female designer was appealing for diversity initiatives, when it came down to it, my work needed to blend into White-dominant culture to be deemed legitimate.

In an attempt to critically examine Eurocentric design, many educators have begun to diversify their teaching materials, often encouraging their students to find ways to represent their identity in their design work. While it's important to create opportunities for students to share their cultures, we must be careful to make sure minority students don't feel tokenized or put on display for their differences.

As educators work to move the needle forward, it's important for industry "gatekeepers" (creative directors, recruiters, etc.) to recognize how differences in culture and identity might show up in the portfolios of Black designers and to confront potential biases in their reviewing standards.

STUDENT ENERGY My students refer to daily life in their branding projects. Poster by Damyr Moore (left); logo by Ravyn McCollins (above); courses taught by Kaleena Sales, Tennessee State University.

Double consciousness When you're Black and working in a predominantly White industry, fears of affirming any racial stereotype can create a pervasive, nagging voice inside your head, reminding you to always represent your people well. This hyperawareness of one's identity as a racial minority in a professional setting makes some Black people question their tone of voice, their hairstyles, their clothing, and more, all in an effort to blend into the majority. This internal battle leaves some people feeling like imposters and others exhausted from the performance. It's a mistake to think that these things have no impact on design. The truth is, the feeling of being an outsider can creep into a person's thought patterns, making some designers second-guess their instincts, potentially muzzling them and suppressing important contributions and insights.

In his 1903 book, *The Souls of Black Folk*, W.E.B. Du Bois explores the concept of Black double consciousness: "It is a peculiar sensation, this double-consciousness, this sense of always looking at one's self through the eyes of others....One feels his two-ness—an American, a Negro; two souls, two thoughts, two unreconciled strivings." Our identity is abstract and ever-changing. The ways in which we're shaped by our world can evolve as the world around us changes and we encounter new experiences. What's important is that as we meet young designers along their journey, we don't impose antiquated ideas about what it means to make good design, or quiet their instincts to fit our expectations. With diverse representation comes a wealth of experiences and perspectives that elevate the design industry and the work we put out into the world.

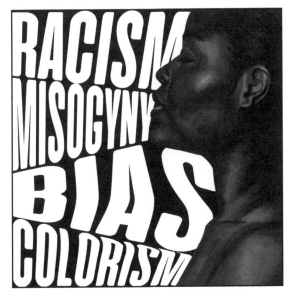

TEACHING TOOL Inspired by AfriCOBRA, I created this work to show my students how to celebrate urban elements in their work. Design and illustration by Kaleena Sales.

meet mythical norm

TEXT BY ELLEN LUPTON AND LESLIE XIA

What does it mean to design "normal" things for "normal" people? Western society defines certain individuals and communities as average and ordinary, while everyone else is something other. People living inside the norm bubble often don't recognize their own special status, because norms aren't supposed to be special. Synonyms for the word *normal* include *standard*, *average*, *typical*, and *ordinary*. Norms are invisible, becoming present only when they rub up against difference.

Graphic designers are in the norm business. We employ legible fonts and familiar interface conventions in order to churn out seemingly neutral, user-friendly messages. We use grids, hierarchies, and tasteful type pairings to unify publications and websites. We produce brand standards and corporate identity manuals to regulate the public image of companies and institutions. Each year, we harvest a fresh crop of sans serif typefaces claiming to deliver content in anonymous, trouble-free text blocks. It's Helvetica's world. We just live in it.

Norms appear throughout design culture. Uniforms and road signs are norms. Icons and emoji are norms. Style sheets, templates, and content management systems are norms. Social media interfaces are norms. At its core, typography is a norm, invented to reproduce text in a consistent, error-free manner. The rules of writing and typography encompass grammar, spelling, punctuation, capitalization, and the correct use of spaces and dashes.

People use graphic design to study and transform social relationships as well as visual ones. The words and concepts we use to talk about design—in both normative and disruptive terms—also ripple through the critical writing about race and feminism. Design is a tool for diagramming and exposing structures of power.

In the 1920s, designers in Europe argued that cubic buildings, sans serif typefaces, photographic images, and functional products could be useful and relevant to people across nationalities and income groups.

Such seemingly neutral forms resisted the nationalist and fascist ideologies that pitted groups against each other. Despite modernism's egalitarian ideals, however, the concept of universal or transnational design solutions presumed a male, Western European subject.

According to poet and activist Audre Lorde, the "mythical norm" is what a given society understands to be generically human. Writing from the perspective of a Black queer woman, Lorde noted that the norm in the US is typically "white, thin, male, young, heterosexual, Christian, and financially secure." The mythical norm is an artifact of White supremacy, upheld by racism and oppression. Lorde writes, "As white women ignore their built-in privilege of whiteness and define woman in terms of their own experience alone, then women of color become 'other,' the outsider whose experience and tradition is too 'alien' to comprehend." White women are complicit in preserving the normative system,

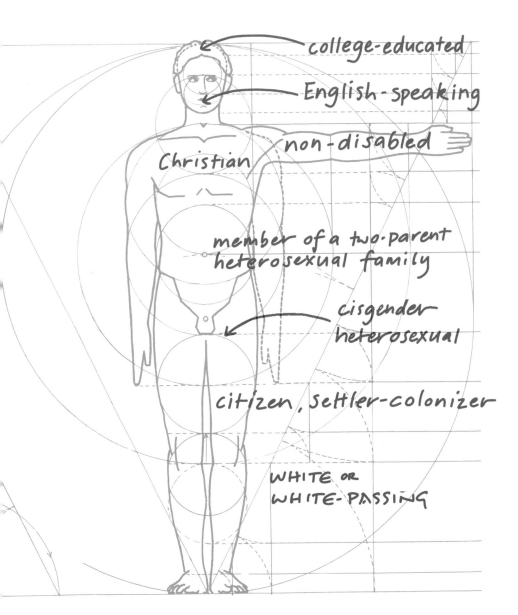

college-educated

English-speaking

non-disabled

Christian

member of a two-parent heterosexual family

cisgender heterosexual

citizen, settler-colonizer

WHITE OR WHITE-PASSING

modern man in his modern bubbles

DIAGRAM BY ERNST NEUFERT
ANNOTATED BY JENNIFER TOBIAS

In 1938, Bauhaus-trained architect Ernst Neufert published a system of standard sizes for products and architecture based on a perfect male body. Harkening back to Leonardo da Vinci's famous Vitruvian man, Neufert's masculine measuring stick sealed the notion that universality stems from the White, male, Western classical tradition. Neufert's book of architectural standards—embraced by Hitler for its "Aryan" normativity—remains widely used today, circulated around the world in multiple languages.

which inflicts ongoing violence—physical, psychological, and economic—on Black people and people of color.

Exclusion from the protective bubble of normativity leads to varying degrees of oppression or inequality. People who embody some or all aspects of the norm tend to treat their ostensibly typical attributes as neutral, invisible, or nonexistent. Being normal seems natural—not a special privilege. It's easy to say "I don't see race" when you live inside the bubble of Whiteness.

Indeed, any norm tends to disguise itself and disappear. Thus, a White, heterosexual, cisgender man may ignore the superpowers bestowed on him by the mythical norm—believing instead that his achievements are wholly earned through hard work, talent, and merit. A White woman may feel the forces of sexism while denying her race-based privilege. Although the norms of Whiteness or maleness may appear invisible to people who are White and/or male, they are oppressively visible to those excluded by their bubbles.

Although norms are deeply embedded in design's professional ethos and official history, protest and resistance are crucial parts of this history, too. Dada and Constructivist artists used diagonal lines, mismatched fonts, and montaged photos to challenge thousands of years of static symmetry. In the mid-twentieth century, industrial designers rejected the Renaissance ideal of the perfect young man and began creating "ergonomic" products, designed to fit more bodies. Disability historian Aimi Hamraie calls this area of inquiry "epistemic activism." New guidelines for human measurements encompassed a wider range of people.

Not all products are ergonomic. The COVID-19 crisis revealed that the gowns masks used in hospitals and care facilities are designed to fit a so-called average male body, making them dangerous for caregivers of smaller stature, including many women.

Writers and thinkers can use the tools of graphic design to study and change social relationships. The words and concepts we use to talk about design ripple through the critical writing about race and feminism. Terms like axis, intersection, and orientation are familiar to graphic designers. Writers and philosophers use these

Space itself is sensational: it is a matter of how things make their impression as being here or there, on this side or that side of a dividing line, or as being left or right, near or far.

SARA AHMED

terms too, creating spatial metaphors for concepts like racism, sexuality, and gender. Spatial ideas such as "margin/center" help people create vivid mental pictures of dominance. These concepts prompt readers and listeners to construct diagrams in the gray matter of the mind. White savior narratives are told from the perspective of White people who become enlightened and help improve the lives of people in marginal groups. Such narratives are said to "center Whiteness," a process of erasing the margins and focusing on the emotional needs and seemingly heroic actions of the dominant group.

Sara Ahmed's book *Queer Phenomenology* unpacks the spatial language of queerness. The phrase "sexual orientation," commonly used to label a person's attraction to people based on their gender identity, suggests how bodies gravitate toward other bodies, as if drawn by a magnetic force. Ahmed wants to rethink how a body's turn "'toward' objects shapes the surfaces of bodily and social space." She states that

queer comes from the Indo-European word meaning "twist." Historically, to be queer meant to deviate from the straight line of social norms. Today, people use the word *queer* to express pride and solidarity.

Design is normative, but it can also be transformative. Binary oppositions lure the mind with their shiny, neatly defined polarities. Just one of many alternative models is the spectrum, which contains endless shades of difference between opposing endpoints. Intersections, twisting paths, and mixed ecologies push beyond the either/or structure of binary categories.

SOURCES Audre Lorde, "Age, Race, Class and Sex: Women Redefining Difference," 1980, in *Words of Fire: An Anthology of African American Feminist Thought*, ed. Beverly Guy-Sheftall (New York: New Press, 1995), 284–91. Ernst Neufert, *Bauentwurfslehre* (Berlin: Bauwelt-Verlag, 1938); Nader Vossoughian, "Standardization Reconsidered: Normierung in and after Ernst Neufert's *Bauentwurfslehre* (1936)," *Grey Room* 54 (Winter 2014): 34–55; Aimi Hamraie, *Building Access: Universal Design and the Politics of Disability* (Minneapolis: University of Minnesota Press, 2017); Sara Hendren, *What Can a Body Do? How We Meet the Built World* (New York: Riverhead, 2020); Sara Ahmed, *Queer Phenomenology: Orientations, Objects, Others* (Durham: Duke University Press, 2006).

margins and centers

DIAGRAMS BY ELLEN LUPTON

Margins and centers are part of the fundamental language of graphic design. Cropping, framing, padding, and gutters are tools for focusing attention and creating relationships such as inside/outside and figure/ground. Borders in the physical world, however, are leaky and porous, not solid and absolute.

margin

(center)

'splaining

TEXT BY JENNIFER TOBIAS

Kim Goodwin helps companies develop human-centered product design strategies. She often finds herself in situations where men eagerly seek to explain concepts to her that she has written about in her own books and research papers. After a male coworker asked her if a particular behavior could be construed as "mansplaining," she designed a chart to help him (and other humans) navigate the flow of conversation. Goodwin's chart may be funny, but it is more than that— it is a helpful guide to seeing how the act of overexplaining can be an annoying (if unintentional) display of power.

The term *mansplaining*, inspired by an essay by writer Rebecca Solnit, refers to situations where a man tells a woman detailed information about a subject she is quite knowledgeable about. When Goodwin shared her chart on Twitter, several men took offense. Why, they asked, does overexplaining need to be called a gender thing? Don't we all want to tell everything we know to everyone?

Well, since the guys asked, Goodwin patiently explained it. Sexism is about power imbalance, and mansplaining anchors the power on the dominant side. Given that men hold dominant positions in many workplaces and throughout society, mansplaining perpetuates top-down communications. Goodwin's diagram shows us when didactic discourse veers into 'splaining—and when it qualifies as welcome peer-to-peer exchange.

Not all conversations are power games. Someone who constantly explains stuff to every person they meet—including those in their own power group—is just irritating, but someone who targets those with less privilege is displaying their dominance.

Variations of mansplaining include Whitesplaining, cissplaining, and richsplaining. What should you do when you are told that you've been displaying your authority in an insensitive way? Well-meaning individuals feel ashamed when they learn they have made a comment that is racist, sexist, ableist, homophobic, transphobic, or otherwise exclusionary. The quickest response is a defensive one: "I didn't mean it that way." This silences the other person and prevents you from understanding the problem.

Try to grasp that person's point of view rather than jumping to your own defense. Research the topic. Seek out sources written by members of that community. Be open. Try to learn. Instead of becoming angry yourself (or worse, bursting into tears and making the whole incident about your own feelings), try to listen and grow.

SOURCES Rebecca Solnit, *Men Explain Things to Me, and Other Essays* (London: Granta, 2014); Erynn Brook, "Is the Term Mansplaining Sexist?" Jun 6, 2018 →theguardian. com/commentisfree/2018/jun/06/is-the-term-mansplaining-sexist-google-autocomplete; Maisha Z. Johnson, "6 Ways Well-Intentioned People Whitesplain Racism (And Why They Need to Stop)," Everyday Feminism, Feb 7, 2016 →everydayfeminism .com/2016/02/how-people-whitesplain-racism/; Ibram X. Kendi, *How To Be An Antiracist* (New York: Random House, 2019); Elle Glenise Pike →wherechangestarted. com; Rachel Cargle →rachelcargle.com.

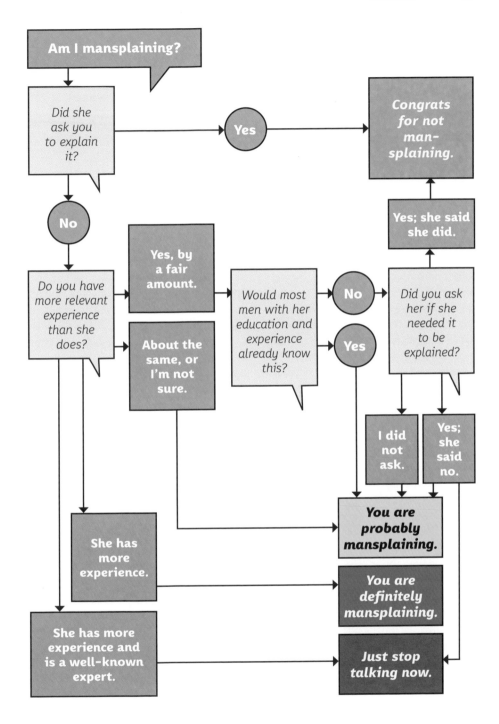

disability theory

TEXT BY JOSH A. HALSTEAD

I was at a stoplight, and you know that feeling you get when someone's looking at you? The hair on your arms starts to bristle, neck gets clammy, chest slightly caves in. Well, I got this feeling when I was at the stoplight. So I looked up. Across the street, there was a man—blue overcoat, red plaid shirt, chocolate shoes, dusty jeans…looking at me. The light turned green. I walked towards him. He walked towards me. As I turned to offer a smile, he cut me off and said, "How about you and your disabled friends find a car and drive out of San Francisco?"

I was born disabled, so atypical interactions in the world are rather typical, but this transaction threw me off. Emotions surged: anger, confusion, a little surprise, but it was relief that soon exceeded the rest. I had been thinking through a presentation scheduled in London the next day. The topic? Critical design and disability. And I'd finished everything but an opener.

Identifying as a graphic designer and disabled has made me an unrepentant questioner of symbols and society throughout my life. This man saw my body as a problem because it's not normal. This surfaces two questions: When did challenging the norm become a problem? And what does it mean to be normal to begin with? After committing myself to these questions, I found out that *normal* is a construct manufactured and fed to society hundreds of years ago. This essay looks at three theories or paradigms for disability: medical, social, and identity-based.

The medical paradigm The origins of the medical (or deficit) model go back to the life of Belgian scientist Adolphe Quetelet (1796–1874). By the age of nineteen, he was a blooming scientific prodigy. He studied statistics, mathematics, movement, and terrestrial magnetism, and he had an intense interest in populations. In 1823, he traveled to Paris to study astronomy.

In his magnum opus, *A Treatise on Man and the Development of His Faculties*, Quetelet introduced the concept of the *homme moyen*—average man—by applying the Law of Error to bodies.

Astronomers were using the Law of Error to plot stars. How? Essentially, find a star in the night sky, take a few guesses about its mathematical location, and average your guesses. The mean (i.e., average) was the most likely location of that star. Quetelet created the *homme moyen* by applying this method to human features such as height and weight, giving us a statistically defined "normal" body. This set the groundwork for concepts like the BMI (body mass index) and the IQ (intelligence quotient) test, both processes of marking deviant bodies against accepted norms.

As the medical model developed, based on statistics, Sir Francis Galton (1882–1911) came on the scene. Galton was a British eugenicist. The pseudoscience of eugenics is associated with the Holocaust. Galton believed that everyone below average should be rooted out of society. In Quetelet's equation, the outliers were neutral. But Galton swapped out the mean, exchanging it for the median, and produced another model of normal. Instead of average and outlier, Galton split populations into quartiles that rank human beings first, second, third, and fourth. The ideal body—

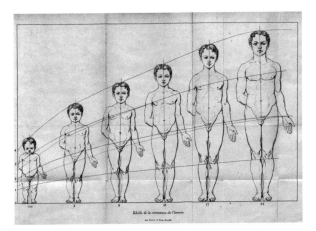

ADOLPHE QUETELET "*Anthropométrie, ou mesure des différentes facultés de l'homme* [Anthropometry, or measurement of the different faculties of man]," 1870. British Library.

that is, a body existing above the median—replaced Quetelet's *homme moyen*.

When it's okay to erase human diversity, you don't plan on diverse bodies being around, and so you don't design for them. Galton created a corporeal split between deficient and desirable, design-worthy and a design afterthought.

The social paradigm We didn't begin to unseat this profound erasure until the 1960s, when architectural guidelines began addressing disabled bodies, marking the beginning of a new paradigm.

Let's imagine that you and I decide to go grab some coffee at a fancy San Francisco coffee shop with a loft and a view of the city. You grab your coffee, you go up one, two, three stairs, and you turn around, noticing I didn't follow you. You look at me, and I look at you. Then, it gets a little awkward. Stairs aren't made for legs like mine. Normal gets concretized in the design of places today; thus, *eugenic logic*, a term coined by disability studies scholar Rosemarie Garland-Thomson, isn't something that simply disappeared after World War II.

These stairs, and countless other examples of eugenic logic applied to the design of spaces and technology, made me become a designer. If I wanted to draw, I had to design ways to do that. If I fell in love with art so much that I wanted to go to art school, I had to design a way to do that. If I went to art school and had to trim a whole bunch of posters, I had to design a way to do that. If I graduated from art school and wanted to practice as a professional, I needed to design a way to answer e-mails. (They don't tell you that in design school.)

I wouldn't be a designer today if my mom, Mari Halstead, who happens to be my favorite designer of all time, didn't invent a way for me to draw. One night we were learning how to say colors for the first time—red, blue, green—and my mom had an idea: Wouldn't it be nice if I could color the colors as we were talking. On the corner of the table were a bunch of rubber bands. After looking at me, then looking at the rubber bands, my mom leapt across the table and wrapped one around my hand. Then she wedged a marker underneath and effectively started my art career. This early prototype worked all right, but it often snapped after long periods of time.

We made our second apparatus with duct tape. This solved the instability problem, but it was painful to remove, so we made a third prototype. My mom got a wetsuit at a garage sale. She cut out a strip, made a U-shape, and created a cuff.

TOM OLIN Photograph, Capitol Crawl, 1990.

This design provided stability and flexibility, and I used it for the next dozen or so years. It allowed me to draw and paint as well as helping with tasks like eating.

This story illustrates the shift to the social paradigm of disability, which separates a person's impairment from a disabling society. Before my mom and I designed the cuff, the pen was the artifact of a disabling society. I was disabled not because I couldn't grab a pen but because there wasn't a pen available that could be fastened to a hand that doesn't grab.

The social paradigm of disability took shape in the 1960s and '70s. The passage of the 1964 Civil Rights Act, led by African American activists, inspired the Disability Rights movement to fight for accessibility in buildings and schools as a civil right, not as a nice-to-have or an afterthought. In 1990, hundreds of protesters gathered in front of the Capitol building in Washington, DC to claim their civil rights. A group broke

off, setting aside wheelchairs and crutches, and crawled up the marble steps. This performative act exposed tangible, physical discrimination and helped instigate the passage of the Americans with Disabilities Act (ADA).

Today, we think of accessibility as the law. What we call *inclusion*, with respect to people with disabilities, is what I'd just consider good QA (quality assurance). If we're going to make things accessible, the people who are using our products and environments should test them and be considered designers themselves.

Mainstream design culture is now taking the social model of disability seriously. Big players such as IKEA and Google are getting on board. The Creatability project, a collaboration between Google and NYU, is creating open-source and accessible tools using AI and machine learning so traditionally excluded bodies can contribute creatively. But we're not going far enough.

Scholar Tom Shakespeare identifies three weaknesses with the social model: it undermines the significance of impairment in shaping lived experience; it represents disabled people as always oppressed; and it promotes the concept of a barrier-free utopia (where everyone has access to everything, all of the time). The social model's strengths are its power and simplicity. For most, conceiving disability as social is paradigm-busting. It does not require new knowledge, just a new frame. But the disability experience is not monolithic: some of us are disabled by society *and* our bodies; some of us find meaning and identity in our bodies as sites for reexamining and reconfiguring selfhood and society; and universal design is, unfortunately, a myth. Although the access needs of individuals often overlap, they sometimes conflict.

If viewed uncritically, the social model has the insidious potential to reify existing power structures and discourage difference. Because the social model focuses rigidly on the environment, nondisabled designers often believe they can apply this model without the help or insight of disabled people. Thus, accessible design can be popularized without authentically engaging with disability communities. Shifting the focus from bodies to society excludes those bodies from the conversation. Designers end up creating objects and services through their own worldviews, consulting a toolkit or checklist to make their solutions accessible to "others." From this angle, the social model doesn't move us far from the medical model. Although we aren't normalizing or rehabilitating bodies, we end up trying to normalize or rehabilitate the environment in lieu of exploring plurality and difference.

Let's return to the cuff example from my childhood. My mother and I designed an apparatus that would allow me to draw. Our solution, however, left social structures untouched. We weren't only designing a useful prosthetic; we were designing a tool to support independent self-expression in a socially acceptable way. Materially, the cuff affirmed the use of an extant tool and hand for self-expression. Symbolically, it reified the colonial notion that photorealistic representation is superior to modes that are more abstruse. Politically, it prioritized independence over interdependence. We designed the cuff to help me fit into an ableist world, and it delivered on that promise.

I highlight this example not to critique assistive devices but to foreground the lost occasion to critically examine society. In a world designed for nondisabled people, we absolutely need products that fit disabled people into an unchanged, unquestioned world. I used such devices to get through grade school. But if our questioning stops here, so does our understanding of disability, design, and society.

"In solidarity with my 7-year-old Black Autistic son and in virtual protest with my Black disabled community, I felt compelled to use my art to bring visibility to the facts. More than half of Black/Brown bodies in the US with disabilities will be arrested by the time they reach their late 20s. We don't see many positive stories or acts of #AutisticJoy among Black/Brown bodies because they don't make headlines. 'To Be Pro-Neurodiversity is to be Anti-Racist': this statement carries a lot of truth, which directly influenced the need to create the graphic."
—JENNIFER WHITE-JOHNSON

This symbol, created by disabled designer Jennifer White-Johnson in 2020, combines a black fist—representing protest and solidarity—with the infinity symbol, which Autistic communities use to depict the breadth of the autism spectrum as well as the larger neurodiversity movement.

The identity paradigm Artist Neil Marcus writes, "Disability is not a brave struggle or courage in the face of adversity. Disability is an art. It's an ingenious way to live." For Marcus, disability is a generative identity, and this has radical implications for design. When we reorient beliefs about disability-loss toward disability-gain, designers can begin to realize that access issues transcend the environment. Becoming an "inclusive" designer requires transformative work from the inside out.

Alex Haagaard is an Autistic designer and disability activist-scholar. In 2019, they created thirty drawings representing aspects of Autistic experience. Haagaard also posted a list of artistic prompts for others in the #ActuallyAutistic community, ranging from "comfort" and "texture" to "uncertainty," "flap," and "movement." After Haagaard posted these prompts on Twitter, a respondent questioned number 15: "glitter." Haagaard explained that their experience is fluid. Although they appreciate low-sensory environments, sometimes glitter is a favorite visual stim.

The respondent said, "Got it!" and posted a link to a glitter-filled room in Tokyo designed by teamLab. You probably wouldn't think of glitter if I asked you to design something with autism in mind. Challenging the disability-as-problem paradigm centers difference. It took one prompt ("glitter") to shift attention from design platitudes to unexpected queer-crip aesthetics. Disability becomes an identity—a standpoint for resisting normalization and amplifying nonconformity.

Downstream access design, like my own cuff example, needs to continue. Not every project presents an opportunity to unseat hegemonic norms and ways of relating with each other and the world. But we need to make space for the identity paradigm. Often, when designers want to learn about disability, their instinct is to interview a doctor or peruse PubMed. Resources like this typically reflect the medical (or deficit) model of disability, which limits creativity. Some projects do require medical data, but it's important to learn from multiply marginalized disabled people, disability activists, and disability studies scholars.

In closing, here are two places to start: hire disabled people and work toward demedicalizing and decolonizing the disability–design nexus. Invite Black, Disabled, Indigenous, Latinx, Mad, Neuroqueer, Trans, Two-Spirit, and other historically marginalized people and communities to share their perspectives with your design program or company (and pay them, please). Not only are marginalized people experts on their own oppression, but they are also designers themselves. Don't assume that a community needs your students or company to organize a design charette—they have likely organized themselves for decades. Inclusive design must dismantle power structures within ourselves and the institutions we occupy as much as those in society. Make no mistake, this is subversive work.

We've learned about the construct of normalcy—what it means to be normal and not normal. We've explored the medical, social, and identity paradigms of disability. After I learned about teamLab's glitter room, I couldn't resist taking a look at their logo. As it turns out, their logo is a star. Ironic. Quetelet, if you remember, manufactured the "average" human by recycling a methodology for plotting stars. So I'll leave you with this thought: the questions we ask become the stars we follow.

Thank you to Emeline Brulé, PhD, Rahul Guttal, Ellen Lupton, and Emily Nusbaum, PhD, for their helpful comments.

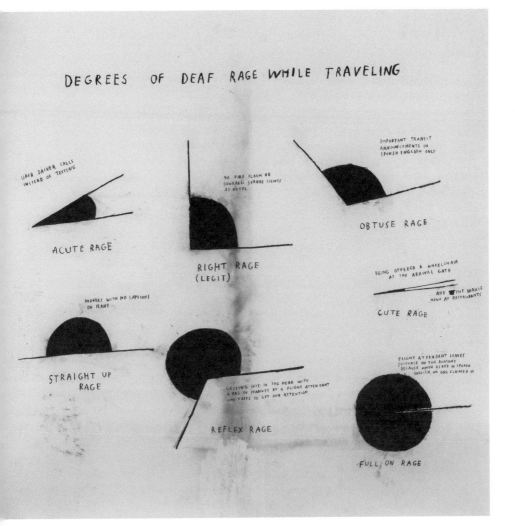

DEGREES OF DEAF RAGE WHILE TRAVELING

UBER DRIVER CALLS INSTEAD OF TEXTING

ACUTE RAGE

NO FIRE ALARM OR DOORBELL STROBE LIGHTS AT HOTEL

RIGHT RAGE (LEGIT)

IMPORTANT TRANSIT ANNOUNCEMENTS IN SPOKEN ENGLISH ONLY

OBTUSE RAGE

BEING OFFERED A WHEELCHAIR AT THE ARRIVAL GATE

AND THE BRAILLE MENU AT RESTAURANTS

CUTE RAGE

MOVIES WITH NO CAPTIONS ON PLANE

STRAIGHT UP RAGE

GETTING HIT IN THE HEAD WITH A BAG OF PEANUTS BY A FLIGHT ATTENDANT WHO TRIES TO GET OUR ATTENTION

REFLEX RAGE

FLIGHT ATTENDANT LEAVES SUITCASE ON THE RUNWAY BECAUSE WHEN ASKED IN SPOKEN ENGLISH, NO ONE CLAIMED IT

FULL ON RAGE

CHRISTINE SUN KIM The pie charts in this charcoal drawing by Korean American artist Christine Sun Kim express anger toward exclusionary design and behavior. Kim's distinctive use of text and materiality come into conflict with the dry, familiar idiom of infographics. *Degrees of Deaf Rage While Traveling*, 2018. Charcoal on paper, 49.2 x 29.2 in. (125 x 125 cm). Courtesy of White Space Beijing and Yang Hao 杨灏.

TRANSCRIPT (from top left)

DEGREES OF DEAF RAGE WHILE TRAVELING

ACUTE RAGE Uber driver calls instead of texting

RIGHT RAGE (legit) No fire alarm or doorbell strobe lights at hotel

OBTUSE RAGE Important transit announcements in spoken English only

CUTE RAGE Being offered a wheelchair at the arrival gate… and the Braille menu at restaurants

STRAIGHT UP RAGE Movies with no captions on plane

REFLEX RAGE Getting hit in the head with a bag of peanuts by a flight attendant who tries to get our attention

FULL ON RAGE Flight attendant leaves suitcase on the runway because when asked in spoken English, no one claimed it

this body is worthy

PROJECT BY HANNAH SOYER AND MARY MATHIS | TEXT BY JOSH A. HALSTEAD

"All bodies are worthy, regardless of what they look like and what narratives they have been forced to live inside of."—Hannah Soyer

After finishing her undergraduate studies, Hannah Soyer started working with her friend Mary Mathis, a photographer, to capture various angles of her body that she felt self-conscious about.

Soon, the project started to expand. She and Mathis conducted workshops inviting anyone who felt that their bodies were outside of mainstream, normative ideals to write phrases on their bodies professing their worth. Participants received photo-graphs of their bodies and wrote about the phrases they chose. *This Body is Worthy* extends past disability to a broader set of marginalized, gendered, and racialized bodies. The project has become a platform that features the work of disabled artists. Proceeds are split between the artists and disability justice organizations.

HANNAH

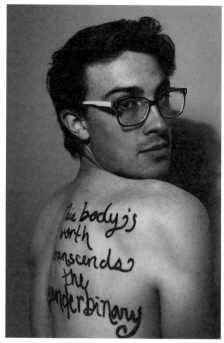

RYAN

PHOTOGRAPHS BY MARY MATHIS

anti-stairs club

PROJECT BY SHANNON FINNEGAN | TEXT BY ELLEN LUPTON

In 2019, artist and designer Shannon Finnegan organized the Anti-Stairs Club protest at the Vessel, a public sculpture conceived by Thomas Heatherwick in New York City. Consisting of 154 staircases, the Vessel resembles a giant vase or basket. Although the Vessel meets accessibility requirements by including an elevator, riding the elevator is not equivalent to traversing the sculpture's elaborate staircases.

Disability advocates argue that public amenities should holistically incorporate inclusive design principles. Designers often fulfill accessibility regulations in a perfunctory way. Participants in the Anti-Stairs Club protest signed a statement vowing to never use the Vessel's stairs. Finnegan designed custom cushions adorned with a crossed-out staircase and a zine printed with letters shaped like stairs. According to Finnegan, "We need to focus on centering disability culture and acknowledging the complexity and nuance of disabled people. I know this will not happen without the presence of disabled people as designers, artists, thinkers, leaders, and creators." Inclusive design is a collaborative process.

SOURCES Shannon Finnegan, "Disability Dreams," *Distributed Web of Care*, Jan 30, 2019 → distributedweb. care/posts/accessibility-dreams/; Emily Sara, "Fighting the Art World's Ableism," *Hyperallergic*, Aug 2, 2019 → hyperallergic.com/510439/fighting-the-art-worlds-ableism/.

PHOTOGRAPHS BY MARIA BARANOVA

voices | shannon finnegan and aimi hamraie

CONVERSATION MODERATED BY EMILY WATLINGTON

SHANNON FINNEGAN	Artist, designer, disability advocate
PRONOUNS	She, her
AIMI HAMRAIE	Associate Professor of Medicine, Health, and Society and American Studies, Vanderbilt University; author, designer, and Disability Justice advocate; author of *Building Access* (2017)
PRONOUNS	They, them

AIMI HAMRAIE Tell us about the Anti-Stairs Club Lounge (see page 43).

SHANNON FINNEGAN The first version was at the Wassaic Project in upstate New York in 2017. Their historic building has seven floors and no elevator. I consider fellow disabled people to be the audience for my work, so I was trying to figure out if or how I could continue making art in an inaccessible space. I decided to make the lounge behind a door with a keypad entry: in order to get the access code, you had to sign a piece of paper promising that you wouldn't go up the stairs to the other six floors of the space. The lounge became a space exclusively for people who were staying on the ground floor, whether out of necessity or in solidarity.

In 2019, I took the lounge to Thomas Heatherwick's Vessel in New York, a monumental structure made up of 154 interconnected stairways. When I saw the plans, I felt Anti-Stairs Club Lounge had to respond. The area around the Vessel is privately owned, which means that the owners have full jurisdiction over what is allowed to happen there. They can forbid protest, so I had to be really strategic. The idea of a lounge still guided the gesture: I created space to gather and rest, providing pillows and snacks. To mark the lounge, I created a newspaper-like version of Kevin Gotkin's essay "Stair Worship: Heatherwick's Vessel" [from the *Avery Review*, 2018]. When you opened the paper up to read it, the exterior functioned as a sign that said "Anti-Stairs Club Lounge." I also made bright orange beanies with crossed-out stairs symbols on them, designating people in the club. Like at the Wassaic Project, to participate in the lounge, you had to refuse the inaccessible space. Participants signed paperwork saying, "As long as I live, I will not go up a single step of the Vessel."

HAMRAIE I'm interested in how this project invites participation as an embodied argument. The same is true of your benches. In both projects, you invite your audience into the piece. The political statement is something that people do with their bodies.

Increasingly, entire neighborhoods are being planned by one developer—including Hudson Yards, which houses the Vessel. We see lots of amenities like sidewalks and benches as public because they're outside a building, but they're still privatized and often especially surveilled or policed. That's why I think your tactics are so interesting as a social movement strategy: you've created something that disseminates critique and knowledge but is also a protest sign that people can casually fold up and take home if the cops show up.

I also love your strategy of physically bringing Gotkin's article to the space. So often, criticism and the object of critique remain completely separate. People who design spaces are often oblivious to what scholars like myself are saying about them. You also present the critique to tourists going to the Vessel to take selfies and insert your argument by having disabled people gather at the site. Can you tell me more about the audience for your work?

FINNEGAN I've been disabled my whole life, but I grew up really isolated from other disabled people. I was encouraged not to identify as disabled, not to seek out the disability community, and not to find disabled role models. That was combined with really horrible media information about disability—the representations I ex-

perienced, and continue to experience, are about tragedy and pity or about overcoming and moving beyond disability. Reading and engaging with the work of other disabled people sparked an incredible shift in my life. Understanding other peoples' experiences helped me understand my own experience and how it's shaped socially and culturally. I want to experience and create those moments when something you've thought about crystallizes or gets validated. I think about disabled people as the primary audience for my work because so often, we're not being spoken to.

HAMRAIE You're also shifting the balance of art that disabled people can access, precisely because so many spaces are inaccessible for us. There's a longer history of accessibility laws being applied and enforced in public spaces than in private spaces. In private spaces—like Hudson Yards, as well as many art spaces—there's a lag in enforcement; it takes something like a lawsuit. So I'm not surprised that the Vessel exists. There is an elevator, so there's this idea that accessibility is an add-on at the end, even though the monument is about valorizing strength and climbing—the justification being, "It's OK because there's an elevator."

Similar arguments are made about buildings that have features called "irresistible staircases"—that's a real phrase! They're supposed to be public health tactics, enticing or even tricking people into taking the stairs. Designers make staircases a building's main event and then hide the elevator in the back. Some of these features have some sort of art installation attached to them: there's one here in Nashville, at the Lenz Public Health Center. When you go up the stairs, LED bubbles light up so that people can see: "Oh! Someone's using the stairs! Congratulations!" There's no art piece that lights up and celebrates somebody using the elevator. The building itself celebrates a certain type of body. Over time, the ADA will have more regulatory guidelines around this type of feature, but at the moment, they're totally compliant, even though they promote inaccessibility and they shame people for taking the elevator.

FINNEGAN I brought Anti-Stairs Club Lounge to Gibney, a dance space in New York. The place used to have a situation similar to what you describe, with the accessible entrance around the corner. But when Gibney remodeled, they asked me to do a project for the opening of the new elevator. I decided to mark the elevator itself as an Anti-Stairs Club Lounge. I installed vinyl lettering on the elevator wall that says "Welcome: Anti-Stairs Club Lounge," and added a removable stool so you can sit in the elevator. I've been thinking about naturally occurring Anti-Stairs Club Lounges—spaces where people who are deprioritizing stairs tend to gather—and how to mark those gatherings as a community.

HAMRAIE Ramps and elevator access for wheelchair users clearly continue to be abysmal in most places. But for so long, "accessibility" has been used to refer exclusively to wheelchair access. If you try to talk to somebody about any access need that's different from that, responses can be catastrophic. People don't always think that different needs—such as strobe warnings, peanut-free environments—are equally valid. That's why the Disability Justice movement is so important—this cross-disability campaign makes an effort to include people with nonapparent disabilities and chronic illnesses and to think about how disability intersects with class.

FINNEGAN Your writing has been so helpful for me in thinking about what we mean

when we say things are "universal" in the sense of being open to "all" or "everyone." Now, every time I read "design for all," it raises a red flag: I'm not sure it's possible to create something that works for everyone, so when someone says that, it signals to me that they haven't considered the limits of what they're doing.

HAMRAIE I was writing *Building Access* right around the time that Michael Brown was killed by the police and the Black Lives Matter movement started. There was a lot of conversation about how the slogan "All Lives Matter" was anti-Black, because it refused to say that Black lives do matter and was intended, instead, to divert the conversation. I thought about how that sentiment shows up in design practices: we constantly hear promises of the most aspirational forms of inclusion and accessibility, and at the same time, we're constantly excluded. What's up with that?

It became really clear that the reason this exclusion keeps happening is that we're not specific enough about our commitments. A flyer for a party might say it's body positive: all bodies welcome. But then you might inquire about a specific form of accessibility and might receive a total refusal or a lot of back-and-forth: then it becomes clear that there is no true intention to really include everyone. That's because we're not thinking about our specificities and differences. One of many critiques of so-called identity politics is that if we say people are different, it's going to divide us and polarize us. But I believe that the kind of false universalization that's proposed as the alternative to identity politics tends to center on the most powerful people. It's important to know as much as possible about all of the ways that we're different.

Universality makes us feel like we have to be perfect and one hundred percent accessible in all these unanticipated ways, so people often aren't fully assessing what kinds of accessibility they are able and willing to provide. As a result, I frequently go to places that I've been told are going to be accessible, and then I have to leave.

Your alt-text-as-poetry workshops seem like a great example of a cross-disability project.

FINNEGAN I've been developing workshops with Bojana Coklyat, an artist who lives with low vision, to think about how to make artwork accessible in nonvisual ways. I've focused on describing visual information online using alt text [tags for images in HTML, often read aloud by software]. The workshop moves away from compliance-oriented, minimum-effort, check-the-box modes of thinking toward creative and generative approaches to writing alt text.

HAMRAIE Alt text and image descriptions are typically approached with objective descriptions that are economical with words. This presumes that there is such a thing as an objective description. Why—especially as an artist—do you think it is important to aestheticize descriptions?

FINNEGAN First, our workshop is different from access consulting: often, people seek consulting in search of concrete guidelines. But cut-and-dried instructions for alt text haven't been worked out yet. The project is getting more people thinking about this issue collectively so that we can start building a tool kit. AI's capacity to generate image descriptions will improve, and we want to have a say in setting the framework for what AI prioritizes.

HAMRAIE While researching for my book, I learned that architectural accessibility and digital accessibility standards emerged almost at the same time. Some groundwork for architecture was laid in the 1960s, but really in the '80s, leading up to the ADA, people were hard at work and in dialogue about both. Many digital accessibility standards overlapped with thinking about flexible designs that factored in user error.

Nowadays, we're thinking more about access to information as something that we are all designers of, so we all have a responsibility. Content producers—these new types of laborers—are responsible for having their audio transcribed or providing image descriptions. We're so used to outsourcing the labor of accessibility to architects and web developers.

FINNEGAN The question of who is responsible for access is something I think about a lot in my workshops. People are often overwhelmed by the task of making images accessible. The idea of access as an ongoing process is really important for me.

HAMRAIE Accessibility often gets subjected to economic calculations—when is it worth it? How much more productive will it make someone? The legal framework for disability in the US is intended to yield productive workers and good consumers.

FINNEGAN We're not quite in a place where the labor of accessibility is valued, and many people—often already overworked—find it stressful when they learn about all this work they don't yet know how to do. I hope the value of that labor is shifting.

SOURCES "Shannon Finnegan and Aimi Hamraie on Accessibility as a Shared Responsibility," moderated by Emily Watlington, *Art in America*, Dec 17, 2017 → artnews. com/art-in-america/interviews/shannon-finnegan-aimi-hamraie-access-art-architecture-1202671288/. © 2019 Penske Media Corporation. See also Aimi Hamraie, *Building Access: Universal Design and the Politics of Disability* (Minneapolis: University of Minnesota Press, 2017).

embodied learning

TEXT BY JOSH A. HALSTEAD

April Coughlin is an educator, scholar, and self-identified "wheeler." Bearing an apparent disability, Coughlin has experienced discrimination throughout her career as a high school and college professor. One morning, a seventh grader in her English class remarked, "We don't have to show you respect like other teachers, because you're in a wheelchair." Shaken, Coughlin searched for a response while suppressing the pain. This student didn't know that she was a first-year teacher. They didn't know she'd been staying up until 4:00 a.m. every night working on lesson plans. And they couldn't possibly know how challenging it was for a new teacher fresh out of grad school to manage thirty-five students. Didn't she deserve a little respect? Apparently not. She was different.

Alas, Coughlin's story is not unique. Lateef McLeod, Sonya Renee Taylor, Tobin Siebers, and many others have written about the politics of corporeal orthodoxy and dissent. In this essay, I join this lineage and foreground embodiment as a tool for self-knowledge and design insight.

To be embodied is to understand ourselves as undivided and reflexive body-mind-spirit-social-relational beings. The body gives us direct access to embodiment and, in so doing, becomes a locus for learning. Internal proprioception (cognizance of the movement and composition of one's own integrated body) grants us access to our emotions, sensations, and desires. To acknowledge these sensory modes of knowledge is to resist binary oppositions like subject/object, mind/body, and nature/culture.

Coughlin was objectified and devalued early in her career for appearing different from other teachers, but she later realized that this experience had shaped her, and she cultivated an embodied pedagogy that challenged dualist modes of knowing. On field trips, she and her students ride the subway together. If an elevator is out of service, the students join in carrying her up and down the stairs. In the process, they learn about physical access and social justice issues firsthand, not merely thinking or reading about the topic but through direct, embodied experience. Coughlin teaches through her body—not in spite of it.

Like Coughlin, I had to learn to value my body unapologetically. When I first moved to San Francisco, I took a longer route to work just to avoid catching a view of my stiff gait in the glossy towers on Market Street. I wasn't exactly ashamed of my body, but I'd internalized the ableist narrative that by graduating from college and moving to a city on my own, I'd somehow escaped disability. My reflection was a constant reminder that I hadn't.

As my career progressed, I had the opportunity to teach an introductory graphic design course at UC Berkeley Extension. Like many first-time teachers, I threw myself into hours of research and preparation. One evening, while building a lecture on postmodern design, I came across Barbara Kruger's 1989 silkscreen *(Untitled) Your Body is a Battleground*. Kruger—artist and fierce feminist—devised this piece for the Women's March on Washington in 1989 in the wake of mounting US antiabortion laws.

BARBARA KRUGER *Untitled (Your body is a battleground)*, 1989. Photographic silkscreen on vinyl, 112 x 112 in. (284.5 x 284.5 cm) Courtesy the artist, the Broad Art Foundation, and Sprüth Magers.

The image became a well-known political symbol for women's rights.

Bodies are not just skin, muscles, and bones, I realized—they are political battlegrounds. How was my disabled body linked to those of women fighting for reproductive freedom? Could disability be an important political identity rather than a fleshy glitch? This marked a turning point in my orientation toward design.

Being embodied is a process of constant becoming. We are always either moving toward or away from embodied presence. When we are closer, we feel connected to our sentient selves, fully in our bodies, aware of our feelings and emotions, fully alive. When we are distanced, we may feel trapped in our thoughts, alienated, ready to snap. Centering is at the heart of the practice of being and becoming embodied. Coming back to our center opens up space in our bodies, affording more options for our actions and decisions.

The first time I was introduced to centering, my teacher, Thomas Loxley Rosenberg, asked me, "What would it take to live life through your legs?" At first thought, there is nothing particularly significant about legs. Stomach, arms, feet—all the same. What he was suggesting, however, was that I try spending less time in my head. Designers often talk about "knowing their users." How could they achieve that without first knowing themselves? Centering helps us come home to embodied presence and, as artist and organizer Kimi Hanauer writes, "embrace groundlessness, multiplicity, fluidity, and change." In the process, we can become designers who are more comfortable with complexity and ambiguity.

SOURCES April Coughlin, "Teaching on Wheels: Bringing a Disability Experience into the Classroom," in *International Perspectives on Teaching with Disability: Overcoming Obstacles and Enriching Lives*, ed. Michael S. Jeffress (New York Routledge, 2018); A. Wagner et al., "Centering Embodied Learning in Anti-Oppressive Pedagogy," *Teaching in Higher Education*, 2015, DOI: 10.1080/13562517.2014.993963; Kimi Hanauer →kimihanauer.com/calling-all-denizens-boston; Gilles Deleuze and Felix Guattari, *A Thousand Plateaus: Capitalism and Schizophrenia* (Minneapolis: University of Minnesota Press, 1987); Rebirth Garments →rebirthgarments.com/about.

how to center the body

To arrive at the present moment, try to drop your awareness to the level of sensation. Notice your heartbeat, breath, temperature, and muscular tensions. Depending on the senses available to you, what do you hear, smell, taste, feel, and see? Is your mood heavy or light? Is it dispersed evenly or collected in a particular area? The following guide uses spatial dimensions (length, width, and depth) as a framework for centering bodily knowledge and agitating the politics of design. This exercise derives from First Nations practices and draws on the somatic teachings of Richard Strozzi-Heckler and Thomas Loxley Rosenberg.

length = dignity

To become aware of your length, begin at the crown of your head and relax your scalp, ears, jaw, throat, shoulders, chest, back, ribcage. Take another deep breath and continue through the rest of your physical body. This is your length, your dignity.

Social forces define our bodies from the outside. Our bodies are raced, sexed, gendered, abled/disabled, and more. For example, I don't inhabit only a disabled body. I also occupy a body that's been policed by gender norms. The effeminate man undermines standards of masculinity. The philosopher Aristotle, in his study of metaphysics, established a tendency in Western society to smooth complexity into transcendental categories—and our bodies, shaped by internal and external forces, wear the scars.

The physical environment shapes us, too. I have an urban body rather than a suburban or rural body. For example, I can't see the horizon from my seventh-floor apartment in San Francisco; my body noticeably shifts when I can see it.

Rebirth Garments is a fashion company tailored to bodies that occupy myriad genders, sizes, and disabilities. The company was founded in Chicago by Sky Cubacub, a nonbinary, queer, and disabled Filipinx designer. They write, "For me, every day is a performance where I bring my body as a kinetic sculpture into the consciousness of the people I interact with….I embody the spirit of Radical Visibility, and Rebirth Garments is my soft armor." Sky is always cloaked in brilliant colors, textured fabrics, and a hint of chain mail. Rebirth Garments embraces the bodies and fashion society often rejects and punishes. Sky amplifies identity and reshapes dignity one outfit at a time.

SKY CUBACUB; PHOTOGRAPH BY
COLECTIVO MULTIPOLAR

width = belonging

Width is the dimension of our social, relational being. The Lakota people say *Mitákuye Oyás'iŋ* (all my relations). Feel the energy around you: people, animals, trees, sun, moon, the cosmos. Notice your body expanding. This is the dimension of belonging. All day, our bodies react to social situations by expanding and contracting, reshaping to fit in.

Philosophers Gilles Deleuze and Félix Guattari wrote, "We know nothing about a body until we know what it can do, in other words, what its affects are, how they can or cannot enter into composition with other affects…" Affect (form and capacities) is shaped in relation to the people and social forces around us. Your network includes your family, friends, neighborhood, institutions, and social norms that enforce various expectations. Services, systems, and labor practices distribute penalties and privileges to people based on their bodies.

Robert Wechsler's project *Meta-Interview* critiques verbal supremacy and celebrates nonverbal bodies. This interactive exhibit invites two people to have a conversation; words and gestures are translated into sound and light. The installation matches movements produced by the eyes, mouth, hands, eyes, or entire body with soundscapes and fluid light patterns.

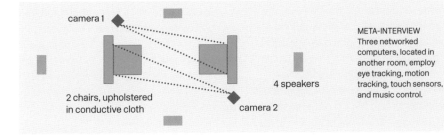

camera 1

META-INTERVIEW
Three networked computers, located in another room, employ eye tracking, motion tracking, touch sensors, and music control.

4 speakers

2 chairs, upholstered in conductive cloth

camera 2

depth = time

Finally, consider the dimension of depth. Lean back slightly and feel the presence of your ancestors, mentors, and past experiences. Notice the back of your head, shoulders, hips, and—when you are ready—the cavern of your heart. This is the dimension of time. Feel yourself emerge at the intersection of past and future—fully embodied in the present moment.

My history included discovering the field of disability studies and learning about the Civil Rights movement and Disability Justice. I became a graphic designer in the seventh grade, the day I created a sticker for my Led Zeppelin cover band. I was sixteen when I took my first design class, at a local art school. My instructor, Wo Jo, fanned out a stack of *Raygun* magazines, designed by David Carson, and I was immediately excited by Carson's spliced, jagged, messy constructions.

Later, I met the artist Neil Marcus, whose performances celebrate the idiosyncratic movements and contours of his own body. Seeing Marcus's collaged, self-published zine *Special Effects* made me think of Carson. Back when I was a teenager, I must have sensed a tacit link between my body and Carson's unruly typographic style.

leaves with you

PROJECT BY SHAINA GARFIELD | TEXT BY JOSH A. HALSTEAD

Designer, activist, and entrepreneur Shaina Garfield acquired a chronic illness early in her career. From its onset, Shaina's new embodiment drew her into a rich, interconnected relationship with the natural world—specifically in response to warm temperatures. From there, she began thinking about the connection between climate change and burial rituals.

Drawing from her knowledge of ecology, Shaina wanted to challenge human exceptionalism—where we place our needs above that of the environment. In her research, she found that, on average, Americans use about 800,000 gallons of formaldehyde in the burial process each year. Why does this matter? When bodies decompose, formaldehyde leaks into groundwater, contaminating ecosystems before returning to the ozone layer and contributing to global warming. Form-

aldehyde is also a well-known and toxic carcinogen.

So Shaina designed a new system: her substitute for formaldehyde is biodegradable macramé. Leaves With You invites family members and mourners to participate in and weave their prayers into the coffin's contour. The ancient practice of tying rope offers space for mourners to be present with grief and healing. The deceased is then returned to the earth in an object of love, allowing ecosystems to continue uninterrupted.

This case study illustrates how disability can be creatively generative—not just a problem for design to overcome. Shaina has since healed considerably from her chronic illness but is grateful for its visit. Being sick and disabled, in her words, "was the inception of my entire life's path."

PHOTOGRAPH BY SPENCER HILL

life | sugandha gupta

TEXT BY JOSH A. HALSTEAD

Textile designer, artist, maker, educator, and disability advocate Sugandha Gupta is currently a high-school fiber-art teacher in New York. She was born in New Delhi, India, in 1987. Her multisensory textiles create access for a broad audience through touch, smell, sound, and sight. Her work combines a variety of textures, materials, and techniques to cultivate embodied learning through sensory engagement. Gupta's pieces have been widely exhibited, and she regularly lectures on the importance of accessible design.

Gupta wasn't always shown respect, however. Growing up with albinism meant being reminded of her difference daily. Neighbors would stop her in the street to ask, "Why are you so pale? Are you sick?" In school, Gupta collided with pedagogy centered on sightedness. At the beginning of college, textiles seemed like an unlikely major; albinism commonly affects eyesight, making it difficult to focus on fine material like thread. "I broke a warp thread on a group weaving loom, and the visiting faculty yelled at me in front of the whole class."

Recalling an early weaving class, she writes, "I hid in my room for two days out of shame and embarrassment." Indefatigable in her pursuit to complete her college education, she found allies in faculty and the chair of the textiles department. Soon, Gupta started embracing her differences and exploring the world through touch.

As a graduate student, she dove into haptics as a potential method for expanding how we learn. Our five senses—sight, hearing, smell, taste, and touch—enmesh to deliver phenomena such as patterns, landscapes, sensations, memories, and perceptions. Maurice Merleau-Ponty writes in *Phenomenology of Perception* (1945), "Sensing is a way of immediate communication with the world as opposed to knowing." Gupta's thesis drew on sensory engagement to question rational knowing and foreground embodied learning. Her wearables and 2D textiles employ felting, sewing, embroidery, weaving, and other techniques. She continues to teach people how to connect with the world and each other through touch.

"The act of making and learning through my senses transformed my work as an artist and an educator. It aided a new perspective of experiencing the world through an intentional use of the senses."
—Sugandha Gupta

SUGANDHA GUPTA; PHOTOGRAPH BY SAVANNAH COLLEGE OF ART AND DESIGN

mother cyborg

TEXT BY ELLEN LUPTON

Donna Haraway's essay "Cyborg Manifesto" (1985) questions binaries that privilege human creatures (especially White, male, nondisabled ones) while othering alternative ways of being, especially those dwelling across categories. The cyborg—a being both biological and mechanical—defies such binaries as human/animal, human/machine, culture/nature, and abled/disabled.

According to Haraway, cyborgs belong to more than science fiction. The cyborgs are here, and they are us! Cyborgs flourish in many domains of design and technology, include AI, VR, bioengineering, and robotics. Countless medical technologies extend the body with devices, animal parts, and structural alterations. Cyborg technologies are as old as design itself. Clothing protects people from hostile climates and alters the shapes of their bodies. For thousands of years, humans have used tools, cooking, and agriculture to change their biological capacity for dominance and survival.

Disabled feminists critique Haraway's essay for promoting the myth of technology as a fix and cure. Jillian Weise, voicing the perspective of the "common cyborg," rejects normative society's glamorization of technology. She writes, "The cyborg is the engineer's dream. The engineer steers and manipulates the human to greater performance. As a common cyborg, I subvert that dream. I do not want to sell any of their shit for them. I am not impressed with their tech, which they call 3C98-3, and which I am wearing, a leg that whirs and clicks, a socket that will not fit unless I stay in the weight range of 100–105 pounds."

Cars, bicycles, wheelchairs, artificial limbs, binoculars, telescopes, reading glasses, hearing aids, and other devices can enhance our mobility or change our sense perceptions. Such products should be codesigned with real users, addressing human needs rather than feeding the drive for profit or the normative urge to hide and assimilate disabled bodies. The designers of assistive devices such as hearing aids and prostheses are beginning to openly celebrate these devices as expressions of identity, beauty, and personal style.

Across human history, gender roles and identities have been subjected to many techniques of body transformation. Circumcision and genital cutting are ancient customs serving a variety of functions, such as affirming membership in a group or marking the passage from child to adult. Such rituals can also reflect cultural fears about sexuality.

Fertility treatments and cloning challenge beliefs about reproduction and gender identity. The first living child conceived in vitro (outside a living organism) was born in 1978. Referred to at the time as "test-tube babies," individuals conceived in vitro are now commonplace. Tech-assisted reproduction methods raise ethical questions, from the fate of frozen embryos to the rights associated with sperm donors, surrogate parents, and the children resulting from these processes.

Cloning occupies the outpost of this ethical frontier. Copying an organism without mixing the DNA of two parent organisms defies natural reproduction and subverts the biological process of evolution. It raises the specter of eugenics and the erasure of difference in favor of racialized and ableist ideals—pushing normativity to its bleakest conclusion.

cyborg bodies

DIAGRAM BY THOMAS CARPENTIER

Architect Thomas Carpentier
created a set of diagrams
critiquing traditional ergonomic
guides. Those traditional guides
provide—and thus normalize—
measurements only for a "typical"
range of human bodies. His project
imagines products and spaces
for an amputee, a bodybuilder,
a cyborg queen, and conjoined
twins. *The Measure(s) of Man*,
degree project, 2011, École Spéciale
d'Architecture, Paris.

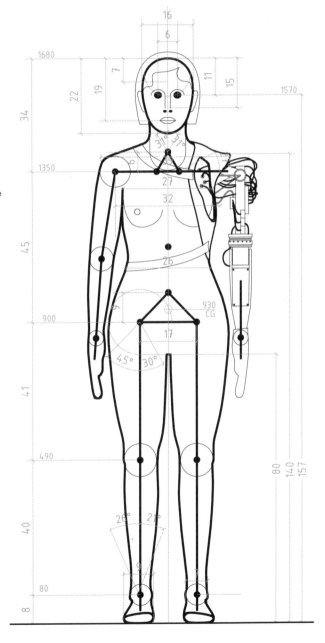

Cyborg technologies appear in gaming, AR, VR, and voice computing. AI systems are trained to recognize people and objects by studying thousands of images fed to them by human operators. Machine learning thus replicates human bias, leading to problems such as racial profiling and wrongful accusations.

Many voice computing systems speak in a female voice, encouraging users (including young children) to view women as passive servants. No matter how rude you are to Siri or Alexa, she takes the abuse rather kindly. Q, a gender-neutral voice assistant, was created by Copenhagen Pride, the Equal AI Initiative, and others in 2019. To create Q, sound designer Nis Norgaard listened to many voices of nonbinary people and then chose one and distorted it to make it sound gender-neutral.

Speculative design uses illustration, modeling, animation, and other storytelling techniques to imagine new, often dystopian futures. Anthony Dunne and Fiona Raby laid out the principles of this experimental practice in their book *Speculative Everything*. Examples of speculative design include proposals for gestating a Māui dolphin in a human womb (designed by Ai Hasegawa) and for using a dog as a living, breathing ventilator (designed by Revital Cohen). Such emotionally charged visions of the future point to the different ways human beings exploit animals—for food, for work, and for emotional support.

The word *robot* comes from the Czech word *robota*, meaning "forced labor." Writer Karel Čapek coined the term in 1920 in his futuristic play *R.U.R.*, or *Rossum's Universal Robots*. Robots are machines for performing autonomous labor. This labor often consists of dangerous or distasteful dirty work, such as housework, sex work, and warfare. Feared as well as embraced,

the robot threatens to take desirable jobs away from humans (and rise up against their capitalist masters).

Musical artist Janelle Monáe addresses this dark history of the robot as an enslaved, not-human being in the fantasy world she designs around her music. Her mythical alter ego Cindi Mayweather belongs to an oppressed class of androids in a magical kingdom called WondaLand, where dominant Wolves harass the robot population. Monáe says, "The android represents 'the other' in our society. I can connect to the other, because it has so many parallels to my own life—just by being a female, African American artist in today's music industry....Whether you're called weird or different, all those things we do to make people uncomfortable with themselves, I've always tried to break out of those boundaries."

Monáe's storytelling builds on generations of Afrofuturist creativity. Sun Ra, Octavia Butler, and Jean-Michel Basquiat envisioned advanced utopian worlds for Black people, an answer to what their lives would be like devoid of colonialism and the effects of White supremacy.

Cyborgs challenge designers to subvert culturally enforced binaries and question the power dynamic between humans and machines.

SOURCES Donna Haraway, *Manifestly Haraway* (Minneapolis: University of Minnesota Press, 2016); Beatriz Colomina and Mark Wigley, *Are We Human? The Archaeology of Design* (Zurich: Lars Müller, 2016); Jillian Weise, "Common Cyborg," *Granta* →granta.com/common-cyborg/; Dalia Mortada, "Meet Q, The Gender-Neutral Voice Assistant," National Public Radio, Mar 21, 2019 →npr.org/2019/03/21/705395100/meet-q-the-gender-neutral-voice-assistant; Anthony Dunne and Fiona Raby, *Speculative Everything: Design, Fiction, and Social Dreaming* (Cambridge: MIT Press, 2013); Dan Hassler-Forest, "The Politics of World Building: Heteroglossia in Janelle Monáe's Afrofuturist WondaLand," in *World Building*, ed. Marta Boni (Amsterdam: Amsterdam University Press, 2017).

cyborg storytelling

SPECULATIVE DESIGN BY AI HASEGAWA

Many cyborg technologies—both real and imaginary—involve gender, sexuality, and reproduction. Ai Hasegawa imagines a dystopian future in which a woman who craves to give birth but doesn't want to become a mother has the option of using synthetic biology to gestate an endangered dolphin.

Dilemma chart (Why don't I get pregnant with...)

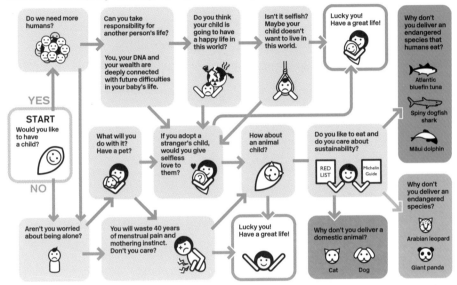

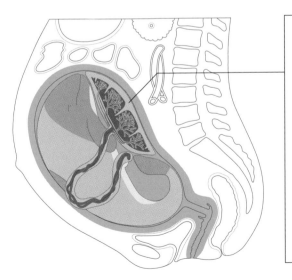

Dolp-human Placenta
The placenta originates from the dolphin rather than from the human host. This avoids the ethical and legal difficulties associated with reproductive research involving human eggs. The dolp-human placenta has been modified to tolerate—rather than reject—cells from another mammal. Additional modifications to the dolp-human placenta prevent the human host from transferring harmful antibodies to the dolphin baby. Instead, the baby will receive antibodies from synthesized first milk just after delivery.

The Māui dolphin is the world's rarest and smallest known subspecies of dolphin. As of 2016, approximately 63 adults existed in the world. Their main cause of unnatural death is entanglement and drowning in fishing nets. Adults measure between 3.9–4.6 ft. (1.2–1.4 m) and weigh up to 110 lbs. (50 kg). The newborn is almost the same size as a human baby, 19.7–23.6 in. (50–60 cm).

binary structures

TEXT BY ELLEN LUPTON AND LESLIE XIA

Philosopher Judith Butler challenged the belief that gender identity is a fixed state of being in her groundbreaking 1990 book, *Gender Trouble*. Whereas many feminist writers at that time sought to define the essence of being of a woman, Butler questioned "male" and "female" as socially constructed categories. She argued that notions of universal womanhood reinforce the binary upon which gender oppression depends. *Gender Trouble* presents two ideas that help us think about feminism, sexuality, and design: first, the concept of the gender matrix, which questions the male/female binary, and second, the concept of gender as performance, a set of repetitive gestures that replicate and enact the gender binary.

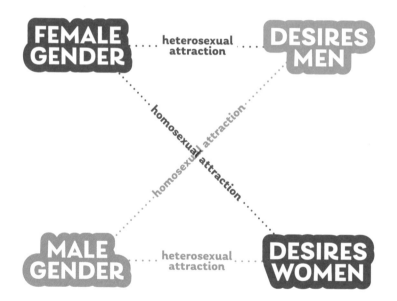

GENDER MATRIX Butler didn't publish a visual diagram of the matrix—readers need to picture this structure in their own minds. Various writers have attempted to draw the matrix; our version appears here. In the matrix, homosexual desire runs counter to the norm of heterosexual desire. The terms society uses to describe desire further reinforce the gender binary. Language matters. Expressions like *homosexual* and *same-sex attraction* draw their meaning from the male/female binary. The concept of homosexuality is relatively new. offering a quasiscientific, medicalized name for attractions that have always existed. The term *compulsory heterosexuality* explains how categories of biological sex map onto forms of sexual attraction.

Let's start with the gender matrix. This oppressive structure sets fixed points of desire and identity. The polarities of sex (biological characteristics) connect to the polarities of sexuality (desire for other people) to produce a person's gender identity (the internal, psychic sense of being male or female) and sexual orientation (being straight or gay). The matrix excludes shifts and nuances of identity and desire.

The gender matrix is embedded everywhere in society, from family structures to dress codes. The matrix requires people to be either male or female, and it dictates desire for the "opposite sex" as the only healthy and natural mode of attraction. The matrix pressures each individual to accept a stable identity and adhere to fixed sexual attractions. While some societies accept gender practices that resist the matrix, others condemn them.

Over time, nonconforming behaviors can break out of the matrix and change the culture. Butler writes, "As the effects of a subtle and politically enforced performativity, gender is an 'act,' as it were, that is open to splittings, self-parody, and exaggeration." When drag performers parody gender codes, they show how fragile these norms really are.

Butler's work rejects rigid definitions of gender and the search for ancient matriarchies and female-only futures. According to Butler, any notion of fixed gender identity upholds oppressive binaries. Furthermore, feminists who insist on a universal, vulva-centered womanhood perpetuate colonialist and racist power structures by ignoring the category of Whiteness. Defining womanhood as a transhistorical, cross-cultural mode of being denies the oppressive force of White privilege.

Building on Butler's philosophical deconstruction of the binary, younger writers and activists developed the concept of fluid gender identity, replacing closed binaries with more open spectrums. Activist Jacob Tobia writes, "As people, our identities change over our lifetimes. This applies to transgender and cisgender people alike. Everyone has a gender that evolves." The way that you embody your manhood or femininity can shift throughout your life and in different settings.

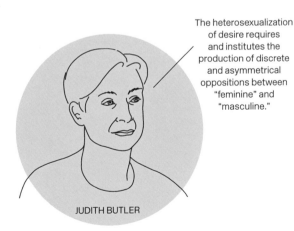

The heterosexualization of desire requires and institutes the production of discrete and asymmetrical oppositions between "feminine" and "masculine."

JUDITH BUTLER

Like Tobia, Butler argues that gender is an unstable phenomenon, "a complexity whose totality is permanently deferred, never fully what it is at any given juncture in time." Not everyone has a fluid experience of gender, however. Many people who are cis, trans, intersex, genderqueer, gender neutral, or nonbinary feel firmly locked into their identity.

Tobia points out that mainstream media enforces the gender binary by defining success for a transgender person as being able to pass as the gender they identify with. Telling a trans person that they look like a "real woman" or a "real man" solidifies restrictive views of gender.

The matrix is limiting and oppressive because it demands each individual to have an essential identity as either male or female and heterosexual or homosexual. Each person enacts and reinforces the matrix by finding their place within it and behaving according to its rules.

When individuals enact the socially constructed attributes of gender (such as "girls wear dresses"), they replicate and reinforce social rules and expectations. According to Butler, the process of "doing" makes the "doer," rather than the other way around. We are what we enact. Performance creates the performer. Norms become visible and dominant because they are repeated across society—by individuals and families as well as by movies, TV shows, fashion, advertising, toys, and so on. Subversive ways of performing gender, such as appearing in drag or adopting a butch or femme persona, disrupt the matrix by switching its polarities.

Butler's phrase "styles of the flesh" refers to varied modes of gender performance. Such styles come from society and are performed by individuals. From valley girls and soccer moms to jocks, nerds, bros, and bears, gender styles are roles to play and identities to wear. People challenge norms by mixing styles and inventing new ones. For example, in popular culture, the fashion model is a pinnacle of body normativity; fashion ideals are subverted and appropriated by drag culture. We model our behavior on performances that we witness and aspire to, and, in turn, our own behavior becomes a model for others.

People perform different ways in different contexts. Think about how your speak-

enforcing the binary

pink is for girls
blue is for boys

SOURCES Judith Butler, *Gender Trouble: Feminism and the Subversion of Identity* (New York: Routledge, 1990). See also Adrienne Rich, "Compulsory Heterosexuality and Lesbian Existence," *Blood, Bread and Poetry* (London: Virago, 1978); Jacob Tobia, *Sissy: A Coming-of-Gender Story* (New York: G.P. Putnam's Sons, 2019); Susan Stryker, *Transgender History, Second Edition: The Roots of Today's Revolution* (New York: Seal Press, 2020).

ing voice, vocabulary, and body language might shift in various settings, such as a college classroom, a client presentation, a hardware store, a family dinner table, or an apartment with friends. For people of color or people who are trans, intersex, gender-queer, gender neutral or nonbinary, the ability to code-switch (putting on a "White voice" or a "masculine voice") can be a matter of survival.

Designers contribute to the social construction of gender when they use stylistic cues to suggest masculine or feminine characteristics. In Western culture, soft colors and loopy scripts typically are associated with feminine values, while hard edges and neutral tones are considered more masculine. These associations are repeated and reinforced over time, making them a legible vocabulary.

When designers make choices about colors, fonts, textures, symbols, motifs, and images, they are performing styles— and sometimes inventing new ones or generating new meanings through shifts in context. To create a zine, poster, or website is to mobilize codes, structures, and technologies that are already in place,

such as typefaces, printers, servers, and platforms. Such systems exist before and beyond the practice of graphic design. No matter how original a new font or logo might seem, some of its elements come from history and culture. The performance of graphic design is never wholly original or fully liberated from rules.

So, too, the performance of gender occurs within and against the matrix imposed by society. In Butler's words, "To enter into the repetitive practices of this terrain of signification is not a choice, for the 'I' that might enter is always already inside….The task is not whether to repeat, but how to repeat or, indeed, to repeat and, through a radical proliferation of gender, to displace the very gender norms that enable the repetition itself." Butler's stunning description of freedom and constraint, originality and repetition, parallels the limits and opportunities of the designer's practice. This practice is embedded in a dense weave of social patterns, from the gender matrix to structures of racism and class difference.

**breaking
the binary**

TYPEFACE | CONFITERIA | JULIETA ULANOVSKY

sex and gender terms

TEXT AND ICONS BY STEPHANIE BORGOVAN

The terms collected here gesture toward the many different ways that people name their sense of gender identity and sexuality. This vocabulary is always changing.

gender
A set of socially constructed associations with biological sex, such as behaviors, appearance, and social roles.

intersex
A variation in sex characteristics which is not strictly male or female. Intersex newborns are often forced into treatments to conform to one or the other.

gender identity
How someone internally identifies with social gender constructs, regardless of their biological sex.

cisgender
Someone whose gender identity aligns with the sex they were assigned at birth.

gender expression
How someone conveys gender, such as through choice of clothing, mannerisms, and preferred pronouns.

transgender
Someone whose gender identity does not align with the sex they were assigned at birth.

biological sex
The division of a species based on reproductive function. In humans, sex is divided into male and female.

gender binary
The idea that gender is divided into two distinct categories that are considered opposites: masculine and feminine.

assigned sex
The classification of a newborn's sex as either male or female based on the appearance of their external genitalia.

masculine
Characteristics and social roles associated with male sex. Examples in many societies include assertiveness, short hair, and patriarchal roles.

feminine
Characteristics and social roles associated with female sex. Examples in many societies include grace, long hair, and matriarchal roles.

 agender
Not identifying with gender constructs, Refusing to label one's gender, gender neutrality, or a lack of gender.

 nonbinary
Gender identities and expressions which do not fit typical cultural associations with only the male and female sex.

 gender neutral
Characteristics and social roles with no associations with what is considered masculine or feminine.

 man
Someone who identifies with the behaviors, presentations, and roles traditionally associated with the male sex.

 demigender
Experiencing only a partial sense of a gender, or only partially relating to the concept of gender more broadly.

 woman
Someone who identifies with the behaviors, presentations, and roles traditionally associated with the female sex.

 multigender
Having the experience of identifying with more than one gender, either simultaneously or intermittently.

 androgynous
Having a combination of characteristics and social roles that are considered masculine and feminine.

 gender fluid
The experience of a variable gender identity, experiencing different gender identities at different times.

typographic binaries

TEXT BY ELLEN LUPTON

Binary categories are under attack. Advocates for racial justice have challenged racial binaries, which marginalize people of color while enshrining White supremacy. LGBTQIA+ activists are dismantling the male/female polarity, which enforces gender norms and compulsory heterosexuality. Environmentalists are unraveling oppositions such as nature/culture and human/animal, which justify human domination and destruction of the planet.

What is the role of binary thinking in Western typography? Invented in Germany in the fifteenth century, printing with metal type became the first form of mass production. Mechanized letters hastened changes in religion, science, literature, law, and commerce. The rapid spread of typography coincided with the age of Western colonial conquest and techno-scientific exploitation of the Earth's resources. Typography—a tool and medium for these world-changing developments—quickly adopted binary structures. All the while, alternative modes of expression have challenged strict polarities.

Consider the opposition of roman and italic. In Western typography, italic type styles are typically viewed as secondary to the roman norm. In semiotics (the theory of signs), this kind of relationship is called *marked* and *unmarked*. The unmarked category is the neutral default (roman), while the marked category stands out as an exception (italic).

This opposition has not always existed in typography. During the first century of metal type, roman and italic flourished as separate dialects, unbound by any binary relationship. Early typefaces were based on handwriting styles, each with different purposes and properties. The printer Aldus Manutius worked in the busy commercial city of Venice at the turn of the fifteenth century. He published many beautiful books, including low-cost, small-scale volumes, using an italic typeface designed by Francesco Griffo. These early italics were inspired by casual, cursive scripts that working scribes could write quickly and inexpensively. Griffo's italic lacked uppercase letters, so roman capitals were inserted where needed. Tall and fluid, Griffo's italics conserved space, making them a cheaper alternative to the romans used in more deluxe printed books.

By the early sixteenth century, roman text became the norm in many regions, while italics were reserved for emphasis. Type families created by Claude Garamond and other type founders included italics whose x-heights and line weights conformed to the dominant roman style. The typefaces of this era also featured uppercase and lowercase characters in matching styles. These relationships—roman/italic and uppercase/lowercase—became standard components of typography.

What is an italic letterform, anyway? Is it a mere shadow of its roman master, or does it assert its own unique personality? The italic alphabets of Garamond and Caslon are quite distinct from their roman partners, despite having strong family ties. Their strokes are more fluid and relaxed, with lilting serifs leading one letter to the next, while their single-story *a*'s and *g*'s are designed to comfortably accommodate the letters' narrow proportions and snug spacing.

Sloped or slanted romans take their cues from a roman template. These italic forms are made by tilting the basic roman character, rather than designing a unique yet sympathetic partner. In many sans serif type families, the italic style is called *oblique*, meaning slanted. Software tools such as Photoshop and InDesign can add a slope to any letter—usually with awkward results.

In traditional typesetting, italics establish contrast with no change in weight. Italic letters (slanted or not) are one way to perform this function; other techniques include underlining, l e t t e r s p a c i n g, or introducing **a new typeface** altogether.

In Western publishing, foreign words are set in italic unless those borrowed words have become commonplace. For example, in written English, the French words "cliché," "café," and "cul-de-sac" are usually set in roman, while less familiar phrases, such as *pompe à chiasse* (diarrhea pump) or *sans-couilles* (without balls), are set off with italics. Some bilingual writers reject this native/foreign language binary. Dominican American novelist Junot Díaz sets Spanish words in roman rather than mark them as other and thus presume that the typical reader speaks only English.

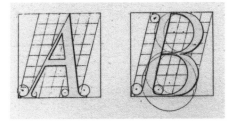

FRANCESCO GRIFFO The roman and italic fonts designed in Venice for printer and publisher Aldus Manutius were conceived as separate designs.

THE BRIEF WONDROUS LIFE *of* OSCAR WAO

unread, so that when she arrived at Idlewild she would not know who it was she should be looking for. La pobrecita.

Just as the standoff between the Good Neighbor and what remained of Family Trujillo reached the breaking point, Beli was brought before a judge. La Inca made her put ojas de mamón in her shoes so he wouldn't ask too many questions. Homegirl stood through the whole proceedings, numb, drifting. The week before, she and the Gangster had finally managed to meet in one of the first love motels in the capital. The one run by los chinos, about which Luis Díaz sang his famous song. It was not the reunion she had hoped for. Ay, mi pobre negrita, he moaned, stroking her hair. Where once was lightning now there was fat fingers on straight hair. We were betrayed, you and I. Betrayed horribly! She tried to push the dead baby but he waved the diminutive ghost away with a flick of his wrist and proceeded to remove her enormous breasts from the vast armature of her bra. We'll have another one, he promised. I'm going to have two, she said quietly. He laughed. We'll have fifty.

The Gangster still had a lot on his mind. He was worried about the fate of the Trujillato, worried that the Cubans were preparing to invade. They shoot people like me in the show trials. I'll be the first person Che looks for.

I'm thinking of going to Nueva York.

She had wanted him to say, No, don't go, or at least to say he would be joining her. But he told her instead about one of his trips to Nueba Yol, a job for the Jefe and how the crab at some *Cuban* restaurant had made him sick. He did not mention his wife, of course, and she did not ask. It would have broken her.

ROMAIN DU ROI In 1695 the official French alphabet known as the Romain du Roi (king's roman) was drawn on a grid; the italics were drawn on a slanted grid. See Jacques André and Denis Girou, "Father Truchet, the Typographic Point, the Romain du roi, and Tilings," TUGboat 20, no. 1 (1999): 8–14.

JUNOT DÍAZ The novel *The Brief Wondrous Life of Oscar Wao*, by Junot Díaz, includes Spanish and English words set equally in roman (Riverhead Books, 2007).

HOME INTERIORS, gravestones, and pottery participated in the material landscape of whitened goods popular in the American South before the Civil War. White paper was a special case because it brought together the racial ideology of unmarked, standardized white skin with the invisibility of paper. The demand for pure, bright, white paper linked racial legibility with print legibility. Thus, READING LANGUAGE and READING BODIES became very close, dependent on common visual techniques.

[—JONATHAN SENCHYNE—]

TYPEFACE | FILOSOFIA | DESIGNED BY ZUZANA LICKO
TEXT ADAPTED FROM JONATHAN SENCHYNE, *THE INTIMACY OF PAPER*

Designers have multiple tools for marking (or not marking) differences. From commercial printers to champions of the avant-garde, designers have questioned canonical binaries within typography and the broader culture. Serif and sans serif typefaces exist on a spectrum. Letters with horizontal stress are bucking the patriarchy of the vertical. Typefaces built with inconsistent parts have been championed by activists and people with disabilities.

Typography's strongest binary is black versus white. Many medieval books are multicolor productions, written on vellum writing surfaces that aren't stark white. According to Jonathan Senchyne, the black/white opposition coincides with the rise of printing. Image and text both expressed this polarity. Wood engravings were produced with type-high blocks, manufactured so that they could print simultaneously with text. Engravings were printed in pure tones of ink—usually black.

Senchyne writes that ultrawhite paper became the ideal printing surface in the eighteenth and nineteenth centuries. While some printers rebelled against the brilliant tones and hard finishes of state-of-the-art paper manufacturing in favor of softer shades and overall tactility, white paper dominated as a standard of quality. White paper was often compared to a virginal White woman, a pure blank page awaiting the writer's mark. Printers' obsession with white paper reinforced White society's fierce devotion to the Black/White racial binary. The supposed purity of the White race could not withstand a single drop of "Black" blood, just as white paper had to be rigorously defended against smudges of wayward ink.

The eighteenth-century English printer and type founder John Baskerville engineered his own inks and his own paper in order to maximize the contrast between black and white. Although some critics condemned the glittering brilliance of Baskerville's work, the hunger for contrast continued unabated.

The typefaces created by Firmin Didot and Giambattista Bodoni at the turn of the nineteenth century have extreme contrast between thin and thick strokes, enhancing the difference between black ink and white paper. Bodoni's *Manuale Tipografico* (1818) describes typography as a system of interchangeable parts: "Analyzing the alphabet of any language, one not only can find similar lines in many different letters, but will also find that all of them can be formed with a small number of identical parts."

Bodoni aimed to eliminate subtle gradations of form in favor of "marking the differences which are required in a most outstanding way." Despite Bodoni's own classical, austere sensibility, his modular approach helped open the profusion of inventive display types created for the burgeoning advertising industry in the nineteenth century.

SCENE I.

JOCASTE, OLYMPE.

FIRMIN DIDOT The severe, abstract typefaces cut by the Didot family in France feature slablike, unbracketed serifs and a stark contrast from thick to thin. Nineteenth-century printers and typographers called these glittering typefaces "modern."

The opposition between serif and sans serif is another binary structure. Typefaces with blunt terminations—now called sans serif—began appearing in the early nineteenth century. Type designers tricked out the alphabet with deep shadows and fancy scrollwork. Serifs ceased to be staid and dignified finishing details; they shed their inhibitions to become expressive elements in their own right. Created for advertising and commercial signs, these display typefaces flaunted curly-topped serifs, chunky slabs, or no serifs at all. These variations were not polar opposites so much as scrappy siblings cohabiting typography's strange new reality.

In the twentieth century, the sans/serif binary took on the weight of ideology. Jan Tschichold, evangelist for rational, machine-age typography, wrote in 1928, "Among all the types that are available, the so-called 'Grotesque' (sans serif) or 'block letter' ('skeleton letters' would be a better name) is the only one in spiritual accordance with our time.…Sans serif is absolutely and always better." Tschichold struggled to find the right terminology. The letters he idealized not only lacked serifs but have uniform line weights as well. His phrase "skeleton letters" describes the monoline, serif-free typefaces that became the backbone of modernist graphic design. (Slicing the serifs off of Bodoni is not what Tschichold had in mind.)

Yet just as italics take multiple forms of expression, the serif is an elusive thing. Typographer John Berry's taxonomy of letter endings suggests that if a serif can be so many things—from a spiky spur to a massive, blocky slab—it might not be a thing at all. Letters that lack serifs also take many different forms. Stems and strokes that swell, bend, pucker, or flair resist neat binary categories.

Attacking the uppercase/lowercase binary, Bauhaus master Herbert Bayer sought to eliminate capital letters and thus reduce the alphabet to its skeletal essence. He argued that unicase fonts require fewer characters, are easier to learn, and would lower the cost of printing. Furthermore, a lowercase alphabet would challenge social hierarchy—all letters would now be equal.

Although the bid to eliminate capital letters failed to become a standard in the West, designers today use lowercase letters in posters, ads, branding, and publications to signify a relaxed, conversational tone. Writer bell hooks spells her name in lowercase to question patriarchal naming systems. Our book *Extra Bold* uses lowercase chapter titles and headings to undercut the power-based concept of typographic hierarchy.

Because of their kingly status, capital letters can signal dignity and importance. In the 1920s, Civil Rights leader and sociologist W.E.B. Du Bois pressed editors and publishers to spell the word *Negro* with a capital *N* in order to confer respect on an oppressed people. Likewise, many publications today capitalize the word *Black* to show respect for Black identity.

What about the word *white*? Historian Nell Irvin Painter advocates capitalizing *Black*, *White*, and *Brown* when referring to race or ethnicity. Capitalizing the word *White* racializes this ostensibly neutral, invisible category. (Some writers prefer to write *white* in lowercase to avoid giving credence to White nationalism.) Painter asserts, "One way of remaking race is through spelling—using or not using capital letters. A more potent way, of course, is through behavior."

experimental alphabets

CHARVET, A TYPEFACE DESIGNED BY KEVIN KARANJA, IS INSPIRED BY ANCIENT AFRICAN TYPOGRAPHY.

TYPEFACE | CHARVET | BY KEVIN KARANJA In 2013, the Nest Collective commissioned Kenyan graphic artist Kevin Karanja to create this typeface, inspired by Karanja's love for Ancient African typography and geometrics. →thisisthenest.com/charveta-typeface-2013

LGBTQpride

TYPEFACE | GILBERT | BY JUSTIN AU This chromatic typeface honors Gilbert Baker, creator of the rainbow flag, a global symbol of LGBTQIA+ pride. Developed by NewFest and NYC Pride with Fontself.

COME OUT!
JOIN THE SISTERS

TYPEFACE | STONEWALL 50 | BY BOBBY TANNAM AND FEELD This typeface, designed to commemorate the Stonewall uprising, celebrates the validity of every person's experience of sexuality and gender. →feeld.co/blog/announcements/stonewall-50-a-typeface-inspired-by-the-birth-of-pride

SOURCES On italics, see Thu-Huong Ha, "Bilingual Authors are Challenging the Practice of Italicizing Non-English Words," *Quartzy*, Jun 24, 2018 →qz.com/quartzy/1310228/bilingual-authors-are-challenging-the-practice-of-italicizing-non-english-words/. On printing and racial binaries, see Jonathan Senchyne, *The Intimacy of Paper in Early and Nineteenth-Century American Literature* (Amherst: University of Massachusetts Press, 2020). On Bodoni, see *Manuale Filosofia: Typeface by Zuzana Licko*, Vol. 1 (Berkeley: The Emigre Fonts Library, 2019). Ruben Pater talks about bell hooks's use of lowercase letters in *The Politics of Design* (Amsterdam: BIS, 2016). On capitalizing the words *Black* and *White*, see Lori L. Tharps, "The Case for Black with a Capital B," *New York Times*, Nov 18, 2014 →nytimes.com/2014/11/19/opinion/the-case-for-black-with-a-capital-b.html and Merrill Perlman, "Black and White: Why Capitalization Matters," *Columbia Journalism Review*, Jun 23, 2015 →cjr.org/analysis/language_corner_1.php; Nell Irvin Painter, "Why 'White' Should be Capitalized, Too," *Washington Post*, Jul 22, 2020 →washingtonpost.com/opinions/2020/07/22/why-white-should-be-capitalized/.

Typographers and lettering artists have always created letterforms that ignore binary oppositions such as roman/italic or serif/sans serif. Systems of typeface classification often banish decorative display faces and cursive scripts to a catch-all anticategory such as "decorative" or "display." Relegated to the junk drawer of typographic history, these designs refuse to conform to such neat categories. Today, many type designers are exploring irregular proportions, flaring strokes, horizontal stresses, and ambiguous stroke endings. These designs embrace typography's ornamental history rather than its modernist, classical, and Eurocentric canons.

The concept of a "type family" is rather patriarchal. A type family is a group of individual styles unified by an originary list of features. Real-life families are less matchy-matchy and predictable. Living families fall apart, break up, and get repaired—with varying degrees of success.

When is a type family nonbinary? Leah Maldonado's experimental typeface Glyph World rejects oppositions such as roman/italic, serif/sans serif, uppercase/lowercase, and bold/light in favor of a weird and open landscape of ideas. The fonts of Glyph World cohabit and coexist without obediently conforming to a master set of rules or filling in spaces on a grid.

JOHN BERRY This diagram challenges the divide between serif and sans serif.

TYPEFACE | CAPUCINE BOLD ITALIC | ALICE SAVOIE

FLARED

TYPEFACE | INJURIAL | SANDRINE NUGUE

blotted

TYPEFACE | MANDEVILLA BOLD | LAURA WORTHINGTON

TYPEFACE | AMPERSANDIST | LYNNE YUN

glyph world

TYPE FAMILY BY LEAH MALDONADO

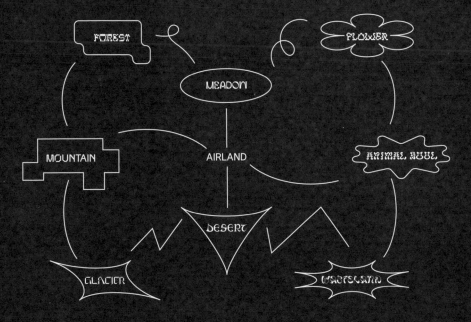

FOREST ▭

MEADON ◯

FLOWER ✿

MOUNTAIN ▢

AirLand

ANIMAL SOUL ✳

GLACIER ◇

DESERT ▽

WASTELAND ✴

a queer year of love letters

PROJECT BY NAT PYPER

A Queer Year of Love Letters is a series of fonts that remembers the lives and work of countercultural queers of the past several decades. The series aims to make the act of remembering these overlooked and delegitimized histories as easy as typing. Better yet: it aims to make the act of typing an act of remembering. That these fonts might be considered typefaces is incidental. They are an attempt to improvise a clandestine lineage, an aspatial and atemporal kind of queer kinship, through the act of writing.

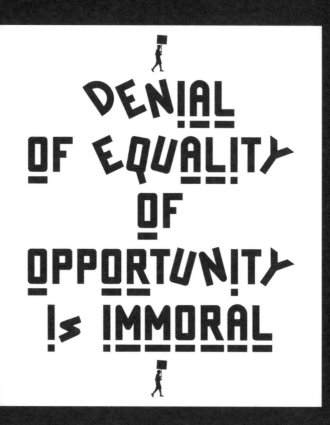

ERNESTINE ECKSTEIN (1941–1992) was ahead of her time. She was the lone Black lesbian at an early gay rights protest in front of the White House in 1965. Eckstein called for a progressive activism that included equality for trans people, anticipating the umbrella of LGBTQIA+ solidarity. The letterforms in this font are based on those Eckstein wrote on her picket sign at that iconic protest: "Denial of equality of opportunity is immoral."

SOURCE *A Queer Year of Love Letters*, 2018–20, Women's Car Repair Collective and Ernestine Eckstein commissioned by Library Stack, 2020 →librarystack.org/queer-year-of-love-letters/.

She KNOWS WHO SHE IS

THE LOLLIPOP GENERATION

ROBERT FORD (1962–1993) published *THING* from 1989 through 1993. The Chicago-based publication foregrounded queer Black and Brown DJs, drag queens, artists, poets, and filmmakers. *THING* proudly proclaimed on its masthead, "She Knows Who She Is." In 1994, Ford died from complications related to AIDS. This font was commissioned by Earth Angel, a Milwaukee club night, in June 2018.

G.B. JONES (b. 1965) is an artist, filmmaker, and musician. In the early 1980s, Jones cofounded the post-punk proto–riot grrrl band Fifth Column and in 1985, launched the queer punk zine *J.D.s* with Bruce LaBruce. Jones's "no-budget" films often depict bad-mannered girl gangs, homo hustlers, and anarchist mischief-makers. This font is based on the title sequence of her 2008 film *The Lollipop Generation*.

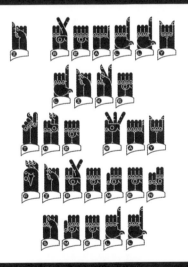

"SHE WOULD TAKE ENGINES APART..."

MARTIN WONG (1946–1999) painted the world in bricks, sweat, and sign language. A gay Chinese American painter in New York, Wong created tributes to the gritty ecstasy of city life, the homoerotics of prison and firemen, and queer Black and Brown love. This font is based on the stylized sign language system Wong employed in his artworks.

WOMEN'S CAR REPAIR COLLECTIVE was one of several initiatives organized by the Lesbian Alliance of St. Louis, Missouri, in the early 1970s. This "service by and for women" offered repairs of foreign and American cars, workshops, and rentals of garage space, books, and tools. This font is based on lettering from a flyer advertising the collective.

voice | shivani parasnis

CONVERSATION WITH ASH HIGHFILL

SHIVANI PARASNIS	Biotechnologist turned graphic designer
PRONOUNS	She, her

Where do you draw inspiration from? I grew up in Mumbai, India, and moved to the US a couple of years ago, so a lot of the work I did at the beginning of my career drew inspiration from what I grew up seeing and experiencing. Currently, the idea of being influenced by the things around me is still the same, but now I feel my work has numerous layers that meld influences from the East and West. I love things and processes that are analog: illustrations on old matchboxes from India, vintage packaging that hasn't changed in a million years, textures from old cassettes and VHS tapes, and lettering and colors from old movie posters.

Tell me about how you begin designing a typeface. I am trying to be more experimental and free in my practice, and drawing interesting letters has been a way to let myself go beyond the usual. I attended a workshop on Korean type design at MICA, where the assignment was to draw Hangul letters using some insane grids. I took the same grids and used them to design Latin letters, and the result was some experimental lettering pieces. Hangul letters are extremely geometric and lend themselves to all kinds of variations, so it was so refreshing to use those modular forms for a totally different script, all based off of the same grid. This process blew my mind, and I pursued the same idea and used it to create a whole typeface for my thesis.

I love the hazy, retro mood of your Risographs. Riso printing is more or less like a hybrid of a copier machine and screen printing. Each color is printed as a separate layer, leaving much room for experimentation. The colors are gorgeous, and the textures produced naturally add beauty to each print run. The Riso is not perfect, and I think that is one of my favorite things about the process. The colors are not always registered correctly; they don't always mimic the file you create digitally, and I love to embrace that imperfection in my work.

What's next for you? I wrapped up my MFA thesis in May 2020 at MICA in Baltimore. I developed a fictional type foundry called Extra Bold Italic, and I designed four typefaces that challenge the binaries in typeface design. Just like binaries related to gender, traditional type design showcases a certain set of either/or binaries, like roman/italic or serif/sans serif. The preference for vertical stress is very Western. I worked on designing typefaces that provide an alternate point of view. The

process was exciting and stressful at the same time, primarily because I had never done type design before. For me, designing the applications of my typefaces was equally important, beyond just creating a typeface and a typical type specimen. I focused on creating content that not only used my typefaces but also followed and advanced my design aesthetic.

Tell us about the typeface you designed for *Extra Bold*. This typeface challenges Latin type design traditions. While some letters are reverse-stressed, some appear monoline and others have a more standard vertical stress. Playful counters and absurd anatomies resonate throughout the font. The typeface was designed for bold headlines.

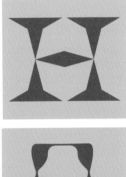

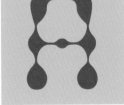

SOURCE Interview adapted and expanded from Ash Highfill, "An Interview with Shivani Parasnis," Femme Type, Jun 15, 2020 →femmetype.com/an-interview-with-shivani-parasnis/.

voice | tré seals

CONVERSATION WITH ROGER PEET

TRÉ SEALS	Graphic designer, typeface designer, entrepreneur
PRONOUNS	He, him

How did you get started on the project of creating fonts? I love branding. Branding makes up about 90 percent of my projects. But in the process of looking for inspiration, I got really bored. Don't get me wrong, graphic design is my passion, but I just wasn't inspired by anything I was seeing on Behance, Dribbble, Pinterest, and even in many design books. It all looked the same, and the fact that people like this monotony really bothered me. I started wondering if I had chosen the wrong career.

This all started in May of 2016. And some time after that, something told me to research the demographics of the design industry. So I did. I found that 84 percent of all designers in America are White (→bls.gov/cps/cpsaat11.htm). And that's when everything started to make sense to me.

I realized that when a single gender and race dominates an industry, there can only be (and has been) one of way of thinking, teaching, and creating. This lack of diversity in terms of race, ethnicity, and gender has led to a lack of diversity in thought, systems (like education), ideas, and, ultimately, creations.

When you hear things like "The majority of women don't see themselves on TV" or encounter advertisements filled with stereotypes of underrepresented cultures, this is why. This is not a recent issue. It's just that now, profits are being affected as the world we live in becomes more diverse. One of the first articles to bring up the issue of diversity in design was written in 1987 by Dr. Cheryl D. Holmes Miller as her senior thesis. Discovering this text inspired me to start creating fonts based on the history of Civil Rights activism. I knew that I couldn't simply diversify design's demographics or educational system. So I tried to figure out a way to introduce a nonstereotypical piece of minority culture into the design vocabulary itself, starting with the basis of any good design—typography.

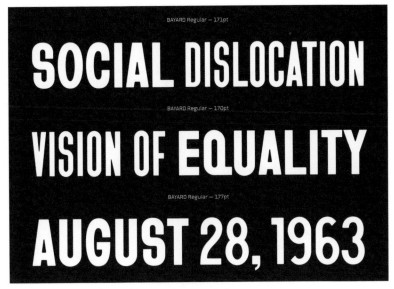

TYPEFACE | BAYARD | TRÉ SEALS | INSPIRED BY BAYARD RUSTIN
AND THE CIVIL RIGHTS POSTERS OF THE 1950S AND '60S

How have you chosen the subjects that you've used so far? Because
I'm tackling the issue of diversity, I try to focus on movements that either
relate to minorities of color or to everyone. During the Memphis Sanitation
Workers' Strike of 1968, over three-quarters of the workers were Black.
A movement that affected everyone was the Anti-Draft movement of the
Vietnam War era.

Next, I look for a piece of ephemera that multiple people have a connection to, from a sign distributed among hundreds or thousands of individuals to a single banner carried by a dozen people.

What's your process? My process is 25 percent research, 25 percent
design, 25 percent research, 25 percent design, in that order. I do this because in one particular instance, I did all of my research in the beginning
and all of my designing afterwards. Not long before I was getting ready to
release the typeface, I found an article from the past decade that prompt-
ed me to cancel the release all together. So, while this process adds up
to 50 percent research plus 50 percent design, breaking it up allows the
process to be more fluid, and that way, I'm continuously finding inspiration and information that may affect the end result.

Have you seen your fonts in use in any interesting contexts?
There are too many to have a favorite. I'm just honored to see them used.

SOURCE Adapted from an interview with Roger Peet, JustSeeds,
Oct 30, 2018 →justseeds.org/civil-rights-fonts/.

History isn't everything that ever happened. It is a selective set of narratives that have been recorded and passed on. Writing history is a process of making connections among people, events, and broad social changes. Official histories focus on a society's most visible and dominant figures—kings, generals, business magnates, and famous artists, inventors, statesmen, and explorers. Today's historians are studying the achievements of overlooked people and practices in order to create de-colonized histories, queer histories, gendered histories, local histories, disability histories, and histories of popular culture.

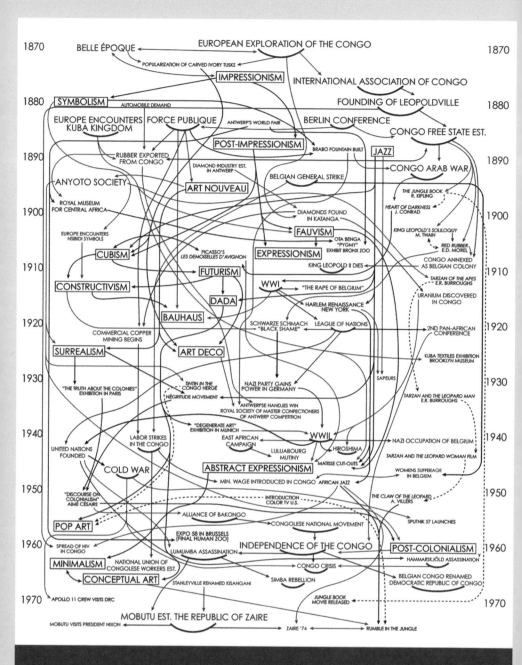

COLONIALISM AND ABSTRACT ART

HANK WILLIS THOMAS *Colonialism and Abstract Art*, 2019. Courtesy maruani mercier gallery © Hank Willis Thomas Studio

TEXT BY ELLEN LUPTON

Every history has a point of view. Alfred Barr Jr. was the founding curator of the Museum of Modern Art. In 1936, he created a timeline leading from Paul Cézanne and Impressionism to his own era. Art created outside the Western world is segregated from the flow of history. Barr's diagram describes a complex narrative with overlapping influences. He drastically simplified this story at the very end, however, where his timeline leads to just two outcomes: "non-geometrical abstract art" and "geometrical abstract art." (In fact, modern art led to many other modes of expression.) Barr's diagram has inspired many redo's, including the work at left by artist Hank Willis Thomas, which tracks the history of the Congo, an African nation that achieved independence in 1960.

Writing history and passing it on to others is a form of power. History validates the people it depicts. Design history—a relatively new discipline—is largely written by working designers with a passion for research and storytelling. New, more inclusive histories are being created by people who are practicing and redefining design from the perspective of varied backgrounds, identities, and abilities.

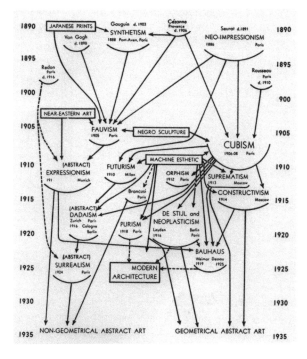

ALFRED H. BARR JR. This diagram appears on the jacket of the exhibition catalog *Cubism and Abstract Art* (New York: Museum of Modern Art, 1936; New York: Arno Press for Museum of Modern Art, 1966). © The Museum of Modern Art/Licensed by SCALA/Art Resource, NY.

Historians often use birth as a metaphor for the origins of social or intellectual transformations, in phrases such as *the birth of civilization* or *the birth of modern surgery*. Like any overbaked metaphor, this one verges on cliché. The idea of birth helps us picture a fertile ground or single point of origin from which something new and original can spring forth. The metaphor also suggests an outcome with a singular identity—like a shiny new baby. (Just add death to the metaphor, and history becomes a narrative arc with a neat and knowable beginning, middle, and end.)

Let's mess with the metaphor of birth as a point of origin. Textbooks of graphic design history—written from a primarily White, Western point of view—focus on the people and events that helped create a certain profession that came to be practiced in the mid-twentieth century in industrialized countries around the world. The modern graphic designer was a white-collar intellectual who orchestrated the work of blue-collar printers, typesetters, and paste-up artists. This archetypal designer was equipped with Bauhaus-inspired views of rational communication. (Learn more about the Bauhaus on page 92, "Life | Anni Albers.")

Key developments in this linear tale include the invention of typography in Germany, the rise of alphabet-based printing and publishing, the Industrial Revolution and its reformers, and the critical rupture of avant-garde movements. All these strands of DNA lead, ultimately, to Baby Helvetica: the crowning glory of a normative, monoline language designed to lubricate the wheels of capital anywhere on Earth.

Our alternative history diagram funnels the backstory of graphic design through the cervix of mid-century modernism. Instead of identifying famous people or art movements, we listed reproduction processes and business practices. What emerges from our picture of history is not a unitary being but a messy reality. While Swiss modernism was creating a scalable design methodology in the 1950s and '60s, the certainty of Western imperialism was falling apart. Youth movements rebelled against war, racism, patriarchy, and the grid. Soon after, desktop publishing mashed design back into production by jamming the scrappy old tools of production into a box the size of a toaster. The unitary identity of graphic design as a singular discourse was a momentary mirage. The embryo did not implant.

In real human biology, most ova never become fertilized at all. A female reproductive system can generate hundreds of cycles over the course of a lifetime—and the vast majority bear no fruit, as the expression goes. The cycle resumes, and after a while, it doesn't. Cycles are loops, not linear progressions. In the words of design historian Sara De Bondt, "History is what gets repeated."

Like fairy tales or movie scripts, history is told as a series of events that lead to a climactic moment, yet in real life, an infinite number of other actions take place alongside the established narrative of history. Questioning the absolute value of minimalism or functionalism can open our eyes to other aesthetic languages. The pages that follow depict some alternative histories. Anyone can add to history through personal research and study.

History is more like a stain than a line. It's an ink blot with no obvious shape. It bleeds out, sinks in, and leaves a mark. Those marks are there to be discovered.

the birth canal of graphic design

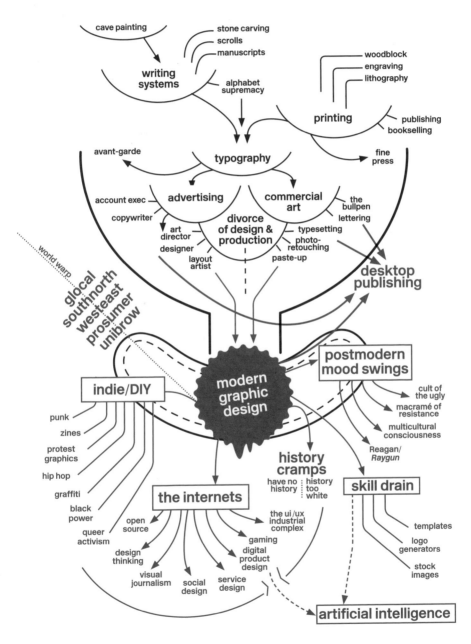

DIAGRAM BY ELLEN LUPTON

how to
be a
historian

The magic of holding an original object conjures the spirits and lives of working women.

lisa unger baskin

Thousands of books and other documents collected by Lisa Unger Baskin show evidence of women at work from the fifteenth century to the present. This landmark collection demonstrates that for centuries, women have worked in printing, publishing, and bookselling as well as in in fields whose knowledge was spread through print, including science, medicine, and politics. Baskin transferred her collection to the Duke University library, making this material available to future historians—including you!

My formal design education is rooted in methods developed by mostly White men.

jerome harris

As a designer, Jerome Harris got his start by mastering Photoshop and creating flyers for Black nightlife scenes in New York, Philadelphia, and Connecticut. He earned an MFA in design from Yale University and found that in his design courses, there was nearly zero discussion of Black design practices. In 2018, to address this gap, Harris curated the traveling exhibition As, Not For, which displays work by Black designers in the domains of music, politics, infographics, and advertising.

andy campbell

Queer X Design (2019) is the first illustrated survey of queer graphic design history. To create this book, Andy Campbell immersed himself in numerous collections, including the Leather Archives & Museum in Chicago. His book tells the story of famous symbols (the rainbow flag) and local icons (Dandy Unicorn, an inclusive symbol of the queer community in Austin, Texas). With a background in art history, Campbell is Assistant Professor of Critical Studies at USC's Roski School of Art and Design. Cover design: Katie Benezra.

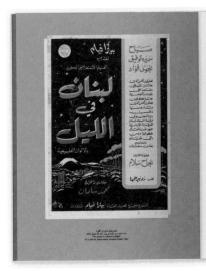

maya moumne and hatem imam

Safar is an independent magazine about the history, culture, and beauty of graphic design in the Arab world. It is published by Maya Moumne and Hatem Imam, who also run a client-based design studio in Beirut, Lebanon. Issue 4 features an article by Zeina Maasri about Arab film posters created in the 1960s and '70s. Designers in Cairo produced posters that circulated across the region, merging Hollywood marketing strategies with local customs. Maasri challenges binaries such as local/global and vernacular/modern.

READ MORE Andy Campbell, *Queer X Design: 50 Years of Signs, Symbols, Banners, Logos, and Graphic Art of LGBTQ* (New York: Black Dog & Leventhal, 2019). Sara De Bondt, exhibition, *Off the Grid: Belgian Graphic Design from the 1960s and 1970s as Seen by Sara De Bondt*, Design Museum Gent, 2019 →designmuseumgent.be/en/events/off-the-grid. Jerome Harris, "Black Graphics: Celebrating Designers of Color," *Afropunk*, Sep 25, 2018 →afropunk. com/2018/09/black-graphics-celebrating-designers-of-color/. Zeina Maasri, "The Print Culture of Film," *Safar*, no. 4 (2019). Naomi L. Nelson et al., *Five Hundred Years of Women's Work: The Lisa Unger Baskin Collection* (New York: Grolier Club, 2019).

life | yolande bonhomme

TEXT BY ELLEN LUPTON

In typography, a widow is a single word stranded on the last line of a paragraph. It turns out that real widows participated in the early print industries. In Paris during the 1500s, some fifty widows operated printing businesses. They were the daughters of printers who learned the family business and went on to marry printers themselves. After the death of a husband, a wife could legally inherit his business. In addition to the widows who owned printing presses, many wives, sisters, and daughters worked in printshops and other family-owned businesses.

Born in Paris c. 1490, Yolande Bonhomme grew up working in her father's printshop. She married the printer Thielmán Kerver, whose press she inherited in 1522. She ran this lucrative business until her own death thirty-five years later, in 1557. Bonhomme published books for markets across France as well as in Germany, Switzerland, and the Netherlands. Her press employed approximately twenty-five workers and contracted work out to other printers located in Paris.

YOLANDE BONHOMME *Institutes of Justinian*, title page and detail of the printer's mark, 1541. Library of Congress.

SOURCES Beatrice Hibbard Beech, "Yolande Bonhomme: A Renaissance Printer," *Medieval Prosopography* 6, no. 2 (1985); Naomi L. Nelson et al., *Five Hundred Years of Women's Work: The Lisa Unger Baskin Collection* (New York: Grolier Club, 2019); Marianna Stell, "Female Printers in Sixteenth-Century Paris," Library of Congress, Aug 20, 2018 →blogs.loc.gov/law/2018/08/female-printers-in-sixteenth-century-paris/; Margaret Lane Ford, "Types and Gender: Ann Franklin, Colonial Printer," in *A Living of Words: American Women in Print Culture*, ed. Susan Albertine (Knoxville: University of Tennessee Press, 1995).

TEXT BY ELLEN LUPTON

Born in 1696, Ann Smith Franklin was an author, printer, and publisher in the American colony of Rhode Island. She married James Franklin, a printer, and inherited the family business when he died in 1735. Like other widowed printers, she was permitted to run the business in order to support her children. She became the official printer of the colony's General Assembly. She also published five editions of the *Rhode Island Almanac*, a collection of weather predictions and clever quips. In 1741, she started selling the more popular publication *Poor Richard's Almanac* instead, created by her famous brother-in-law, Benjamin Franklin, who apprenticed in her family's shop when he was a teenager. Ann Franklin published popular British novels, sermons by local ministers, and her own newspaper, the *Newport Mercury*. Her daughters were skilled at setting type, and her son helped run the business. A Black man, who was enslaved by the Franklins, also worked in the printshop.

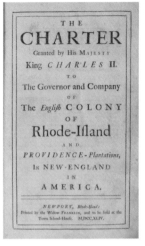

ANN SMITH FRANKLIN

ILLUSTRATION BY JENNIFER TOBIAS

life | sojourner truth

TEXT BY JENNIFER TOBIAS

Born into slavery in New York's Hudson River Valley, Sojourner Truth (1797–1893) was an abolitionist, feminist, preacher, and singer. She became a free woman when slavery was outlawed in New York in 1827. Her autobiography, as stated on the title page, was "published for the author" in 1853.

In addition to selling her book at events, Truth sold photographs of herself, which were less expensive to produce. Called *cartes de visite* (calling cards), these popular, affordable photographs were printed from negatives in multiples and then trimmed and mounted to cards. Authors, actors, and politicians commonly sold *cartes de visite*. As historian Nell Irvin Painter points out, Truth crafted her representation in photographs. In the image below, she wears tailored clothing and sits beside a vase of flowers and a table draped with an embroidered cloth. Truth masked her right hand, which had been injured during her enslavement. In contrast, some former slaves posed for photographs unclothed, revealing such ravages of slavery as a deeply scarred back. While these dramatic images stirred the passions of White abolitionists, Truth preferred to highlight her humanity and dignity as Black person.

Truth said in her speech "Ain't I a Woman?" that she was both a former slave and a woman—and that both groups deserved full rights. Truth believed that all women and all Black people are entitled to voting rights, while her contemporary Frederick Douglass prioritized the rights of Black men. This conflict divided feminists as well. Many White feminists objected to the Fourteenth Amendment, which granted citizenship to men born in the US—but not to women—in 1868.

I Sell the Shadow to Support the Substance.

SOJOURNER TRUTH.

SOURCES Nell Irvin Painter, *Sojourner Truth: A Life, A Symbol* (New York: W. W. Norton, 1997); Naomi L. Nelson et al., *Five Hundred Years of Women's Work: The Lisa Unger Baskin Collection* (New York: Grolier Club, 2019).

SOJOURNER TRUTH The activist and author produced portraits like this one for sale at lectures and events. She describes this photograph as a "shadow" of her person.

TEXT BY JENNIFER TOBIAS

William Wells Brown (c. 1814–1884) was born into slavery in Kentucky and hired out as a teenager to work for a newspaper publisher in St. Louis. Working at the press, Brown learned to read and write through the process of sorting and setting type. He also learned about the business of publishing. Brown later became a free man and a prominent novelist, playwright, and historian. In addition to fighting slavery, he supported women's right to vote and prison reform.

Brown was an active public speaker on the lecture circuit in the US and Europe. He carried printing plates in his luggage, which he used to publish his book in different locales. These plates, called "stereotypes" or "clichés," were cast from the original typeset forms of individual metal letters, assembled when the book was first prepared for publication. Printers created stereotypes in order to free up the costly metal type for other projects. Stereotypes weighed less than metal type, making them relatively portable. Printers could republish a book from the plates without repeating the laborious and expensive process of typesetting.

With this origin in the printing process, today the word *stereotype* refers to a simplified, derogatory view of a group of people. Stereotypical ideas about race, gender, or ethnicity are repeated again and again in culture with little effort at understanding, just as stereotyped printing plates can be used repeatedly and at low cost. A stereotype about race or gender is a shorthand way of simplifying and flattening identity. A cliché is also a lazy habit of language, a clever phrase beaten down by overuse.

SOURCE Jonathan Senchyne, "Bottles of Ink and Reams of Paper: Clotel, Racialization, and the Material Culture of Print," in *Early African American Print Culture*, ed. Lara Langer Cohen and Jordan Alexander Stein (Philadelphia: University of Pennsylvania Press, 2012).

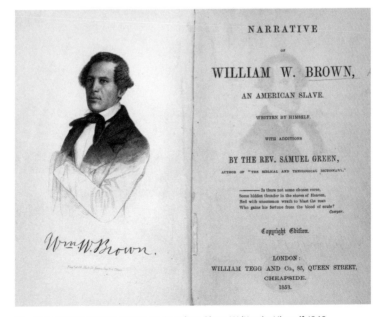

Narrative of William Wells Brown, An American Slave, Written by Himself, 1849.

life | angel de cora

TEXT BY JENNIFER TOBIAS

Artist, designer, writer, and educator Angel De Cora (1871–1919) sought to integrate Native American heritage into the contemporary design practices of her day, especially in the field of publishing. Declaring in 1911 that the "Indian's artistic conception is well worth recognition," she believed that "designing is the best channel in which to convey the native qualities of the Indian's decorative talent."

De Cora, born Hinook-Mahiwi-Kalinaka, "fleecy cloud floating in place" or "woman coming on the clouds in glory," belonged to a prominent Ho-Chunk (Winnebago) family in Nebraska. They raised her to have "the general bearing of a well-counseled Indian child," steeped in her family's traditions. She recalled, "A very promising career must have been laid out for me by my grandparents, but a strange white man interrupted it."

Lured by the anonymous man's promise of a trip on a train, De Cora was stolen from her family and brought to the Hampton Institute in Virginia. The school, founded to teach practical arts to emancipated African Americans, expanded its mission to forcefully assimilate Native children.

De Cora went on to study at Smith College and then joined a new commercial art program at the Drexel Institute in Philadelphia. She studied with the illustrator Howard Pyle before ultimately rejecting his pedagogy. "I am an Indian," a colleague recalled her saying. "I don't want to draw just like a white man."

In 1906, De Cora accepted a mandate to reconceive the art program at the Indian Industrial School in Carlisle, Pennsylvania. Her conditions: "I shall not be expected to teach in the white man's way but shall be given complete liberty to develop the art

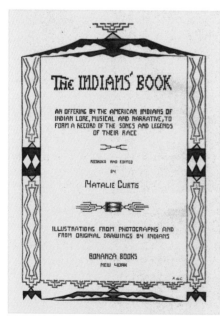

APACHE TITLE-PAGE

ANGEL DE CORA Title page and lettering for Natalie Curtis, *The Indians' Book*, 1907. When De Cora presented a sample of her lettering design to the publisher, the in-house designer said, "Get that girl to do all the lettering in the book and you will have something unlike anything that's ever been done with the alphabet before." Drawings by Native artists represent each chapter's culture.

of my own race and to apply this, as far as possible, to various forms of industries and crafts." She introduced progressive art education methods and integrated "Indian history, not as the white historian has pictured it in words, but as some of us have heard it from the Indian storytellers by the light of the campfire."

Following the closure of Carlisle in 1918, De Cora contracted the so-called Spanish influenza in 1919, succumbing to the global pandemic at age forty-nine.

Through her life of advocacy, teaching, and publishing, De Cora envisioned a future for Native Americans in design: "The only difference between me and the women on reservations is that I have chosen to apply my native Indian gift in the white man's world." She looked forward to the day when "America will be proud to have her Indians make beautiful things for all the world."

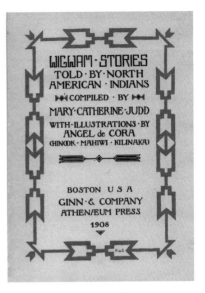

ANGEL DE CORA Title page for Mary Catherine Judd, *Wigwam Stories*, 1908. The title page credits the artist in both in her colonized and Native names.

SOURCES Angel De Cora, "Autobiography," *The Red Man* 3, no. 7 (Mar 1911): 278–85 →carlisleindian.dickinson. edu/publications/red-man-vol-3-no-7; Linda Waggoner, *Fire Light: The Life of Angel De Cora, Winnebago Artist* (Norman, OK: University of Oklahoma Press, 2008); Elizabeth Hutchinson, "Modern Native American Art: Angel De Cora's Transcultural Aesthetics," *Art Bulletin* 83, no. 4 (Dec 2001): 740–56 →jstor.com/stable/317723.

life | anni albers

CONCEPT AND TEXT BY SARA TORRES

This interactive biography of a woman artist explores the
life of Annelise Elsa Frieda Fleischmann, born in Berlin in
1899 to an affluent family. As a teenager, she likes painting,
but art is more than a hobby for her. Follow her life and make
choices as she attempts to become an artist.

1. become an artist

The Expressionist painter Oskar
Kokoschka lives nearby. Will you stay
at home or knock on his door and
introduce yourself?

stay home?

Become a bourgeois painter. Entertain
guests at home and show them
your lovely, untroubled art. As you
superficially discuss with your guests
those modernists pushing the envelope,
you have a lump in your throat, knowing
you'll never become a modern artist.

knock on the door?

Take your paintings with you and pay
a visit to Oskar Kokoschka.

yes! the door opens

The artist stares at you with disgust. You tell
him you love painting and want to become his
apprentice. He laughs and slams the door.
　You came to this place to become an
apprentice and what you got was a more
important lesson: getting someone to train you
as a serious artist is going to be tough. Although
knocking on Kokoschka's door is a humiliating
experience, this choice allows you to continue the
Adventure of Modern Art.

2. enroll at the bauhaus

You are now twenty-three and in luck. The government has given women equal access to study, and a very cool school called the Bauhaus is accepting female students. However, nothing is perfect. Women have to pay more than men—150 marks for men and 180 marks for women! What should you do?

refuse to pay more than men?

No! If you decide the situation is unfair, good for you! For a few weeks you are admired by your female colleagues, who make the pragmatic choice: they pay, they get an education, and they work in a male-dominated art world. As for you—stubborn, brave, bold fighter for equality—you are simply a few decades ahead of your time. Alas, you never become a modern artist.

agree to pay more than men?

Yes! If you decide to pay more because you have enough money, you accept the status quo. You surf a male-dominated school without making much noise. Nobody ever apologizes to you, and you don't expect them to. After all, you are grateful to be allowed to continue participating in the Adventure of Modern Art!

ILLUSTRATIONS BY JENNIFER TOBIAS

3. choose your course at the bauhaus

You made it! You are in the Bauhaus! It is time to choose what you want to study. Alas, female students don't have many choices. Though the Bauhaus preaches inclusivity, women are allowed entrance into only a couple of classes, including the bookmaking studio and the weaving workshop. Which do you choose?

bookmaking?

Sadly, the same year you enroll in the Bauhaus, the bookmaking workshop is shut down. You never acquire the skills and are not given the choice to enroll in a different class. You lose your place in the Adventure of Modern Art.

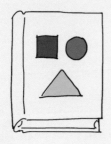

weaving?

Yes! Choosing the weaving workshop will please Bauhaus founder Walter Gropius, who believes that men can think in three dimensions while women can only handle two! Years later, you will challenge that notion by creating free-hanging textile room dividers, described by many as three-dimensional sculptures. Suck it, Walter Gropius!

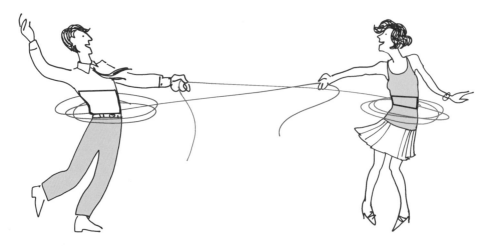

4. love and war

At the Bauhaus, not everything is about weaving. There are parties! You meet Josef Albers! You marry him in Berlin in 1925. But complications lie ahead. In 1933, Adolf Hitler comes to power in Germany and the Bauhaus is pressured to shut down. The Nazi terror campaign targets Jews, disabled people, Roma, Poles, Soviet prisoners of war, homosexuals, Jehovah's Witnesses, Afro-Germans, and people with ties to any of these groups. Your family has converted to Christianity, but you have Jewish roots. An opportunity comes up in the US: Josef is invited to teach at a new experimental school called Black Mountain College in North Carolina—a place you know nothing about. There, you could become just your husband's wife and lose everything you have built in Germany. But the risk of persecution by the Nazis is real. What do you do?

stay in germany?

After Hitler is declared Führer, people like you are subjected to laws restricting your rights, and you see anti-Semitism rise in Europe. You lose all chances to get a job because your grandparents were Jewish and you are seen as racially impure. You live in constant threat of being sent to a concentration camp, and you seek options to leave the country. Chances to escape are limited.

go to america with josef?

Black Mountain College gives no grades and has no required courses! You find it "truly interesting." You teach weaving, make extraordinary weavings, and develop new textiles. You write essays on design that reflect your passionate vision. You are Anni Albers, and you have won the Adventure of Modern Art!

life | charlotte perriand

TEXT BY ELLEN LUPTON

Charlotte Perriand (1903–1999) designed some of the most influential furniture of the twentieth century. In 1927, she was a young woman working independently in Paris, designing furniture and interiors. Portfolio in hand, she approached the Swiss architect Le Corbusier and asked him for a job. He turned her down with a sexist quip.

Soon after Corbusier refused to hire Perriand, he visited an installation she had designed, which recreated her attic apartment in Paris. The room gleamed with metal and glass. Nickel-plated copper stools surrounded an anodized aluminum bar. There were cushions—but they were leather. Corbusier hired her, and she worked in his studio for the next decade, together with Pierre Jeanneret.

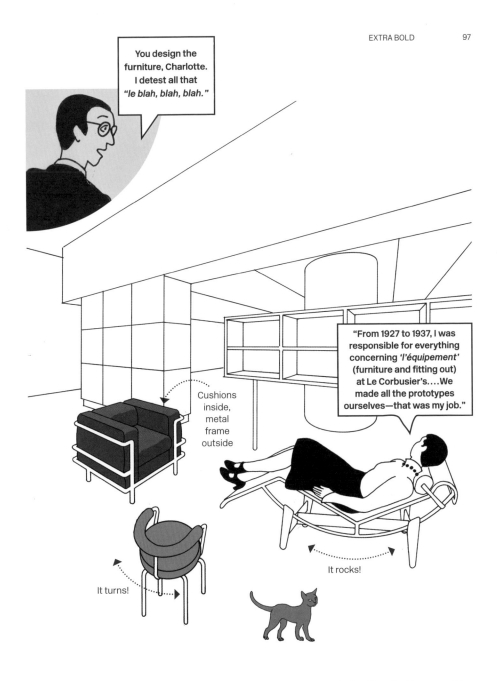

In Paris in 1929, Perriand exhibited an interior for modern living with Corbusier and Jeanneret. Perriand is considered the primary author of the stunning furniture pieces on display, including an upholstered leather cube supported by a metal grid, a swivel chair inspired by office furniture, and a reclining chaise fitted with pony skin. These iconic objects were manufactured in 1930 with the names of all three designers (Corbusier, Perriand, and Jeanneret). In the 1960s, Corbusier marketed them exclusively under his brand, LC ("Le Corbusier").

After World War II, Perriand offered to collaborate with Le Corbusier on Unité d'Habitation, an affordable housing project. He refused to fully collaborate; instead, he invited her to design the kitchen—which he believed was appropriate work for a woman and mother.

"I would be very happy if you could contribute to the practical structural aspects of the settings which are within your domain, that is to say the knack of a practical woman, talented and kind at the same time."

Prefab modular kitchen

Perriand designed Les Arcs, a ski resort, when she was in her sixties. The staggered building steps down the side of the mountain, blending with the snow.

SOURCES Jacques Barsac et al., *Charlotte Perriand: Inventing a New World* (Paris: Editions Gallimard, 2019); Martin Meade and Charlotte Ellis, "Interview with Charlotte Perriand," *Architectural Review*, 1984→architectural-review.com/essays/interview-with-charlotte-perriand/8659677.article?v=1.

Pillow by Donna Wilson, who designs cushions, creatures, knitwear, and home accessories with craftspeople in the United Kingdom.

Although Perriand embraced machine-age materials, she came to value craft and individual makers.

ILLUSTRATIONS BY JENNIFER TOBIAS

feminism in india

TEXT BY TANVI SHARMA

In India, the presence of women in graphic design is largely undocumented. However, one area where women were ardently involved is the design of political posters.

After 1947, when India entered its postcolonial period, leaders and citizens began exploring graphic design as a tool for achieving social change. The Indian Constitution granted equality and freedom from discrimination based on gender, and women from all walks of life began questioning the country's traditional, patriarchal society. Collectives formed across India and published iconic imagery to bring attention to a variety of causes, from domestic violence to the practice of female feticide, which uses sex determination tests to favor male offspring. Posters served as conduits to get people acquainted with issues of marginalization under caste, class, religion, sexuality, age, ability, and gender and to suggest new ways to distribute power.

The posters shown here, created in the mid- to late twentieth century, question gender oppression. As with many collective and craft-based enterprises, most of the creators of posters from India's feminist movement are unknown. These women didn't become famous designers, in part because design was not yet an industrialized or formalized occupation, much less a source of personal fame or prestige. They produced their work to communicate ideas in simple and direct ways, often using pictures instead of words to transcend the barriers of literacy in a multilingual, multicultural society.

The visual artifacts that have survived from this history bear witness to the cause of the oppressed. The posters shown are archived and documented online by Zubaan Books, a feminist publishing house based in New Delhi. Zubaan initiates research and outreach projects concerning gender, feminism, and the women's movement.

GOVERNMENT Written in Oriya, the headline of this poster says, "When women become aware." The illustration shows the transformation from a traditional power structure in an Indian village to a female-centered one. In the first scenario, the *panchayat* (village government) is controlled by the husband of the woman *sarpanch* (elected decision-maker). His wife, the sarpanch, is sitting on the ground next to him. After the "pattern of change" occurs, the situation reverses: the panchayat is headed by the woman sarpanch and her husband is sitting in the back, at the corner of the house.

DOMESTIC VIOLENCE Written in Bangla, the text of this poster reads, "No ten-armed Goddess ever toiled as I do for free. Yet, insults, biting sarcasm and the stick seem to be my only destiny."

FEMALE FETICIDE Written in Gujarati, this one-color poster says, "Stop killing my daughters before their birth. Stop sex determination tests."

SOURCE More than 1,500 posters from the Indian women's movement can be viewed and studied at →posterwomen.org.

life | ed roberts

TEXT BY JOSH A. HALSTEAD

Ed Roberts (1939–1995) politicized the social paradigm of disability in the US. Roberts contracted polio at an early age and used an iron lung to support breathing. In 1962, he was denied admission to UC Berkeley because dorm rooms were not designed to accommodate his iron lung. After a good fight, Roberts and his family and friends found a space on campus, and he went on to complete his undergraduate and graduate studies in political science.

During his transition from undergraduate to graduate degree programs, he also transitioned from a manual wheelchair to an electrically powered one. He soon found that curbs, which then had no ramped cutaways, or "curb cuts," prevented him from getting around campus independently. He often had to find alternate routes, something not required when he used a manual chair with an attendant.

So Roberts and a group of disabled classmates—the Rolling Quads, as they cavalierly named themselves—lobbied the City of Berkeley to install curb cuts across town. The City agreed and gradually started installing curb cuts in choice locations. From 1972 to 1976, Berkeley's disabled population spiked from about 400 to 5,000. Why? Berkeley was the most accessible place in the US—with respect to infrastructure but also with respect to culture. Disabled people fostered a place where disability was a political identity worth celebrating.

In the 1960s, Berkeley and the Bay Area were hotbeds of Civil Rights activism. Roberts and his friends demanded rights for disabled people. Their first big action launched on April 5, 1977, when a cross-disability coalition occupied ten federal offices across the US to demand that Section 504 of the Rehabilitation Act be signed without being watered down. Stated with full force, the act made it illegal for any entity receiving public financial assistance to discriminate based on disability. They won. The Rehab Act was signed, paving the way for other rights-based legislation like the Americans with Disabilities Act of 1990/2008. These changes too required protest. Elevators, ramps, and closed captions are enjoyed by society because disability communities demand change over and over and over again.

I had to struggle so hard to do what I wanted to do that I just thought, Why don't we struggle together? Many of us have made individual changes in our lives that have ended up affecting thousands, even millions, of people.

ILLUSTRATION BY JENNIFER TOBIAS

TEXT BY JOSH A. HALSTEAD

"At age 13 I began learning co-counseling. Theories of liberation and oppression. This enriched my thinking. My world. I could live. I could give. I could love. I had a brush with which to touch-up the world. Ideas popping. I was radicalized. I had a vibrant self. I had expression. I had raves."—Neil Marcus

Poet, playwright, dancer, actor, and artist Neil Marcus (b. 1954) helped launch the disability arts movement. With wit, humor, and physical movement, his play *Storm Reading* challenged normative ideas about disabled people. Other works include *Cripple Poetics: A Love Story* (with Petra Kuppers) and *Special Effects: Advances in Neurology*, a zine he authored, illustrated, and edited from the mid-1980s through the mid-'90s. Each issue features graphics, punk-rock typography, and concrete poetry, mixing stories from Berkeley's independent living movement with philosophical reflections. Distributed via mail, *Special Effects* encouraged disabled and nondisabled readers alike to make art in their own image.

Marcus drew inspiration from the Black Is Beautiful and Gay Liberation movements in the late 1970s. Moving north from Ojai, California, to Berkeley, he received a crash course in identity politics. Reflecting on that time, he states, "As a disabled person, I was struggling with the issues of self-pride. 'Hiding' [my body] in a 'closet.' Struggling with all the issues of other people labeling me….Here was a whole movement happening all around me that was addressing all of it. And being quite 'in your face' about it." His work continues to be loud, proud, and subversively charming. Now coauthoring an autobiography, Marcus has produced a rich legacy of creativity, political action, and community building.

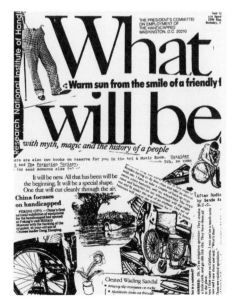

NEIL MARCUS Pages from *Special Effects.*

international symbol of access

ELIZABATH GUFFEY, CONVERSATION WITH STEVEN HELLER

Elizabeth Guffey's book *Designing Disability: Symbols, Space, and Society* explores the history, theory, and politics of the International Symbol of Access (ISA), designed in 1968. Guffey, who is the author of numerous books and articles about design and society, spoke with Steven Heller about her research about the iconography of accessibility.

As a disabled person, were you especially motivated to research the evolution of the International Symbol of Access (ISA)?
The cerebral palsy is unchanged, but my own abilities (walking, standing, etc.) have become more acute and limiting as I've grown older. Just walking across a room takes a lot of effort for me. And so, my own awareness has changed. I understand how able-bodied people may perceive these issues, but I also live as a disabled person today. And this has made me keenly aware of the symbol and its relation to reality.

You write, "When I began writing this book, I was under the illusion that this would be a short article about a design that shaped my life for many years." What did you learn that expanded your coverage?
I thought I knew everything about the symbol, but even I was surprised to learn that it represented an entirely new way of thinking. It was designed in 1968 and only gained acceptance in the US and Europe starting in the mid-1970s. There are probably lots of people who remember a time when the symbol simply didn't exist. But now several generations have grown up with the little wheelchair figure and take it as a normal part of life. I think that familiarity and general acceptance represents a step forward for us a society.

I was surprised to learn about North American and European approaches toward disability itself. The wheelchair symbol is actually a graphic compromise between these two camps. In North America,

international symbol of access
The disability rights movement in the 1960s demanded barrier-free architecture. Organizations and designers created various wheelchair symbols, some including human figures. The icons signaled broader visibility for people with disabilities.

1968 Designed by Susanne Koefoed, seminar organized by the Scandinavian Design Students (SDO).

1969 The head was added by Karl Montan, Rehabilitation International, to humanize the symbol.

disabled people and their advocates often argued that disabled people are just like everyone else—if they could only operate on a level playing field, disabled people could easily assimilate. To begin with, they sought changes in the built environment. They didn't want to live separate from others but asked for accommodations like ramps, railings, wider doorways, etc. There was a big push to install elevators in subway stations and equip buses with wheelchair lifts in order to make public services accessible to everybody.

In parts of Europe, however, you find a different argument—namely that disabled people are, in fact, different from other people; it's been suggested that treating disabled people the same as everyone else is inhumane. That line of thought suggested that disabled people need separate transportation, special housing, and other types of help. The British had a slightly different approach. For many years the British National Health Service not only provided mobility-impaired people with free wheelchairs, but also little three-wheeled cars that could accommodate only one person and their chair. These were called "invalid tricycles," and they came with special privileges, like being able to park on the sidelines of athletic fields and watch games from the car. I was surprised to learn that the wheelchair symbol in use today combines these ideas.

How did this image come about? It started as a stylized schematic of a wheelchair; following the North American approach, it was intended to direct disabled people to legally mandated accommodations. But others insisted that the symbol should look less abstract and more human. This comes closer to the Northern European approach. And so, a circle (representing a head) was placed on the wheelchair's back. Thus, a symbol of a wheelchair became the familiar "person in a wheelchair."

pointing forward The wheelchair icon was designed to indicate accessible entrances, routes, and facilities within buildings. In its many iterations, the International Symbol of Access (ISA) points to the right, serving as a directional sign.

1965 From *Building Standards for the Handicapped*, National Research Council, Canada.

1967 Symbol designed by Paul Arthur & Associates for Expo 67.

How did the wheelchair become the universal sign for access? This always confused me. I am disabled but don't use a wheelchair. In fact, wheelchairs are necessary for a very small subset of individuals with mobility disabilities, to say nothing of the range of disabilities that don't involve physical mobility at all. For years, that symbol troubled me. Over time, I grew to harbor a vague grudge against it. Can only wheelchair users park in special spaces? Am I allowed to sit in the specially designated seats at an airport or theater? Each time I used one of those accommodations, I would ask myself if I was "disabled enough" to use them. But, as I've aged, I find that I really have no choice—I need that extra help and really can't stand around pondering this.

Researching this history helped me see this as more than a communications problem. The modern wheelchair, like the symbol, is actually a very recent invention. The wheelchair was a game-changer for many disabled people. Newly mobile wheelchair users became the first group to advocate for equal rights. The chair seemed a good embodiment of the drive for equal access.

You use the term *misfit design*. What does this mean, exactly? *Misfit* is a word with many meanings. On the one hand, the wheelchair symbol announces a basic misfit between disabled bodies and the built environment. Ramps, elevators, and other accommodations are included as add-ons to help disabled people function in spaces that were not designed or fitted for them.

But also, disabled people have often been cast as social misfits. By the nineteenth century, many disabled people were segregated from society, left uneducated, and lived their entire lives at home or in special schools, hospitals, and care facilities. Still others were poor, beggars, or lived on the margins of society. They had trouble fitting in socially.

At the same time, the wheelchair symbol itself is something of a misfit design. Remember that it underwent a kind of retrofit. It was originally meant to represent a wheelchair, but the requirement to humanize the symbol led to the addition of a large circle representing a head. The result is not a successful design—I would call it a design misfit.

1967 Symbol designed by Selwyn Goldsmith, *Designing for the Disabled.*

1969 Symbol designed by Selwyn Goldsmith, Peter Rea, and students at the Norwich School of Art. The circle over the chest represents pulmonary conditions.

2010 Accessible Icon Project, developed by Sara Hendren and Brian Glenney.

I recall Paris Metro signs that reserve spaces for *"invalides."* **I think it once said "war invalids." At what point were people with disabilities considered part of society that demanded consideration?**

The years after World War II were a major turning point for disabled people. On the one hand, societies throughout history have felt a debt to wounded war veterans—a debt that was sometimes but not always paid. But World War II also saw a higher level of medical care than had ever been possible in the past; more soldiers were able to survive previously fatal injuries. And so, veterans with disabilities became more common. These medical advances also meant that more civilians survived life-threatening conditions. The mortality rate for polio, for example, dropped dramatically at this time, too.

You have to remember that many of these survivors were not born disabled. They took for granted that they had the same right to education, jobs, and housing as their fellow citizens. Those veterans with spinal cord injuries, the many polio survivors, and a host of other people seemed at the time like miracle patients.

But they were also raised with different expectations for their lives. They never had the sense that they were undeserving or deficient. They didn't believe that being disabled meant that they also had to give up the right to live full and active lives. They believed they still had something to contribute, and they asked society to recognize this.

1965 No Barriers logo, from *Architectural Barriers: Progress Report*, President's Committee on Employment of the Handicapped.

SOURCES Interview adapted from Steven Heller, "Making Inaccessibility Accessible," Design Observer, Jan 4, 2018 →designobserver.com/feature/making-inaccessibility-accessible/39739. Illustrations adapted from Elizabeth Guffey, *Designing Disability: Symbols, Space, and Society* (London: Bloomsbury, 2018).

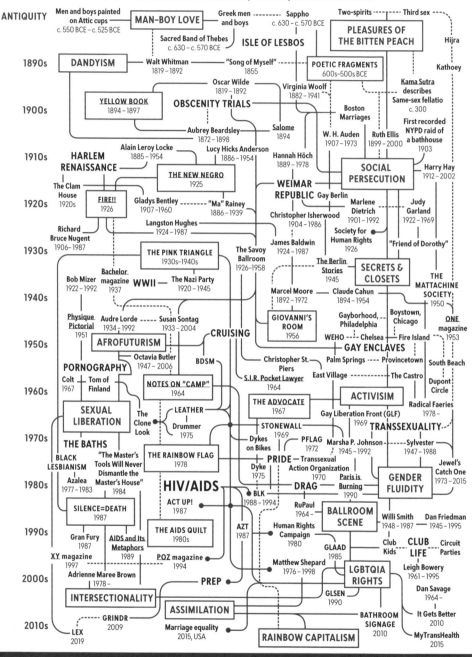

ANTIQUITY

Men and boys painted on Attic cups
c. 550 BCE – c. 525 BCE

MAN–BOY LOVE

Greek men and boys

Sappho
c. 630 – c. 570 BCE

Two-spirits

Third sex

PLEASURES OF THE BITTEN PEACH

Hijra

Sacred Band of Thebes
c. 630 – c. 570 BCE

ISLE OF LESBOS

1890s

DANDYISM

Walt Whitman
1819 – 1892

"Song of Myself"
1855

POETIC FRAGMENTS
600s–500s BCE

Kathoey

Kama Sutra describes Same-sex fellatio
c. 300

1900s

Oscar Wilde
1819 – 1892

Virginia Woolf
1882 – 1941

YELLOW BOOK
1894 – 1897

OBSCENITY TRIALS

Boston Marriages

First recorded NYPD raid of a bathhouse
1903

Aubrey Beardsley
1872 – 1898

Salome
1894

W. H. Auden
1907 – 1973

Ruth Ellis
1899 – 2000

1910s

HARLEM RENAISSANCE

Alain Leroy Locke
1885 – 1954

Lucy Hicks Anderson
1886 – 1954

Hannah Höch
1889 – 1978

SOCIAL PERSECUTION

Harry Hay
1912 – 2002

THE NEW NEGRO
1925

The Clam House
1920s

WEIMAR REPUBLIC

Gay Berlin

1920s

FIRE!!
1926

Gladys Bentley
1907 – 1960

"Ma" Rainey
1886 – 1939

Marlene Dietrich
1901 – 1992

Judy Garland
1922 – 1969

Christopher Isherwood
1904 – 1986

Langston Hughes
1924 – 1987

Society for Human Rights
1926

"Friend of Dorothy"

Richard Bruce Nugent
1906 – 1987

1930s

James Baldwin
1924 – 1987

THE PINK TRIANGLE
1930s–1940s

The Savoy Ballroom
1926–1958

The Berlin Stories
1945

SECRETS & CLOSETS

THE MATTACHINE SOCIETY
1950

Bachelor magazine
1937

Bob Mizer
1922 – 1992

WWII

The Nazi Party
1920 – 1945

1940s

Physique Pictorial
1951

Audre Lorde
1934 – 1992

Susan Sontag
1933 – 2004

Marcel Moore
1892 – 1972

Claude Cahun
1894 – 1954

Gayborhood, Philadelphia

Boystown, Chicago

ONE magazine
1953

CRUISING

GIOVANNI'S ROOM
1956

WEHO

Chelsea

Fire Island

1950s

AFROFUTURISM

Octavia Butler
1947 – 2006

BDSM

GAY ENCLAVES

PORNOGRAPHY

Christopher St. Piers

Palm Springs

Provincetown

South Beach

Colt
1967

Tom of Finland

NOTES ON "CAMP"
1964

S.I.R. Pocket Lawyer
1964

East Village

The Castro

Dupont Circle

1960s

SEXUAL LIBERATION

The Clone Look

LEATHER

THE ADVOCATE
1967

ACTIVISIM

Radical Faeries
1978 –

Drummer
1975

Gay Liberation Front (GLF)
1969

TRANSSEXUALITY

1970s

THE BATHS

BLACK LESBIANISM

"The Master's Tools Will Never Dismantle the Master's House"
1984

THE RAINBOW FLAG
1978

STONEWALL
1969

Dykes on Bikes

PFLAG
1972

Marsha P. Johnson
1945 – 1992

Sylvester
1947 – 1988

Jewel's Catch One
1973 – 2015

Azalea
1977 – 1983

PRIDE

Dyke
1975

Transsexual Action Organization
1970

Paris is Burning
1990

GENDER FLUIDITY

1980s

HIV/AIDS

BLK
1988 – 1994

DRAG

SILENCE=DEATH
1987

ACT UP!
1987

RuPaul
1964 –

BALLROOM SCENE

Willi Smith
1948 – 1987

Dan Friedman
1945 – 1995

1990s

Gran Fury
1987

AIDS and Its Metaphors
1989

THE AIDS QUILT
1980s

AZT
1987

Human Rights Campaign
1980

CLUB LIFE

Circuit Parties

GLAAD
1985

Club Kids

XY magazine
1997

POZ magazine
1994

Matthew Shepard
1976 – 1998

LGBTQIA RIGHTS

Leigh Bowery
1961 – 1995

2000s

Adrienne Maree Brown
1978 –

PREP

INTERSECTIONALITY

GLSEN
1990

Dan Savage
1964 –

ASSIMILATION

BATHROOM SIGNAGE
2010

It Gets Better
2010

2010s

GRINDR
2009

Marriage equality
2015, USA

RAINBOW CAPITALISM

MyTransHealth
2015

LEX
2019

GAYS, QUEERS, FAGS, DYKES, SISSIES, AND ABSTRACT ART

INFOGRAPHIC BY POLYMODE (SILAS MUNRO, BRIAN JOHNSON, AND BEN WARNER)

Queer artists, designers, writers, and philosophers have always existed—often in hiding, sometimes in the open. Design and creativity have played powerful roles in movements to make gay sexuality and diverse gender identities visible and accepted within the broader culture. Artists have also sought to keep queerness queer, by resisting assimilation and embracing difference.

In centuries past, dandies used their witty banter and impeccable taste to challenge and define the style of their eras, paving the way for the camp sensibility, which built new forms of art, life, and expression from styles that had been disgraced or discarded by intellectual elites. During the Harlem Renaissance, expressing non-normative sexuality opened up new worlds for Black artists, writers, designers, and musicians. Believers in Gay Pride turned the rainbow into a global symbol of LGBTQIA+ identity, while AIDS activists took back a Nazi symbol of persecution to speak their rage against a deadly epidemic.

The timeline at left appropriates Alfred Barr Jr.'s famous diagram of modern art to illustrate the clashing ideas, persecutions, and uprisings that have shaped queer history. Key terms from this timeline are defined on the next two pages, followed by profiles of individuals who contributed to queer history, using design to explore identity and forge ideas—intellectual, critical, political, and aesthetic.

Maybe design is a queer practice (odd, strange, different). Designers seek to look at problems from different angles and to see any page, room, product, or process as something that could be changed, improved, or tossed aside. Designer Misha Black has said,

> Designing has always felt gay to me…because it's inherently deviant—it requires imagining that something other than the mainstream offering, the existing thing in front of you, might be great and necessary.…Instead of thinking about getting people to accept LGBTQIA+ people into society as normal, we need to focus on getting people to accept radical paradigm shifts as preferable.

With the Earth in crisis, willingness to live differently may hold the key to human survival.

key terms from queer history

the advocate Still published today, the *Advocate* is the oldest, longest-running LGBTQIA+ publication in the US. It was founded in Los Angeles in 1967 by PRIDE (Personal Rights in Defense and Education). Like the Stonewall Riots, it was inspired by a police raid on a gay bar.

the aids quilt A participatory project begun in 1987, this ongoing memorial quilt consists of hand-sewn panels inscribed with the names of people who have died of AIDS. The names include famous people such as Willi Smith along with thousands of other sons, daughters, and friends lost to the epidemic.

assimilation Some activists see the ultimate goal of the movement for LGBTQIA+ rights as the assimilation of queer identities into the mainstream. This has begun to be achieved through laws such as the US Marriage Equality Act. Similarly, European Jews in the nineteenth century sought to avoid persecution by assimilating with the dominant Christian culture—and yet, anti-Semitism persisted, with devastating results. Forcing immigrants or Indigenous people to give up their language and culture is an additional means of assimilation.

dandyism Beginning in eighteenth-century France and England, men from modest backgrounds who sought to dress and speak with aristocratic elegance were called dandies. Oscar Wilde, a famous dandy and author of *The Picture of Dorian Gray* and other novels and plays, used brilliant turns of phrase to critique bourgeois propriety: "An idea that is not dangerous is unworthy of being called an idea at all." Wilde was tried and convicted in Britain for "gross indecency" (homosexuality) in 1895.

fire!! This 1926 magazine was published by writer Wallace Thurman out of his own apartment. While other publications of the Harlem Renaissance purveyed messages of social uplift, *Fire!!* explored Harlem as a site of nonnormative sexual activities: prostitution, same-sex love, and interracial desire. The magazine's opening manifesto echoed the rhetoric of the Italian Futurists: "FIRE…melting steel and iron bars, poking livid tongues between stone apertures and burning wooden opposition with a cackling chuckle of contempt."

gender fluidity Judith Butler's 1990 book *Gender Trouble* critiques the male/female gender binary and questions heterosexual normativity. Butler defined gender in terms of performed social roles rather than fixed biological categories.

giovanni's room This tragic novel about a young man confronting his desire for other men was written in 1956 by James Baldwin. The narrator is an American living in Paris, where Baldwin lived while writing the novel. The main character, after proposing marriage to his girlfriend, falls in love with an Italian bartender in a gay bar. The novel is about the pain and suffering of living a double life.

harlem renaissance This flowering of Black culture in the 1920s was fueled by queer artists, including singers Gladys Bentley and Bessie Smith and writers Langston Hughes and Alain LeRoy Locke. Gay oppression still continued, however. Prominent Harlem minister Adam Clayton Powell decried "the growing scourge of sexual perversion," and W.E.B. Du Bois fired the business manager of *The Crisis* magazine after he was arrested in a subway restroom for having sex with another man.

intersectionality Legal scholar Kimberlé Crenshaw used the metaphor of a traffic intersection to establish the theory of intersectionality. A Black woman standing in an intersection can be harmed by discrimination on account of both her race and her gender. Today, the concept of intersectionality encompasses overlapping collisions of race, gender identity, class, religion, and other social factors, whose crossings yield unique experiences of privilege and oppression.

lgbtqia+ rights Questioning the male/female gender binary has spurred challenges to binary views of sexual orientation as well. The inclusive acronym LGBTQIA+ (lesbian, gay, bisexual, transgender, queer/questioning, intersex, asexual) asserts that forcing people to identify as either "homosexual" or "heterosexual" is itself a heteronormative idea, imposing society's dominant sexual pattern over all other possible forms of identity and attraction.

the new negro In 1925, philosopher Alain LeRoy Locke published this collection of essays, poems, and short stories by leading figures of the Harlem Renaissance, with illustrations by Aaron Douglas. Locke believed that Black culture should shed its historic burden of oppression and find a new voice.

"notes on 'camp'" Cultural critic Susan Sontag's 1964 essay "Notes on 'Camp'" celebrated the appropriation of extreme beauty and stylized sentimentality often associated with gay style. The essay made the young critic famous and brought critical attention to a derided sensibility.

pink triangle When the Nazis rose to power in 1933, they enforced laws against homosexuality and arrested some 100,000 gay men, forcing them into concentration camps and making them wear pink triangles on their uniforms. More than half of them died between 1933 and 1945, and many remained imprisoned in Germany until the 1970s, when the law against homosexual acts was finally revoked.

pleasure of the bitten peach Mizi Xia was the lover of Duke Ling of Wei in China, c. 500 BCE. One day as they walked together in the royal garden, Xia picked a ripe peach and ate a single bite. It was so delicious, he gave the rest to the duke, who praised him for this pure expression of love. At the time, same-sex relationships were tolerated as long as the men involved also married and had children.

poetic fragments The poet Sappho lived on the Greek island of Lesbos during the seventh century BCE. Her poems, existing today only in fragments, are powerful tributes to erotic love: "Once again Love, that loosener of limbs / bittersweet and inescapable, crawling thing, / seizes me."

rainbow capitalism With the worldwide popularity of Gay Pride parades, corporations have latched onto to queer populations and their enthusiastic allies as marketing opportunities. Although gay-themed advertising campaigns may help mainstream audiences become more comfortable accepting their gay neighbors, "rainbow capitalism" has been critiqued for placing profit over meaningful support for at-risk populations and those who suffer from violence, trauma, and discrimination.

rainbow flag This symbol for the LGBT movement was designed by Gilbert Baker in 1978 to represent the diversity of the gay community. The first flags, used at Gay Pride events in California, were hand-dyed and stitched by volunteers. The rainbow flag was added to the international emoji set in 2016.

secrets and closets In the 1930s, the term *coming out* referred to gay men presenting themselves to their peers in drag balls. These spectacular parties emulated traditional debutante balls, which introduced young women to elite society. Coming out in this sense didn't necessarily mean that one's identity had been previously hidden. These events, however, were noted in mainstream newspapers, so participation could reveal a person's gay identity to a broader public. *Coming out of the closet* later came to mean revealing oneself to friends, family, and beyond.

sexual liberation When the Stonewall Riots erupted in New York in 1969, homosexual acts were illegal nearly everywhere in the US. Cross-dressing was also illegal. Police regularly raided gay bars, arrested the clientele, and collaborated with the Mafia to blackmail wealthier patrons. This time, the community fought back, creating a public riot and launching the Gay Rights movement. Many of the protestors were trans people of color. This event took place alongside sweeping changes in beliefs about sexuality during the 1960s.

silence=death The Silence=Death Project, an activist collective in New York City, created a poster in 1987 featuring a pink triangle and the phrase "Silence=Death." The poster was used extensively by ACT UP, an organization calling for bold political action during the AIDS crisis.

social persecution In the 1910s and '20s, activists and revolutionaries challenged laws against homosexuality in Europe, the US, and the Soviet Union. In Berlin, Dr. Magnus Hirschfeld cofounded an institute dedicated to sexual health and coined the term "transsexualism." Such efforts fought against the continued criminalization of queer sexuality and nonconforming gender identity.

the yellow book This British art periodical was published in the 1890s. Its principal art director was Aubrey Beardsley, whose voluptuous illustrations defied Victorian sexual etiquette. Beardsley, who illustrated Oscar Wilde's *Salome*, was fired from the *Yellow Book* when Wilde appeared to arrive with a copy of the magazine at his trial—in fact, Wilde was carrying a French novel with a yellow cover.

SOURCES Andy Campbell, *Queer X Design: 50 Years of Signs, Symbols, Banners, Logos, and Graphic Art of LGBTQ* (New York: Black Dog & Leventhal, 2019); Misha Kahn, quoted in "Designing with Pride," *A/D/O Journal*, Jun 25, 2019 →a-d-o. com/journal/pride-month-lgbtq-design; Matthew N. Hannah, "Desires Made Manifest: The Queer Modernism of Wallace Thurman's *Fire!!*" *Journal of Modern Literature* 38, no. 3 (2015): 162–80; Anna Pochmara, *The Making of the New Negro: Black Authorship, Masculinity, and Sexuality in the Harlem Renaissance* (Amsterdam: Amsterdam University Press, 2011).

life | walt whitman

TEXT BY ELLEN LUPTON

The poet Walt Whitman was born in 1819 and died in 1892. He was deeply involved in the design and production of his books, including *Leaves of Grass*, published in many editions during his life. The early editions are abundantly erotic, celebrating the physical and emotional love of man for man, man for woman, and man for self.

Whitman learned to set type at age twelve at a newspaper in Brooklyn. He worked in a series of print shops during the 1830s and '40s, setting type and doing presswork; he also edited several newspapers and started his own paper, *The Brooklyn Freeman*. For Whitman, writing, editing, printing, and publishing formed a continuous chain of manual and mental labor. He believed that his skill as a "practical printer" authenticated his role as an American working man.

Whitman self-published the first two editions of *Leaves of Grass*. His friend Andrew Rome printed the first edition in Brooklyn in 1855. Whitman fully controlled the book's design, from choosing the typefaces and the binding to laying out the pages and setting some of the type.

Typography was intrinsic to Whitman's writing process. He said, "The way books are made—that always excites my curiosity: the way books are written—that only attracts me once in a great while." Whitman's focus on the printing process was unusual at the time. He liked to sit in the press room while his books were being printed. Each of the six editions of *Leaves of Grass* has multiple versions because Whitman revised and corrected his work as the proofs came off the press—from fixing typos to altering the page sequence or changing titles.

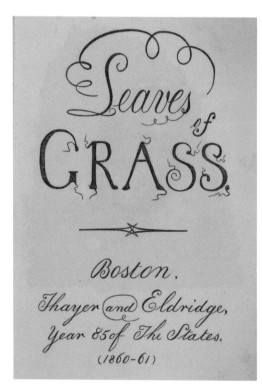

WALT WHITMAN The title page of the third edition of *Leaves of Grass* (1860) features extraordinary lettering by Whitman. The inspiration comes from medical drawings of sperm cells, depicted as tadpole-like creatures with tiny heads and long tails. The joyfully drawn curlicues clinging to the ends of the letters seem to be seeking fertile ground—or just comfort and delight. One sperm cell swims free, becoming the period at the end of the book's title. The poems inside the book make lavish references to sperm: "love-flesh swelling and deliciously aching, / Limitless limpid jets of love hot and enormous, quivering jelly of love, white-blow and delirious juice, / Bridegroom-night of love, working surely and softly into the prostrate dawn. . . ."

The sexual intensity of *Leaves of Grass* diminished in later editions, as Whitman became more famous and took on the role of the nation's poet.

SOURCES Ed Folsom, *Whitman Making Books/Books Making Whitman: A Catalog and Commentary* (Iowa City: University of Iowa, 2005). See also Gary Schmidgall, *Walt Whitman: A Gay Life* (New York: Dutton Adult, 1997).

TEXT BY ELLEN LUPTON

Born in Springfield, Illinois, in 1899, Ellis became the first woman in Michigan to run her own printing company. Ellis, whose mother died when she was twelve years old, lived openly as a lesbian throughout her life. She brought girlfriends home as a teenager, and her father accepted her sexuality without judgment.

In 1937, Ellis moved to Detroit with her partner, Ceciline "Babe" Franklin. They started the Ellis and Franklin Printing Company in the front room of their house. Ellis later recalled, "I was working for a printer and I said to myself, if I can do this for him, how come I can't do it for myself?"

Ellis and Franklin's home was both a letterpress printshop and a vibrant gathering place—known as "The Spot"—for Detroit's African American queer community. Ellis and Franklin offered assistance to young people in need of food, books, or a place to stay. The couple parted ways in the 1960s.

When Ellis was seventy years old, the Stonewall Riots erupted in New York City, bringing new power and visibility to the fight for LGBTQIA+ rights. Ellis joined the burgeoning movement, appearing at national events and speaking out for gay and lesbian equality. On her one-hundredth birthday, Ellis led the annual dyke march in San Francisco in 1998. She died at age 101. Today, the Ruth Ellis Center in Detroit carries on the legacy of this remarkable activist and businesswoman by serving the city's at-risk LGBTQIA+ youth.

RUTH ELLIS In her printshop, Ruth Ellis produced letterheads, fliers, posters, and raffle tickets for churches and businesses using a platen press, also called a jobber. This type of press was commonly used in small printing establishments.

SOURCES Terrance Heath, "Over the Course of 101 Years, the Nation's Longest-Lived Lesbian Was Always Out & Proud," *LGBTQ Nation*, Feb 13, 2019 →lgbtqnation.com/2019/02/course-101-years-nations-longest-lived-lesbian-always-proud/; Jason A. Michael, "Ruth Ellis: A Century Worth of History," *Pride Source*, May 2, 2003 →pridesource.com/article/11497.

life | claude cahun and marcel moore

TEXT BY JENNIFER TOBIAS

"Neuter is the only gender that always suits me," Claude Cahun famously declared in their "anti-autobiography" *Aveux non Avenus* (Disavowed Confessions, 1930), produced with their lifelong partner and collaborator Marcel Moore. On the cover, the title forms a cross or addition sign, suggesting plurality and complexity. The word *non* (no) appears repeatedly in the form of an *X*, referencing the book's paradoxical title as well as the unknown or undefined.

The photomontages inside the book experiment with surrealist themes such as the uncanny double or twin, the mirror, and disembodied eyes and limbs. Several montages include photographs of Cahun and Moore, each taken by the other.

Pioneers of gender transcendence and creative collaboration, Cahun (born Lucy Schwob, 1894–1954) and her stepsister Moore (born Suzanne Malherbe, 1892–1972) manifested their beliefs in a lifetime of publishing. Born to wealthy families, the two took on gender-ambiguous names in 1915. In Paris in the early 1920s, they joined the city's salon culture with its vibrant gay and lesbian scene. Moore designed posters and postcards promoting the exotic dancer Nadja (Beatrice Wanger). Cahun's four-part manifesto "*L'Idée-maîtresse*" (The Mistress Idea, 1921) describes their all-encompassing commitment to the "mistress" of queer love: "The love that dare not speak its name lies like a golden haze upon my horizon....I am in her; she is in me; and I will follow her always, never losing sight of her."

Gender fluidity is integral to Cahun's writing, Moore's illustrations, and Moore's photographs of Cahun performing gender identity by donning costumes, makeup, and styling. As critic Tirza True Latimer points out, their practice anticipated the photographs of gender play created by other avant-garde artists, including Marcel

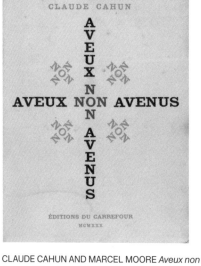

CLAUDE CAHUN AND MARCEL MOORE *Aveux non Avenus* (Disavowed Confessions) (Paris: Editions du Carrefour, 1930). Collection of National Gallery of Australia, Gift of Galerie Zabriskie, Paris 1994, NGA 94.176.

Duchamp, who posed as Rrose Sélavy, a female persona.

Cahun and Moore belonged to several anti-fascist groups in France. Fleeing Nazi encroachment in 1937, they moved to a comfortable house in Jersey, an island off the Normandy coast. When Nazis occupied the island in 1940, the pair applied their talents to producing and distributing resistance leaflets. These handwritten or typewritten works were reproduced on cigarette paper or in colored inks on toned paper. Moore translated illicit BBC Radio reports into German; Cahun rendered the translations into couplets or conversations, borrowing the persona *Der Soldat Ohne Namen* (The Soldier Without a Name).

Cahun and Moore, then in their early fifties, disguised themselves as elderly women and distributed the leaflets at German gathering spots and a cemetery for German soldiers. They slipped flyers onto car windshields and into soldiers' coat pockets. Scholar Katherine Smith explains, "Their flyers brazenly requested '*Bitte verbreiten,*' or 'please distribute,' which recipients apparently obliged: three hundred fifty flyers, representing about one-seventh of the press run, were confiscated throughout the island."

Caught one day with an unusually large supply of cigarette paper, Cahun and Moore were imprisoned and sentenced to death in 1944. German authorities were slow to prosecute the case because they didn't believe that two elderly women could deploy a sophisticated counter-propaganda operation without male assistance. Cahun and Moore were saved by Nazi fear of public outcry and, ultimately, by the liberation of the island in 1945.

After the war, the pair returned to Jersey. Mortality became the focus of Cahun's self-portraits prior to her death in 1954. Moore's late-life activities are shadowy; she died by suicide in 1972.

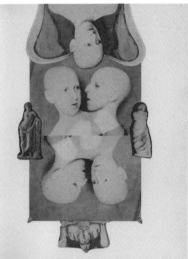

SOURCES Tirza True Latimer, "Entre Nous: Between Claude Cahun and Marcel Moore," *GLQ: A Journal of Lesbian and Gay Studies* 12, no. 2 (2006): 197–216; Katherine Smith, "Claude Cahun as Anti-Nazi Resistance Fighter," Grey Art Gallery, New York University, 2015 →greyartgallery.nyu.edu/2015/12/ claude-cahun-as-anti-nazi-resistance-fighter; Louise Downey, "Claude Cahun: Freedom Fighter," National Portrait Gallery, May 9, 2017 →npg.org.uk/blog/claude-cahun-freedom-fighter.

life | susan sontag

TEXT BY ELLEN LUPTON

Susan Sontag (1933–2004) chronicled and critiqued the cycle of styles, asking how art forms become symbols of revolution one day and signs of ordinary consumerism the next—or, conversely, how popular banalities morph into signifiers bearing ineffable emotional complexity. According to Sontag, popular culture constantly ingests and regurgitates its creative offspring.

Sontag wrote "Notes on 'Camp'" in 1964. She defined camp as a coded sensibility—commonly embraced by queer communities—that exaggerates familiar notions of beauty and elegance until they become a parodic commentary on themselves. Camp is stylized, ironic, and quotational rather than authentic, heroic, or original. It embraces artifice over nature and androgyny over fixed gender roles. In camp, "It's not a lamp but a 'lamp'; not a woman but a 'woman.'"

Less well known is her 1970 essay "Posters: Advertisement, Art, Political Artifact, Commodity." She wrote that posters assimilate radical artistic ideas into an easy-to-eat medium. Nineteenth-century lithographs sold cookies, booze, nightclub acts, and the city itself, creating "urban, public space as an arena of signs: the image- and word-choked façades and surfaces of the great modern cities."

Sontag was reticent about her private life. She announced her bisexuality in 1995 but rarely spoke publicly about her relationships with women. The photographer Annie Leibowitz was her longtime companion. After her death in 2004, lesbian activist Sarah Schulman said, "Sontag never applied her massive intellectual gifts toward understanding her own condition as a lesbian, because to do so publicly would have subjected her to marginalization."

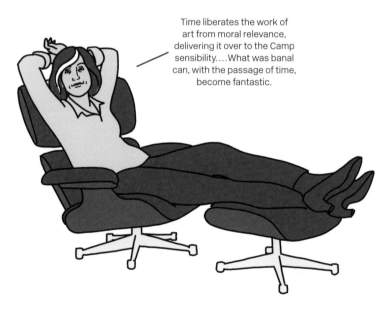

Time liberates the work of art from moral relevance, delivering it over to the Camp sensibility.…What was banal can, with the passage of time, become fantastic.

SOURCES Susan Sontag, "Notes on 'Camp,'" in *Against Interpretation and Other Essays* (New York: Farrar, Straus and Giroux, 1964); "Posters: Advertisement, Art, Political Artifact, Commodity," in Dugald Stermer, ed., *The Art of Revolution: 96 Posters from Cuba* (New York: McGraw-Hill, 1970); Patrick Moore, "Susan Sontag and a Case of Curious Silence," *Los Angeles Times*, Jan 4, 2004 →latimes.com/archives/la-xpm-2005-jan-04-oe-moore4-story.html. Our portrait is inspired by a photograph of Sontag relaxing on her Eames lounge chair, a mid-century symbol of power and status.

TEXT BY ELLEN LUPTON

Willi Smith (1948–1987) designed drapey, sporty, billowy, relaxed clothes intended for everyone, not just elite members of society. He grew up in Philadelphia with his grandmother, who raised him after his parents divorced and labored as a house-keeper to send her gifted grandson to col-lege. Parsons School of Design dismissed Smith in 1967 for having a relationship with a male student. Smith's brilliant talent took flight within New York City's downtown art scene, where he collaborated with artists while designing sportswear for a main-stream fashion company.

Smith founded WilliWear Ltd. with Laurie Mallet in 1976. WilliWear clothing was practical, experimental, and affordable. Anyone could walk into a department store and buy his jackets, shirts, skirts, or pants, whose loose lines fit varied body types.

Smith also released his designs as sewing patterns for Butterick and McCall's. People could buy these paper patterns for a few dollars and make their own WilliWear. Recalling the Philadelphia neighborhood of his childhood, where women made clothes for themselves and their families, Smith believed that home sewing enabled people to truly make his clothing their own.

Smith collaborated with artists Barbara Kruger and Jenny Holzer to emblazon T-shirts with provocative slogans. He com-missioned graphic designer Bill Bonnell to create experimental visual branding, and he published *WilliWear News*, a big news-print poster that folded down into a zine.

Smith suddenly became ill in 1987 and died of AIDS at age thirty-nine. The world lost a generous and gifted visionary, who created art for daily use.

The more commercial I become, the more creative I can be because I am reaching more people.

SOURCES Alexandra Cameron Cunningham, *Willi Smith: Street Couture* (New York: Cooper Hewitt, Smithsonian Design Museum and Rizzoli, 2020). In our fantasy portrait, Willi Smith relaxes on furniture designed by his friend Dan Friedman (1945–1995), a graphic designer and furniture designer who was part of the downtown art scene where Smith thrived. Smith's apartment contained his rich personal collection of art, artifacts, and photography, including several furniture pieces by Friedman, who also designed WilliWear's Paris showroom.

ILLUSTRATIONS BY JENNIFER TOBIAS

Jobs are relationships between employees and employers, governed by rules of fairness and accountability. People living in modern societies put enormous value on jobs. We identify with our jobs, hate our jobs, wish we could get different jobs, and wait to go home from our jobs. People spend a large part of their education preparing for jobs that may not exist in the future. Our careers, however, include more than just jobs. Designers and artists create work outside the parameters of traditional employment. Some of life's most meaningful work isn't paid, from caregiving to activism and self-publishing. This chapter looks at some of the different ways designers work, from paid positions to independent production.

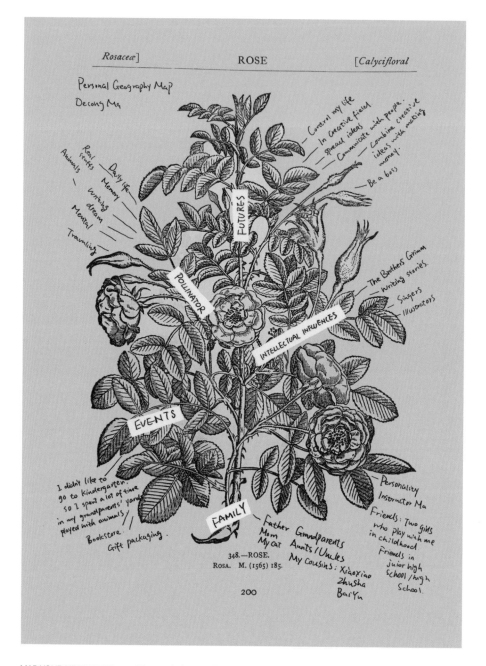

Rosaceæ]   ROSE   [*Calycifloral*

Personal Geography Map
Decong Ma

FUTURES
— Control my life
— In creative field
— Special ideas
— Communicate with people
— Combine creative ideas with making money.
— Be a boss

Real stuffs
Animals
Daily life
Memory
Writing dream
Mental
Travelling

POLLINATOR

The Brothers Grimm
writing stories.
Singers
Illustrators

INTELLECTUAL INFLUENCES

EVENTS

I didn't like to go to kindergarten, so I spent a lot of time in my grandparents' yard, played with animals.
Bookstore.
Gift packaging.

Personality
Instructor Ma
Friends: Two girls who play with me in childhood
Friends in junior high school / high school.

FAMILY — Father Grandparents
Mom Aunts / Uncles
My cat My cousins: XiaoXiao
                            ZhuSha
                            BaiYu

348.—ROSE.
ROSA. M. (1565) 185.

200

MAP YOUR NETWORK Try making a mind map when you are preparing to search for a job or internship or considering a career change. This collage is built on a vintage botanical illustration. Designer Decong Ma has diagrammed her family ties, intellectual influences, life events, inspirations, and future goals.

SOURCES Marcus Fairs, "Karim Rashid Says Unpaid Internships Are Better Value Than 'Exploiting' University Courses," Dezeen, Apr 2, 2019 →dezeen.com/2019/04/02/karim-rashid-unpaid-internships-row; Alex Greenberger, "Association of Art Museum Directors Calls for End of Unpaid Internships," *ArtNews*, Jun 20, 2019 →artnews.com/art-news/news/aamd-resolution-paid-internships-12824.

ILLUSTRATION BY DECONG MA

internships

TEXT BY ELLEN LUPTON AND TANVI SHARMA

Internships provide crucial work experience and can sometimes lead to job offers or lasting professional relationships. Design internships are offered by studios, publishing companies, and marketing agencies as well as by in-house design departments at corporations, universities, hospitals, and community organizations. Internships aren't just for students; many entry-level design positions are posted as temporary internships. A design intern might have to run errands and take notes as well as perform an endless array of digital duties—from scanning and photo retouching to drawing logos and tweaking type.

In many countries, including the US, commercial businesses are required to pay interns. In the US, exceptions are made when students receive college credit for the internship. (In this problematic situation, students pay tuition for doing work that benefits a business or organization.) Interns may be paid a stipend or honorarium lower than the minimum wage; some companies cover transportation.

Unpaid internships do have defenders. In the opinion of product designer Karim Rashid, working for free as an intern is more beneficial to the worker then paying tuition to a university. Hosting an intern takes time and effort. Inexperienced interns need guidance. Internships can help less-skilled workers to enter the field.

Although US law allows not-for-profit organizations to offer unpaid internships, the practice is controversial. In 2019, the American Association of Art Museum Directors (AAMD) encouraged museums to pay all interns because unpaid positions favor people from prosperous backgrounds.

Tanvi Sharma shares her experience as an intern here and on the following pages. The pressure on students to find internships can be overwhelming. Be open to other experiences as well, such as community service, activism, writing and publishing, or teaching kids at a local school.

Tanvi Sharma explains how to get the most from an internship

→ The network of designers and artists you have been exposed to in any capacity is a good place to start looking for an internship. If someone isn't advertising open positions, e-mail them anyway.

→ Reach out to people in the industry who were in your position a couple of years ago. I was fortunate enough to have peers who could recommend me for internships that they ended up turning down.

→ During your internship, request time with your advisor to have conversations about your personal growth and trajectory.

→ If you can, take up personal projects on the side that align with what's going on in your workplace. Ask for feedback.

→ Conduct short, informal interviews with people you are meeting at work and learn what you can in casual conversations. Ask questions. Connect with these new colleagues on social media and stay in touch. Your future self will thank you.

→ I invited some friends to start a collaborative spreadsheet where we could keep each other accountable for follow-ups. Your peers will have your back.

voice | tanvi sharma

CONVERSATION WITH ELLEN LUPTON

TANVI SHARMA	Designer
PRONOUNS	She, her

Tell us about your background. I'm from the outskirts of New Delhi, India. I was born and grew up there, majoring in natural sciences in my last two years of high school. I came to the US as an international student at MICA [Maryland Institute College of Art] in 2016. It was my first time out of the country. I started out as a painting major but switched to graphic design in my junior year, as I found a community in graphic design that was relatively open to challenging itself and finding new ways to problem-solve.

However, graphic design does suffer from the same mindset painting did—it is fixated on a particular idea of what the audience and community looks like. The aesthetic choices that we were taught to make did not reflect the social diversity that I experienced or the visuals I grew up with. I am still learning to reconcile the two.

What internships did you have while you were a student? In my time as a student, I interned twice. The first was with Matt Bollinger, a painter, stop-motion animator, and professor at SUNY Purchase College in upstate New York. It was an unpaid internship, and although I benefited a lot from Matt's wisdom (and free meals), I spent the summer not being able to afford rent, and I relied on my friends who were studying in the city to lend me their couches for a couple weeks at a time.

I worked as an assistant animator on the stop-motion animation film *Three Rooms* that Matt was then working on. I developed the concept, strategy, and execution plan, and I explored alternative methods developing and crafting animated experiences. When not animating, I was organizing the studio space or doing assigned readings.

The second internship was with Zach Lieberman, a designer, coder, cofounder of the School for Poetic Computation, and professor at MIT Media Lab. During the internship, I contributed to a myriad of projects and also worked on my own generative art project. I helped design a website for Zach, assisted in documentation of ongoing work, and helped develop generative motion graphic tools built in openFrameworks. I got paid the minimum wage in New York.

How did you get your internships? In my junior year, after I switched my major to graphic design, the pressure to get an internship among my peers was intense. Somehow, the pipeline to employment seemed such that if you're seeking an internship and don't get one, your chances in the industry dwindle. This expectation prevents equity of opportunity.

I found my internships by reaching out to people I wanted to work with and learn from. My faculty at MICA happened to be connected with my internship advisors and helped me with recommendations.

Describe a low point as an intern. Ah, once the apartment where I was couch surfing got bedbugs. That sucked! That said, initially, it was tough to feel comfortable with not meeting the expectations I set for myself or resisting the urge to compare my experience with that of others. Why am I not getting access to the same opportunities as other (more privileged) students, despite having the same skill set?

Oftentimes, students don't share with each other the challenges they face entering the industry due to a fear of being perceived as not trying hard enough or being a good fit.

Describe a high point as an intern.
Both of my internship advisors are also professors. Knowing how to teach and mentor is definitely an art. It was an absolute thrill to work with people who have a passion for teaching and would send me home with books to read and resources to tap into. The mental shift to doing work for a class versus for a client can be a juggle if you're not used to following detailed instructions, as opposed to subjective exploration. Given that, my supervisors encouraged and challenged me to bring my perspective to projects. I appreciated that.

Now that you have graduated, you are looking for an internship again. Tell us about that. I didn't imagine I'd be looking for more internships postgraduation. It's tough to be an international student in the current climate, as most companies won't be issuing work visas for the near future. I'm currently looking for full-time employment so I can stay in the US for another year and build on my experiences. In all honesty, I am skeptical of the process. The trajectory to employment is skewed; even equal-opportunity employers have their biases. With more and more hiring happening through algorithmic sifting, who is to say that a group would not prefer someone they don't have to sponsor in the future? How is embracing diversity reflected in the hiring decisions?

starting out

TEXT BY ELLEN LUPTON

Working in a small or midsize design studio or agency is a dream job for many designers. Typically, studios attract varied projects from a range of clients. In a company that employs just a few designers, a junior designer will likely report directly to the firm's founder and creative director. In a company with a bigger staff, an entry-level designer might report to a senior designer or account manager—a layer between the junior employee and the commander in chief. Alternatives to these hierarchical studio structures include worker-owned cooperative businesses, single-person shops, and studios organized as nonprofit organizations.

Some studios clearly define the duties of new employees. Others allow a designer's responsibilities to change and grow depending on their abilities—and what's needed by the company that week or that month. Bigger companies tend to have more formal hiring practices.

Some entry-level studio positions are dominated by production tasks such as making clipping paths in Photoshop, entering data into spreadsheets, or building presentation decks. Other positions are more creative from the outset. A junior designer might be asked to develop ideas for a pitch or work on a team with a group of designers, brainstorming ideas and collaborating to develop the best ones.

Many entry-level studio jobs are defined as internships, an arrangement that allows the company to pay a low wage and provide zero benefits. (In many US states, an intern can be paid less than the legal minimum wage.) Such internships sometimes serve as a trial period that could end in a permanent or semipermanent position. Other entry-level positions are defined as freelance or contract work. This means that the worker is an independent contractor rather than an employee of the company—like an Uber driver. Contract workers can also be hired by a staffing agency, which pays the worker. This limits the company's responsibility for providing benefits such as health insurance or paid vacations. It also means that the company isn't committed to a long-term relationship. Like an internship, a freelance gig can be a path to a permanent position. This is not always the case, however; many companies keep contractors revolving on and off their staff to avoid making full-time hires.

Designers work long hours at many studios. When there's a big deadline, everyone jumps in. Leaving early is not an option. Some companies exist in permanent crisis mode. If the studio head likes to take on too many projects and thrives on andrenaline, late nights are likely to be the norm.

Are entry-level jobs like these worth the long hours and low pay? Most professionals can't work this way indefinitely. It's tough to survive in London, New York, or Seattle as a permanent intern. Some young workers get financial help from their parents for a few years out of school. With luck, perseverance, and a hearty dose of privilege, an early period of hardship might give way to a permanent position with appropriate compensation. (Doctors, lawyers, and celebrity chefs endure similar trials by fire.) For some, the intensity of studio work can yield creative growth while building a base of practical knowledge and work experience.

graphic hierarchy

$104K	# CREATIVE DIRECTOR
$83K	**ART DIRECTOR**
$66.5K	*Project Manager*
$67.5K	**MULTIMEDIA DESIGNER**
$54K	*Graphic Designer*
$53K	**ILLUSTRATOR**
$47.5K	*Digital Asset Manager*
$41.5K	DESKTOP PUBLISHER/LAYOUT ARTIST
$37K	*Production Assistant*

SOURCE Midpoint salaries for starting employees in the US, adapted from Robert Half/The Creative Group, 2018 Salary Guide →compensationreport.com/report/robert-half-creative-group-2018-salary-guide. Actual salaries vary from region to region and from business to business.

TYPEFACES | CHOLLA AND ODILE | BY SIBYLLE HAGMANN

IKEA string
lights,
designed
by Sarah Fager

Have you thought about how many trees we will kill printing this envelope?

BYO
coffee

Keurig
cups

cordless
mouse

task
rabbit

two-person shop

Ana is a designer at Kwik Kom, a small firm headed by Josh, a lone account executive. They work together in a one-room office lit by a single bulb. Josh talks all day on the phone with his clients—low-end law firms and long-haul trucking companies. The work is banal, but Ana is in charge of all the design and production, so she is learning technical skills.

small studio

Darius is an intern at WeDoGood, a firm whose clients are not-for-profit organizations. Projects are led by the three creative directors, each working with a team of two or three designers. Darius is the most junior person, so he gets stuck with a lot of production work. His first independent project is a direct-mail piece for an environmental group.

Bauhaus pendant lamp, designed by Marianne Brandt

Bespoke chandelier, designed by Lindsey Adelman

On-staff barista

Nespresso

mouse killer

therapy Chihuahua

famous studio

Charlene is a freelance contractor at Five Famous Guys. The guys who run this company are so famous, some young designers would work there for free. That's not legal, so instead, they work there for almost free. Most of the designers do freelance work to pay the rent. They work until 9:00 p.m. almost every night (long after the FGs have left for the day).

ILLUSTRATION BY JENNIFER TOBIAS

branding agency

Yue is a junior designer at BrandHaus, a company with eighty employees and offices in New York, London, and Cleveland. No one at BrandHaus wants to work in Cleveland, but the wages go further there. Yue reports to an account manager, and the account manager reports to a creative director. BrandHaus will sponsor Yue's visa if she moves to Cleveland.

voice | farah kafei

CONVERSATION WITH ELLEN LUPTON AND JENNIFER TOBIAS

FARAH KAFEI	Designer, Doubleday & Cartwright
PRONOUNS	She, her

Tell us about your first year out of school. What was your first job?
My first year out of school was overwhelming—there were so many
drastic changes going on. You go from having been a student for the last
sixteen years of your life to not knowing what the next year or two might
look like. You go from having a month break in the winter to spend with
family or do whatever to spending New Year's Eve in the office. After graduating from Pratt in Brooklyn, I started an internship at a dream studio,
Sagmeister & Walsh. I was there for almost a year, and while I learned a
lot, it wasn't the right fit for me. I realized I didn't know much about working in the design industry or what I really wanted from it. When I started
looking for the next thing, that first experience made me open-minded
about where I could work and more selective about what I was looking for
from a job.

Where do you work now? I work at Doubleday & Cartwright in Williams-
burg, Brooklyn, a creative studio in the sports, art, and culture sphere.
We work with brands like Nike and Red Bull on culturally leaning projects.
Coming out of school, I really loved branding and identity work, but working at DD&C has introduced me to art direction. My day-to-day doesn't
necessarily look like what we studied in school. It includes story mining,
research, strategy, and looking for photographers or directors. That's
some of what I did when I had the opportunity to work on an editorial
series for Nike Women. We ended up shooting a short doc in Mexico for
one of the stories we found, about team Carta Blanca, a group of incredible grandmas who have been ballin' together for over seventy years!
Working on that as an art director was fun, new territory to explore.

Tell me about 100s Under 100. My friend Valentina Vergara and I met Carly Ayres through our senior thesis, which explored the underrepresentation of women in design history and as professors in design classrooms. We invited Carly to participate in a panel discussion that we held to try and bridge that gap a little, and she ended up becoming a friend and mentor. After graduating, Carly was helpful in connecting us with designers and referring us to jobs. She really believed in us and made us feel powerful! Valentina and I started attending these incredible events she organized called 100sUnder100 #show-n-tell. These talks are a physical manifestation of an online community that she started several years ago through Slack. She had been producing the #show-n-tells for some time and wanted to move on, but didn't want them to stop, so she asked Valentina and me if we'd like to take the reins! These informal events give creatives of all kinds the space to talk about their ideas, process, hobbies, work, or anything they're passionate about to an audience of creative peers. There's always drinks and mingling before and after the talks, which is a great opportunity to meet other people in a low-pressure and non-networky kind of way.

What advice do you have for someone entering the field? Never underestimate yourself. Recent grads are made to feel that with little experience, we have to be overworked and underpaid, and we are constantly being made to prove ourselves. Experience obviously matters, but young people bring different skills to the table. We haven't been molded by years of working in the industry, which can mean fresh perspectives and new ways of thinking. We have an invaluable connection to our generation, which is often the target audience for major clients. As young creatives, we add a lot of value to a team! In film or music, you don't hear, "She's only twenty, what does she know?"

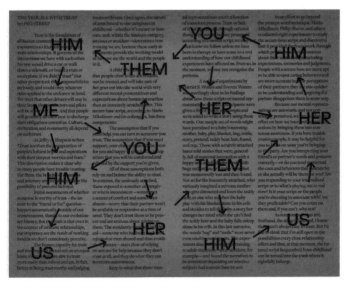

FARAH KAFEI AND ADAM BLUFARB Zine, *Push & Pull.*

voice | valentina vergara

CONVERSATION WITH ELLEN LUPTON AND JENNIFER TOBIAS

VALENTINA VERGARA Freelance designer

PRONOUNS She, her

Tell us about your education and background. I was born in Bogota but grew up in Miami. In 2014, I moved to New York to study at Pratt Institute. During senior year, when my best friend Farah and I were choosing our senior thesis professors, we noticed there were few women as options. We couldn't shake the fact that our student body (which was around 75 percent female) was not reflected by our faculty. It was difficult to find a female mentor who could understand us and give us insight.

We started questioning everything. Why is this happening? Why are the people at the head of classrooms not reflective of the student body? Why, in our four years of design education, didn't we learn about more people like us in our field? These questions uncovered hard truths, and Led By Example was born. We worked closely with department chair Jessica Wexler, who became our mentor throughout the whole project.

Led By Example is a graphic design–focused campaign that rallies for placing more women at the head of our classrooms and for including more women in the history of design. As part of the campaign, we organized an exhibition called *Missing Pages*, where we researched ten designers working from around 1900 to the present day. Our goal was to educate ourselves, our peers, and our professors and ultimately to create the physical and metaphorical space for ourselves that had been missing throughout our education. For the exhibition, we printed our research on large pages that mimic pages scanned from our "missing textbook." We also produced and held a panel discussion called "Against All Odds" with industry professionals, where we conducted a deep-dive conversation about diversity in our field.

What happened after graduating? Upon graduating, I immediately started freelancing. I had a variety of jobs at small studios, agencies, and in-house design departments. I picked up a lot of skills freelancing—most importantly, how to negotiate my rate. My first freelance job was in-house at an underwear company, which gave me insight about working for a brand.

Later, I worked for a small studio focused on art and design clients. For the first month, the position was an internship that paid a small stipend. In the beginning, I was offered an unreasonably low stipend for a city as expensive as NYC—which wouldn't even cover rent. But I negotiated, and the second offer was about $1,400 a month, which was still low, and I ended up working forty-plus hours a week. If I did the math, I was getting about $3 an hour. I figured I'd stay, however, for the experience and because it's the expectation to work for low wages when you're just starting out.

Honestly, this wasn't the best environment for me personally, but I did learn a lot. I got to work on projects from brainstorming to research to the final product. Plus, I gained a mentor from working closely with the senior designer. To this day, she still answers my questions about negotiating rates for freelance projects. After a few months at this studio, I decided to look for something that better suited my goals. The year before, I had interviewed about a freelance position at the Museum of Arts and Design (MAD) and, coincidentally, when I started looking for a job again, MAD was looking for an in-house designer. The creative director reached out to me and suggested I apply for the job—and I got it!

Tell us about working at the museum. As an in-house designer, I had to follow brand guidelines, but I still got to work on a range of projects—from animations and branding exhibitions to redesigning the entire website. The job provided an amazing work-life balance, which was very important to me after my previous job, and it also allowed me to take on freelance projects after hours. Being the only designer at MAD pushed me to learn new skills outside of my comfort zone, furthering my career in ways I would not have imagined.

Eventually, though, I reached my fullest potential there, and I decided it was time to move on. I am currently exploring other sectors, meeting new people, and continuing to grow. I still reflect on what a good mentor my creative director at MAD was, especially given that he was a man. Because I'd had such sour experiences with male professors at Pratt, I had thought that the best mentors were going to be the people who shared my identity. But the reality is that gender is just a construct and every situation is different. I've learned that not all women are going to support you. Society often pits women—and marginalized people in general—against each other. But the truth is, there is power in numbers, and uplifting and empowering each other is the best way to begin to dismantle this extremely flawed system.

Why did you like your museum job better than working in a small studio? A work-life balance is important for staying sane. Some people are completely fine with studios and agencies that expect you to stay until 9:00 p.m. or later every day, but personally, I don't think I can be the best version of myself as a designer/creative if I'm not in the right headspace. I also don't want to eat and breathe work all the time. I think there needs to be a balance in life to be able to keep being creative.

design leaders

CONVERSATION WITH ELLEN LUPTON AND JENNIFER TOBIAS

For many designers, the first requirement for success is finding stable employment with appropriate compensation in a healthy, inclusive workplace. This success can take a surprising number of forms. Designers work in small studios and big agencies as well as start-ups and cultural institutions. They teach in colleges and universities. They run their own practices and sell their own products. Many nine-to-five designers have side hustles. Successful designers reinvest in the profession by speaking, publishing, running workshops, becoming mentors, sharing their work, and being open to learning and critique.

Among women designers, few have achieved influence and admiration at the scale of Paula Scher. In the early 1970s, she landed a job at CBS Records in New York before founding her own studio, Koppel and Scher. When she joined the New York office of Pentagram in 1991, she was the only woman among fourteen male partners in New York, London, and San Francisco. At a global partners' meeting in the early 1990s, she showed her partners a series of posters she had designed for the Public Theater; some of her London colleagues walked out, appalled by her clashing type styles. She put aside their modernist disdain and kept working—and her posters for the Public Theater ended up attracting prominent commissions from museums and concert halls.

Achieving stratospheric success requires years of hard work as well as confidence, courage, and lots of talent. Until recently, it was difficult for any woman to rise to this level of prominence, and nearly all "famous" designers in the West were White. The status quo is beginning to shift as more people who are marginalized by sexism and/or racism take positions of influence in design and across society.

Being a design goddess is hard work. Scher is constantly asked to speak at conferences and to field requests for jobs and internships, and her work is subjected to constant scrutiny on the internet. We asked Scher if she had encountered obstacles as a woman. She said, "Sure, almost from day one. But having obstacles wasn't an oddity. When I did notice people perceiving me as weaker or less powerful—particularly when I was young and the clients were older—I overcame it by being funnier or faster or using whatever I had. Everybody has obstacles. If you expect to receive wonderful treatment and you don't receive it, then I guess it is very disappointing. If you have no expectation of it, then it doesn't really matter."

For many designers, becoming a leader means creating work that gets seen, shared, and understood by one's peers or by a broader public. This can happen in ways large and small. Designer Shira Inbar says, "Put yourself in the conversation and publish your work and ideas. Don't be too precious about waiting for something to be perfect before showing the world. No one cares. Post things. Share things. Look for ways to participate through your work." Blogging, speaking at events, and joining local design organizations are all ways to participate in the larger design discourse throughout your career.

ILLUSTRATIONS BY JENNIFER TOBIAS

voice | amy lee walton

CONVERSATIONS WITH MAURICE CHERRY AND ELLEN LUPTON

AMY LEE WALTON	Product designer, Netflix; formerly at Mapbox
PRONOUNS	She, her

MAURICE CHERRY: You were a cartographer at Mapbox. What's the secret of making a good map? A good map should have a good use case. It's important to be thinking about why a person would be using a map. If you are making a map for navigation, you want to make sure that certain things are highlighted, like larger-scale motorways and road networks. If you're making a map for skiing or hiking outdoors, you want to make sure that you differentiate different types of paths. You want to put as much detail as you can into a map, so that you can cater what you're pulling out and enhance the map for that use case.

How has technology made cartography better? Print maps have been around for hundreds of years, and they are really well done. A lot of surveying was done during the Industrial Revolution, and map designers knew the land very well. They used watercolors and other manual techniques to indicate different terrains. A great thing about digital web maps is that you can kind of see things at many different levels. You can look at the global view of the map on your phone or on your computer. You can zoom all the way in to street level and see your street or the alley by your job, or you can see all the Starbucks on the street where you work.

Explain what Mapbox does. Mapbox provides building blocks for developers to create apps that help people navigate the planet. Mapbox does things from designing map styles that developers can plug and play and use in their apps to creating APIs that developers can use to calculate different directions for walking or driving or cycling.

What did you learn at Mapbox? I learned how to frame problems and projects. I love the details, I love the minutiae and digging very deep into it. I learned a lot about taking a step back and looking at something from a higher level and thinking about why it's important.

How did you get started? As a youth, I would make greeting cards. I would hand-draw them or collage them or create something in the computer. I've always felt comfortable with computers. My dad worked in technology, and my undergrad at University of Cincinnati was in Information Systems. The fact that I look at JavaScript or Processing as a kind of paintbrush has helped me bounce back and forth between designing and programming.

At Mapbox, how could you use design and technology for social good? Mapbox believes in open source. Satellite data should be available to everybody. It shouldn't be something proprietary that only a few people can afford to even touch, because this is everyone's world, right? A lot of information is locked down. There's been a history of people in the Western world controlling the dissemination of maps and information. Being able to align myself with a company that has those types of core beliefs is really important.

ELLEN LUPTON: Describe the scope of your work at Mapbox. I was there for five and a half years. Initially, I was a senior designer, working on the Mapbox Studio tool, which helps people create map designs. After I started using that tool and designing maps with it, I began digging deeper into cartography and actually working with the data. That included using a little bit of SQL and a lot of command line. Next, I joined the brand marketing team, where I was making cool maps and posting about them on our website, speaking about them at events, and creating workshops.

While doing this work, I saw an opportunity. A lot of designers wanted to be able to put maps inside of their prototypes early in the design process. I started to create components that could be plugged into Figma and other design tools. I was responsible for making this product happen, from managing a team of engineers and convincing my boss to give me the budget to hire some people to speccing out what the engineers needed to build.

Now you are a product designer at Netflix. What do you do there? Netflix has various social media channels in different regions. Someone might be focused on *The Irishman*, while someone else is focusing on a new series or on different audiences. I am working on a new tool that is going to help those teams manage all those different channels. The users come from both inside Netflix and from the external studios who upload media to Netflix.

Essentially, it's a posting tool. If you are posting something on Instagram, you go into the Instagram app, upload your photo, add a caption, and post it. Then, you will see how many people liked it and engage with them by liking their likes or adding a comment. I am creating a tool to streamline this process for all these different channels across the different platforms, such as YouTube and Instagram.

To do this work, you need to zoom in and out—like a cartographer. You work closely with engineers and product managers—people who are not designers. You learn so much when you start to see what matters to them and what keeps them up at night.

SOURCES Excerpted and adapted from an interview with Maurice Cherry, Revision Path, Jun 2016 →revisionpath.com/?s=Amy+Lee+Walton; additional conversation with Ellen Lupton, Jan 2020.

voice | elaine lopez

CONVERSATION WITH ELLEN LUPTON

| ELAINE LOPEZ | Designer, activist, associate professor in graphic design |
| PRONOUNS | She, her |

Tell me about the AIGA Chicago Diversity and Inclusion Hiring Survey.
In 2016, I became one of two leads for the Diversity and Inclusion Initiative.
At the panel discussions and events that we organized, many leaders
in the design community would confess that they had a difficult time
hiring BIPOC (Black, Indigenous, and People of Color). They were usually
from independently run design studios with under twenty people, who
don't have the same resources as large agencies with human resources
departments. I wanted to learn more about why they were having a hard
time. Are BIPOC designers not applying to postings, or are their portfolios
not compatible with the work of these studios? Each of these issues has
actionable solutions for AIGA, and I wanted to conduct some research to
better understand the problem.

I leveraged my experience in human-centered design and developed
questions for a survey with the help of Maris García, a design researcher.
I then e-mailed the top fifteen design studios in Chicago at the time and
asked questions around hiring practices. When hiring designers, where
do you post the position? Do designers from diverse cultural backgrounds apply to your job postings? I then sorted their responses and
included them verbatim in a report that I shared back with each studio
and the rest of the AIGA Chicago board.

What is the core insight from the survey? The Chicago design community lacks diversity in its professional networks. This problem begins in
school. If BIPOC students do not have access to study graphic design
(for lack of information or financial resources), then the classroom is not
representative of the population. The networking that happens in school
is critical to your success in this industry. Once you enter the workforce,

you are surrounded by predominantly White people, and so your connections continue to become homogenous. When an opportunity at an independent studio becomes available and they reach out to their network for references, the people who are recommended will usually not be BIPOC. Studios need to work to actively recruit outside of their networks, change the culture of their workplaces to be more inclusive, and adopt inclusive language in their job listings instead of waiting for it to happen by chance. Having a diverse network or workplace should not be seen as a chore. Knowing and collaborating with people who are different than you is a gift, and we are lucky to live in a country with such rich diversity. Not only will the work you make together be stronger, but you will have a richer life experience.

Why did you decide to go to grad school?
When Donald Trump was elected, I decided I needed to take a step back and study the effects of White supremacy on the field of graphic design to develop action-able solutions. I also wanted to study and make work about my Cuban heritage. Even though I grew up in Miami, I never had the opportunity to really understand the complexities of US and Cuban relations beyond the books I read in my spare time. I realized I could only make this work within the context of academia because paid projects about specific cultures are rare in the design industry.

I applied to five top programs and was surprised when I was accepted into RISD. I assumed I was not talented enough to be accepted into these programs, because of my own internalized biases. When I arrived, I was disappointed to find that I was one of two US-born BIPOC in the graphic design MFA program. This strengthened my re-solve to educate myself on the root causes of inequality within the design community.

What do you think? What should we do?
The lack of diversity in this field is urgent and critical. Every year that goes by with-out aggressive measures to eradicate rac-ism and other forms of structural oppres-sion in the field of design further reinforces the issues of White supremacy within the design community. As professors, we need to be aware of and well versed in global events. As our classrooms become increasingly diverse and representative of the global population, we need to be curi-ous, sensitive, and humble to the needs of every student. It was so powerful to learn about my culture in graduate school, and I hope more designers have the opportunity to do so. This is how we expand the field of design—by adding more voices and perspectives.

Tell me about Signs of the Times. The elec-tion of Donald Trump led me to radically change my life. I put my career on hold to attend graduate school at age thirty-three, and I wanted to capture the stories of oth-ers who had made drastic changes, too. On the day of the midterm election in 2018, I reached out to the contacts in my phone and asked, "How has your life changed since the election of Donald Trump?" Each response was powerful, and it didn't feel right to neatly typeset them on a tabloid-size poster—a gesture that frequently speaks only to other designers. I wanted a broader audience for these responses, so I chose a common medium: lawn signs. The phone number on the signs directs a caller to a voicemail that asks how the caller's life has changed since the election of 2016. I have answered the calls a few times and have had conversations with strangers about the changes in their lives. To me, this is at the heart of how design needs to evolve. Instead of just shouting messages at people, we need to learn how to be facil-itators of dialogue and communication.

voice | irene pereyra

CONVERSATION WITH FARAH KAFEI

IRENE PEREYRA	Designer, Anton & Irene
PRONOUNS	She, her

Tell me what you do. I'm a designer at my own company, Anton & Irene. I've had various job titles in the past, like creative director and UX director. When Anton Repponen and I started our own studio, we deliberately chose to call ourselves designers rather than directors. I manage clients, which is technically a project manager's or producer's job. I handle finances, which is technically what an accountant or CFO does. I give interviews about the studio. I do design, all the way from concept to the terms-and-conditions page. Everything is touched by either Anton or me, from traditional director stuff to what would usually be considered junior designer and production work. Having full visibility in every part of your business keeps you honest as a designer. It's very easy to lose your skills if you stop doing hands-on design. It's like a muscle. You have to keep flexing it.

How did you become a designer? There's an inherent designer-like ability that I always had and always will have. I'm incredibly organized. I'm very detail-oriented. I consider how things look, how they work, and whether or not they could be done better. If I'm in a line, I think, "Why is there a line? Maybe this could be more efficient." I can very quickly take big pieces of information, disassemble them, and put them into categories and groupings and figure out where the structure is in this big ball of yarn. I'm also quite concerned with aesthetics. You can train those muscles, but people who are good designers and make it their life's work have to be obsessed with those things naturally.

I went to school for graphic design in 1999. Back in the day, there was no real web emphasis. A bunch of amateurs were on the internet. The design community was still focused on print, posters, and typography.

Toward the third or fourth year, I realized that I had been obsessed with the internet since I was about thirteen, when I first saw it around 1996. In the beginning days, you had to know how to code to get online. The internet felt very Wild, Wild West. We were little hackers in this world of illicit activity. I remember downloading the first episode of *South Park* in the mid-'90s, and it took two and a half days.

We were doing experiments on the web, but we couldn't bring that into our studies, which were based on formal design principles like color theory and the like. In my third or fourth year, I thought, "Eh, I don't really care so much about that." So I decided to get a master's in communications design at Pratt, which I only chose because when I interviewed there, I asked, "Well, what's this master's about?" And they said, "Whatever you want to do. You choose a thesis topic, and you just do it." There was no program.

Has your gender identity ever been an obstacle? Yes and no. For the past fifteen years, I was usually the only woman in the room, especially the only female director. At my previous job, I was basically the only one hiring women, because all the other directors were male, and they hired dudes. There were very few women In the digital tech world. As the only woman in the room, I was kind of treated like a novelty. "Oh, here's this woman who actually knows a lot about this stuff." Because of that, I was invited to a lot of conferences. I was also lucky that my first real job was with a mentor—an incredibly talented man—who didn't give a shit about gender, so I was promoted to director very quickly.

Recently, however, at a conference, I was introduced to the audience by the male organizer in a sexualized way. It was meant to be funny, but basically he alluded to how nice it would be to see me in a bikini. Dude, you can't do that anymore—or ever, really.

There have been multiple instances, mostly with clients, where men would come on to me inappropriately. I had to turn down advances with male clients or laugh off an awkward hug. I don't think my male counterparts had to deal with that so much. I wish that would stop happening. And if there would be 50 percent women in the room, it would spread out a little bit more. If you're the only woman in the room, the men focus on you.

I will say, though, it has gotten a lot better in the past three to five years. More women have been getting into the field. I have more female clients, which is great.

Yet I'm a part of an era before that shift happened. I also think that as a woman, there's always been the myth that female directors can be bitches or women elbow each other to get ahead. In my teams, I have never seen that, but I know it exists because other female directors say it's been a problem for them. If there are ten spots in a room, with two for women and eight for men, then the competition among the women is far greater.

Today, there are maybe four spots for women. Ideally, it would be half, but it's still not the case, especially in director roles. Also, most female designers I know become the super-capable senior designer or super-capable art director but not the creative director. I think we raise girls not to have the space to take on leadership roles. Being a good leader is something you have to learn. So, if you haven't been in leadership positions before, then it is harder to be a leader suddenly in your design career.

voice | leslie xia

CONVERSATION WITH ELLEN LUPTON

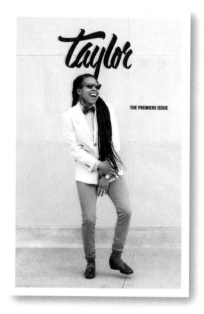

LESLIE XIA	Art director, Foundry 360, Meredith
PRONOUNS	They, them

How did you discover graphic design? I first got interested in art when I was in high school and went to the precollege program at the Cooper Union. I ended up going to MICA in Baltimore for college. At first, I didn't really know what I wanted to do—I dabbled in sculpture, fibers, and painting. Then, I took an Intro to Design class during my freshman year. Growing up, I always loved magazines. I loved the service elements and the fashion elements. They helped me create a sense of identity for how I wanted to look, and they offered a lot of life advice. One of my first graphic design assignments at MICA was a feature layout. That project made me realize that I love design and editorial.

I grew up reading *J-14*, a magazine for young girls. As I got older, I started reading *GQ* and *Esquire*. I cared a lot about fashion and styling, and I loved menswear. But these magazines constantly sexualized women, and the content wasn't really for me. I loved the style, but I knew there could be so much more. During my senior year, I decided to build that vision.

For my senior project, I wanted to create a magazine for someone who is nonbinary and queer and interested in menswear but is not a cis man. I sought out illustrators and photographers from MICA and decided to create *Taylor*. For this huge collaborative project, we had people shoot food and shoot drinks and create fashion styling. *Taylor* became a culmination of everything I had learned about being queer, but it also included different lifestyle elements that weren't particularly for men or women.

I sold *Taylor* online, and after graduation, I shipped copies out to design directors and designers who I admired. It opened a lot of doors. Design directors reached out to say, "Let's grab coffee," because they liked the drive and energy of this project.

What was your first job after MICA? I was a junior designer under Florian Bachleda at Fast Company. I worked on the iPad edition, the new website, and the print edition. The team included a lot of women, and Florian is half Thai. I felt really welcome in that work environment.

Where else have you worked? As an associate art director at *Men's Health*, I collaborated with editors, and I commissioned illustrators and photographers for the lifestyle sections of the magazine. Occasionally, I worked on feature stories. The best part has been working with illustrators to give energy to our pieces. I work on food and drink sections, too, which I love. It is definitely parallel to the magazine I produced for my MICA degree project. Now I'm an art director at Foundry 360.

How is activism part of your practice? The personal is political. So many things matter to me as a nonbinary person of color. I want to help move dialogue and spark conversation. During my senior year at MICA in 2015, a Black man named Freddie Gray was killed under police custody, and it became a movement in Baltimore. There was an uprising, and many people protested at MICA to show solidarity with the community. For our graduation ceremony, I helped letter a patch that said "Black Lives Matter," and it was worn by every graduating student and by the faculty and administration.

The next year, when I was working at *Fast Company*, Philando Castile was shot and killed by a police officer in Minnesota.

That was another pivotal moment for me. I collaborated with eighteen other illustrators and designers to letter the names of folks who had been killed through police brutality. We were able to Kickstart the project and produce 25,000 stickers to distribute throughout the US and other countries. The project memorialized these people we've lost, so that we can continue to remember them and their lives and the injustice that is felt by Black and White people every day.

How has your gender identity influenced your career? At *Men's Health*, I came out as nonbinary, and I wanted to push our editors at *Men's Health* and *Women's Health* to think about the binary and whether or not we are upholding gender stereotypes within the content that we produce. How do we move toward where society is going, especially with millennials and younger people, who are increasingly queer? How do we restructure ourselves, and how do we make content that is interesting to them without enforcing the binary or putting people in corners or tokenizing them?

Share some advice for new designers. Networking is important, and so is being active on many platforms. Instagram is such a great place to connect with other designers and photographers. Right now, it's possible to break through without relying on institutions or companies to be the gatekeepers to your career. It's easy for people to share their content online now, like the way that I produced my magazine at MICA. That all happened by connecting with people. If you have the passion and drive for it, you can reach out to others and work together on something big like an independent magazine and then use it to jump-start your career. Things can happen online so much easier now.

voice | njoki gitahi

CONVERSATION WITH FARAH KAFEI

Cards labeled: STORIES, THOUGHTS, TENSIONS, SCENARIOS, QUESTIONS, BELIEFS. Center card reads "If the police stop you, should they have to tell you why?"

NJOKI GITAHI	Senior design lead, IDEO
PRONOUNS	She, her

What is a project that you are especially proud of? A couple of years ago, the New York Civil Liberties Union asked IDEO to help them create a campaign about overpolicing in New York City. They had conducted a huge survey with people across the city about their experiences with police, and they had talked to the police about their experiences in the force. They wanted to put out the survey results and engage New Yorkers and their elected officials in an interesting way. We thought, "How do we get people to actually talk about the topic rather than being told what to think?" We needed to design a nontraditional type of campaign.

Our goal was to help people both express their experiences and take action. We also wanted to influence officials about making policy changes. The interactive campaign we designed, called "A Listening Room," is a mobile pop-up station that can be set up in different places across the city. The listening part has two sets of chairs set up underneath a frame on either side of a table. The idea is to get two people, ideally with different experiences, to sit down and engage in a personal conversation about policing as well as things like trust and safety.

It was important to have a presence in neighborhoods that don't experience overpolicing. If you live on Manhattan's Upper West Side, you may never see a cop unless he's actually helping you. If you live in Brownsville, you might have an opposite experience. We didn't want to put the burden on the people living that negative experience to constantly have to talk about it, to make them be the ones to do the work and advocate. How could we galvanize others to understand what it's like and speak up about it? People living in neighborhoods without overpolicing also tend to have more wealth and power. They might have more direct contact and influence with elected officials and be able to push for policy changes.

To help get the conversations going, we designed a deck of cards with prompts like "Tell me about someone you associate with the word *trust*" or "You're lost in a neighborhood, and you've got your phone, but you also see a policeman on the corner. What do you do?" The idea was to have a conversation about how and when people feel safe around the police. One person might feel comfortable asking a cop for directions. Someone else might say, "Hell, no. I'm not talking to a cop. I've got my phone and Google Maps, and I'm all set."

We also designed policy-related stickers people could take or apply to a postcard we sent to the mayor, saying things like "If the police want to read my e-mail, they should have to get a warrant." We sent hundreds of postcards to the mayor.

Tell me about the team. There were three core team members: me (the communication design lead), Randy Plemel (an environmental designer, who also led the project), and Rafael Smith (an industrial designer). We designed and tested many rough prototypes. Rafa and I went to Union Square and asked passersby to play early versions of the card game. Rafa built three different physical versions of the space.

How did you become a designer? I was in art club in high school, but I also loved math and science. I've always loved making things, but my college did not have a design program—only fine arts. I ended up majoring in geology. After graduating, I worked at the American Museum of Natural History as a collections manager. I discovered that I enjoyed visually organizing things and helping my boss draw figures for his papers. I realized this thing called graphic design encompasses the stuff I like to do. I took an intensive summer class at Parsons and then applied to grad school. I went to Yale for an MFA.

Has your gender identity ever been an obstacle? Maybe not an obstacle, but it's something I've always been aware of, especially in spaces like geology and science. In undergrad, I had amazing female teachers in geology—that's one reason I pursued that major. At the museum, all the curators were men, with women studying and working under them. At times, at lunch, someone would say something sexist or tell a story that made me uncomfortable. I would wonder if they were seeing me for my full potential. My name is gender-ambiguous in this country, so sometimes I meet someone who says, "I didn't know if you were male or female." Then I wonder if I would've been treated differently if that weren't the case. I've walked into situations and seen someone's demeanor change, and I can tell that I've been underestimated just by their mannerisms or the things they're asking. Then, when I start talking or showing my work, they start sitting up straighter and paying more attention. So I'm always prepared, always making sure that I don't leave a shadow of a doubt in terms of my capabilities. It's exhausting to constantly do that.

Have you ever experienced racial or ethnic discrimination? More often, I see an expectation of representation. People start talking about something related to Black communities and then turn to look at me. "What do you think?" I'm like, "I don't know. Just because I'm Black doesn't mean I know every experience there is of being Black." I can't separate my gender identity from my race, and because my race is so visible, those experiences where I feel uncomfortable or underestimated— I don't know if it's because I'm a woman or because I'm Black. Maybe both!

voice | sabrina hall

CONVERSATION WITH VALENTINA VERGARA

SABRINA HALL	Interactive art director, Scholastic
PRONOUNS	She, her

Tell me about your background. I am a first-generation Afro-Latina. My parents immigrated here from Costa Rica, and my brother and I were born and raised in the Bronx, New York. I studied graphic design at the School of Visual Arts. I love graphic design, but as my career has grown, I've learned a lot about the lack of diversity in our field. When I studied graphic design, every person I learned about was a White male or a White woman. I always thought to myself, What would it have meant for me as a student to learn about someone who looked like me?

What are some projects you are especially proud of? I lead an initiative at Scholastic prioritizing accessibility for our online products. When we design for disabilities, it makes a better product for everyone. As we all get older, our vision is going to change, for example. We should base design on this kind of inclusivity as well as on aesthetics, and I work with my team to do things outside of "just okay." The UI components need to be accessible to every kind of person.

Another project I'm proud of is co-leading the AIGA New York mentoring program with my dear friend Anjali Menon. We paired students from the High School of Art and Design with illustrators, art directors, photographers—anyone who's a member—to build lasting relationships. They're paired for at least two years, and we planned and coordinated all the activities and workshops. This program truly has impact. The students get access to different experiences and to someone who is there for them. The mentors learn so much, too. I started out as a mentor, and I coordinated the program for five years.

Good mentorships create a safe space for everyone to grow together. It's an act of kindness by both parties. I've had conversations with many of my mentees where I say, "That's a great question. I don't know." It's important to convey your experience but encourage the mentee to figure out their own ideas.

Mentorship is critical because there are so many social unknowns and doubts in the design field, so many things you don't learn in school, such as how to speak about your work and how to stand up about cultural differences. Mentorship is having somewhere to learn with someone who is open-minded and able to listen: to have a growing professional relationship.

How did you decide that you wanted to become a designer? I always loved art. I went to a specialized junior high school, where I had to take a drawing test to get in, and my parents were really focused on education. I got into Bronx Science, which was a great experience. In high school, an art teacher said, "You can do this full-time." They told me about the School of Visual Arts and graphic design. My parents let me go, which was a big deal. My parents made a lot of sacrifices to help me go. When my mom came here from Costa Rica, she had to go through the entire teaching certification process all over again, even though she already had a master's degree. As first-generation immigrants, you feel like you have to prove yourself. My parents were really supportive because they wanted me to have better opportunities.

What about unpaid internships? I strongly oppose unpaid internships because of what they mean for people of color, for underrepresented and marginalized groups, for people from different socioeconomic backgrounds. They pose a high bar of entry into a field that's already challenging to enter. Unpaid internships limit students of color, like myself, who couldn't afford to work for free. You are already paying for school, and then you are paying for a job to count for credit, but it's money you have already paid. So the connections that are made there, the foundations that can help people really start their career, are exclusionary. I also think there should not be unpaid labor in design. People should get paid for their work. College students have brilliant ideas.

When I was in school, I had a paid internship at Carnegie Hall. It was the most diverse group of people, and they taught me so much. I worked on designing a mouse pad, and they showed me how to prep files correctly. I made such wonderful connections because of that internship.

Have you ever experienced racial or ethnic discrimination in the workplace? I have to be mindful of how I answer that because I don't want to shout out any specific person or place. Yes, there were moments I have experienced discrimination. There have been moments where unconscious bias was behind some unkind comments. Learning to be compassionate and kind has helped me overcome those moments.

voice | shira inbar

CONVERSATION WITH VALENTINA VERGARA

SHIRA INBAR	Senior designer, Pentagram
PRONOUNS	She, her

Tell me about your background. I was born in Michigan. When I was three, my family moved to Jerusalem. My mother is Israeli, and my dad is American. I grew up there, speaking both English and Hebrew, and I moved back here in 2012 for grad school at Yale University School of Art.

What is a project that you're especially proud of? *Eye on Design*, published by AIGA, is the first project I worked on that had only women on the team. I had never worked with an all-women team before, so this was refreshing and new. I felt like certain pressures were lifted. There was a free exchange of ideas, which made it fun to collaborate. I'm proud of this work because it was a team effort, and I was invited to be part of the editorial process. In addition to the design work, I contributed to the larger discussion.

I don't think that graphic design is an inherently male field. Women have been working in design for a long time but have received less recognition. One of typography's foundational texts is "The Crystal Goblet," by Beatrice Warde, claiming that typography should be invisible and completely committed to the content, as opposed to being expressive and autonomous. I find it interesting that a woman advocated for invisibility in design. Perhaps she was feeling invisible herself. Designers often aspire to invisibility because this approach seems objective. We're often taught to serve, solve problems, make things work. The *Psych* issue of *Eye on Design* explores a different perspective, looking at how designers question the seamless, invisible, and utilitarian design experience and use their skills to subvert expectations.

How did you become a designer?

My mother is a linguist, researching how people talk—how the words are said in terms of tone, volume, and behavior. Graphic design is a visual performance of speech. Visualizing language creates new meaning. I used to draw on scrap paper from my mom's research. She transcribed conversations and placed symbols over words to mark the intonation. If somebody stretched out a word, a symbol indicated that. By drawing on this scrap paper, I discovered that visual symbols could signify how one speaks.

I learned about graphic design when I was eighteen, while volunteering at the Hotline for Refugees and Migrants in Tel Aviv. I worked with migrant families on visa applications. There I learned that typographic layout and hierarchy have an impact on people's lives. Although the applications I prepared were perfectly typeset and organized, many were denied. Something wasn't working, and I wanted to ask why, and what role did my work have in this system. This pushed me to think about design in a way that doesn't only focus on solutions. I always want to ask questions.

Tell me about House of Yes. A friend

organized weekly film screenings at a club called House of Yes. I joined him, and we started to expand the screenings: for example, we would pause the movie and then a band would perform. And then there's a question, "What's projected while that's happening? How do we transition in and out of the film?" I would create projections for each event. Finally, I was asked by the club to come on Saturday night and project some of my own work.

Has your gender identity ever been an obstacle? Although I was raised by women who love their work and never let their

gender be an obstacle, I have experienced times in which I felt that being a woman made things a little harder. I recall my first job in the US, right after school. Back then, I wasn't aware of the emphasis corporate culture here places on "work attire." I came to work on the first day feeling excited and a bit nervous. I had never met the creative director, since we had only spoken on the phone. When he came to meet me, he seemed a bit surprised and disappointed. I think that I didn't look like what he might have expected. There was nothing edgy about my appearance. I wasn't wearing black, and I probably looked like a fish out of water in the polished lobby of the Times Square building.

During my work there, my appearance was never mentioned, and I ended up learning a lot from this creative director, which I'm thankful for. However, the experience of that first impression stuck with me, and every day I felt like I was starting out from a point of disadvantage. This insecurity impacted my work and my ability to open up. I often wonder, If I had not been a woman, would my appearance have played such a big role? Would there have been less expectation to look a certain way? This experience has taught me a few things. Of course, I learned the importance of first impressions. However, the more important lesson is to pay attention to how I greet people and look at *them* for the first time. I'm not that junior person anymore: I'm often the person who welcomes others, whether it's people at work or people I teach. I try to remember how it was when I was in their place and to be as welcoming and open as possible. My expectations should never burden anyone's experience; it is my responsibility to channel those expectations into a process of learning and growth.

workplaces

TEXT BY ELLEN LUPTON

What does it mean to "go to work"? Once upon a time, belonging to the managerial class required the ritual of leaving one's domestic sanctuary and commuting to an office—a place dedicated to desks, data, and the occasional idea. Since the 1960s, professionals such as lawyers, accountants, and designers have been called "knowledge workers." These college-educated people went to work in gleaming downtown towers or low-slung suburban office parks. In the twenty-first century, the rising freelance economy has called for new kinds of workplaces, while COVID-19 forced global changes in how, where, and if people work.

In the mid-twentieth century, many offices featured an open plan instead of walled-off rooms for each worker. Open plans saved space and expenses while keeping employees visible to their bosses. The powerful people occupied the corners, protected by glass doors and elegant receptionists.

In the late 1960s, cubicle systems took over, enabling managers to pack more people into one big room. Cubicles—while offering some privacy—became symbols of boredom and isolation.

Open offices came back into vogue in the 2000s. Design leaders extolled the virtues of people working together at common tables with no barriers or social hierarchy. Cubicles were seen as inhuman and outdated, belonging to less enlightened times. Yet open offices proved imperfect. Noise and lack of privacy drove people to arm themselves with head-phones and to request days at home for tackling the most demanding projects.

Working at home has its own problems. The practice of coworking helps free-lancers move their practices out of their houses and apartments. Coworking offers opportunities to network and collaborate as well as to plug in a computer for a few hours or semipermanently. Coworking also lets small companies save money.

Coworking organizations like WeWork became a huge real estate industry in the 2010s, feeding on the growing freelance economy, which depends on work for hire on a temporary basis. The same technologies that make it easy to hire a car, order a burger, or commission a logo make it easy to rent a desk for a few hours in New York, Seattle, or Seoul. Membership in these clubs is expensive, however, making coworking a domain of privilege.

Meanwhile, although many workers desire more flexible home/office arrangements, companies are uncertain about the value of remote employment. People working in a room together can be more creative (and more accountable) than people beaming in from home. COVID-19 triggered the mass migration of knowledge-class workers back to their bedrooms and dens—and brought surging demand for new tools for collaborating as well as new standards for brick-and-mortar offices. Cubicles returned with a vengeance, armored with Plexiglas sneeze guards.

SOURCES Nikil Saval, *Cubed: A Secret History of the Workplace* (New York: Doubleday, 2014); Cal Newport, "Why Remote Work Is So Hard—and How It Can Be Fixed," *New Yorker*, May 26, 2020 →newyorker.com/culture/annals-of-inquiry/can-remote-work-be-fixed.

open office The classic open offices of mid-century modernism often looked great, thanks to the work of legendary designer Florence Knoll. Her company manufactured sleek and functional desks, chairs, sofas, and filing systems (many of them designed by Knoll herself) and innovated the practice of helping businesses to arrange their furniture and spaces.

cube town Vast office spaces carved into cubes are famous symbols of soul-crushing office life. Manufacturers brought them back in 2020, hoping to build safer, less populated spaces for the COVID era.

collective Some coworking arrangements are started by friends sharing space and expenses. Coworking has collectivist roots, originating as a communal practice allowing independent workers to share resources.

parents' basement Will your parents let you work in their basement? Do your parents even have a basement? Lucky you. Be polite and help with the dishes, and you might land a deal on rent-free office space.

home office Working at home isn't always easy. Kids and roommates can be more distracting than coworkers. The burden of maintaining a home office space falls largely on workers, who have to carve out functional real estate from their own tight quarters and make it work within the bustle of home life.

third places Tired of working at home? Cheap respites from your couch include a café, church basement, or community center. Many libraries have maker spaces and media labs, as well as free access to tables, internet, and—get this—books.

ILLUSTRATIONS BY JENNIFER TOBIAS

the house of work

Re:working

Can you find…
→ three birds
→ one dog
→ one cat
→ one stray sock
→ socialist ideals

cubicle town

collective

server farm

café

mind the pay gap

Exit

parents' basement

SCHOOL

daycare: the missing perk

ON AIR

open-plan office

staff coffee bar

package management

ON
OFF

working from home

WFH WTF

third place

public library

storage unit

catacombs

gates of hell

HELLCOME

working from home

TEXT BY ELLEN LUPTON

In 2020, vast numbers of office workers, from accountants to creatives, stopped commuting to company-owned office spaces and started working from their homes—or the homes of their parents, friends, or relatives. The norm looks nothing like Barbie's DreamHouse—a skylit atelier equipped with a hot tub, pink toilet seat, and spiral slide. Typical conditions are cramped, makeshift, and crowded with other people.

The bed—once reserved for sex, sleep, and folding laundry—has become a workplace. Even before the COVID crisis, many people were spending multiple hours a day working from their beds. According to Beatriz Colomina, the bed is a slice of "horizontal architecture," and it is often the largest open area in a tight living space. Today's bed is a place to plug in and power up—before passing out from exhaustion.

Despite its drawbacks, working from bed with proper pillow support may be safer for your neck and back than hunching over a laptop at a kitchen table. The laptop should be elevated on some kind of tray, however, and you will want to move around frequently rather than putting in an eight-hour day in one position. An ideal work-from-home situation includes a variety of places to work (and a three-story slide).

spreadsheet

ILLUSTRATIONS BY JENNIFER TOBIAS

designing your home studio

Computer setup Your laptop is a portal to the world of working adults. Even if you spend most of your day in bed, try to sit in an actual chair during meetings.

Camera height Photographers recommend aligning the camera near the top of your head to avoid emphasizing your nostrils and extra chins (if the camera is too low) or your bald spot and fading hair dye (if the camera is too high). Angling the camera a bit downward also helps to create a flattering view. Looking slightly up at a camera makes your eyes seem more open and alert. If necessary, elevate your laptop on a box or stack of books.

Lighting Set up a task light behind your computer shining toward your face at a 45-degree angle. (You can also use a circular light created for this purpose.) Avoid any kind of backlight, which will put your face in shadow, as well as strong side lighting. Lower window blinds as needed.

Eye contact, sort of To sustain the illusion of eye-to-eye human connection, look at the camera rather than at your own apalling face. If possible, drag the little talking-head windows up near your camera, or tape a picture of a pet or loved one to the back of your computer to attract your eye. It's hard to stay focused on a nearly invisible, deliberately camouflaged camera lens.

Quiet, please Speaking of adorable, your yappy dog is super-annoying. Either lock him in the closet with your pet skeleton or mute your microphone.

Fidget alert Twirling your hair or tugging your ear lobes will distract colleagues from your message. If fidgeting keeps you sane, try fondling a stress ball or other intriguing toy out of sight in your lap.

Simple background Obviously, no one wants to see your socks, your porn, or your rumpled bed. Clean up! You are at work!

SOURCES Beatriz Colomina, "The 24/7 Bed," *Work, Body, Leisure,* ed. Marina Otero Verzier and Nick Axel (Berlin: Hatje Cantz, 2017); Anne Quito, "Working from Your Bed Is Better than Slumping at the Kitchen Table," *Quartz,* Mar 18, 2020 →qz.com/work/1820072/steelcase-ergonomics-expert-on-how-to-work-from-home-comfortably/; Anne Quito, "We're All Distracted by How Terrible We Look on Video Calls. Here's How to Fix It," *Quartz,* Aug 22, 2016 →qz.com/637860/video-call-tips-for-skype-and-facetime-steelcase-researchers-are-solving-your-appearance-barrier-on-video-calls.

ILLUSTRATION BY JENNIFER TOBIAS

wage gaps

TEXT BY ELLEN LUPTON

According to AIGA's 2019 Design Census, graphic designers identifying as women earned 80 cents for every dollar paid to men. This ratio was similar to overall US employment data. The 2019 Design Census showed that women were more likely than male designers to earn less than $25,000 a year and less likely than men to earn $150,000 or more. The 2019 census also found a pay gap between LGBTQIA+ designers (most of whom earn $35,000–$49,000 a year) and non-LGBTQIA+ designers (who typically make $50,000–$74,000). The survey did not track salary differences by race.

How are wage gaps measured? Studies of employment in the US find that men and women working in the same jobs tend to earn similar pay. Thus, two junior designers or two account managers employed at the same company will likely receive similar salaries. However, if the company employs more men than women in its higher-paid positions (such as creative director) while employing more women in lower-paying positions (such as junior designer, social media manager, or administrative assistant), then a pay gap will exist at that company. In 2019, calculating such differences across all full-time occupations in the US shows women earning 82.3 cents for every dollar earned by men.

Income gaps divide women in the US who identify as White, Black, Asian, and Hispanic or Latina. Asian women have the highest median income, while Hispanic women have the lowest median income. These differences can be attributed to racial discrimination, educational attainment, and immigration status.

When we compare the pay of men and women in identical jobs with identical amounts of experience, the pay gap seems to diminish. However, pulling back to look at broader patterns—from who gets hired and promoted to how many hours people work—reveals an even bigger gap: 49 cents to the dollar. How is this possible? Because women are less likely than men to get promoted, men outpace women in earnings as their careers mature. Women are more likely to leave the workforce for extended periods to care for children or other family members, especially during a crisis such as the COVID-19 pandemic. Such parents return to work with fewer years of experience and holes in their résumés. A study found that women who left the workforce for a single year during a fifteen-year period had earnings 39 percent lower than women who were continuously employed.

Because women are more likely to work in low-paying, minimum-wage, and/or part-time jobs, their earnings as a group are lower than those of men. Part-time jobs often lack health insurance, retirement benefits, or paid vacations and sick leave.

Some women stay home with children or elderly parents or take lower-paying or part-time positions by choice. The interplay between choice and opportunity is ambiguous, however. If it's easier to find employment as a temporary worker, a person might tend to move in that direction. A mix of individual choice and structural opportunity—as well as the feminization of unpaid care work—can guide people along a path of lower earnings.

symmetry

asymmetry

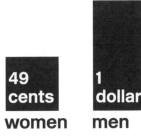

MEDIAN INCOME IN THE US, 2017

SOURCES Archie Bagnall, "AIGA Design Census 2016: Investigating Design's Gender Pay Gap," Aug 8, 2017 →medium.com/aiga-orange-county/aiga-design-census-2016-investigating-designs-gender-pay-gap-4516a9d4ad98; AIGA, *Design Census 2019* →designcensus.org/; Institute for Women's Policy Research, "The Gender Wage Gap by Occupation, 2019" →iwpr.org/iwpr-issues/employment-and-earnings/same-gap-different-year-the-gender-wage-gap-2019-earnings-differences-by-gender-race-and-ethnicity/; Annie Lowrey, "Women May Earn Just 49 Cents on the Dollar," *Atlantic*, Nov 28, 2018 →theatlantic.com/ideas/archive/2018/11/how-big-male-female-wage-gap-really/576877/.

AVERAGE WEEKLY INCOME IN THE US, 2017

hiring for diversity

TEXT BY LESLIE XIA

So you've been hunting for the right job, applied to numerous openings, reached out to potential recruiters through LinkedIn, exchanged a few e-mails with design directors, and—finally—you've done it: you've scored an interview! What are your next steps, and how do you know if the company you are interested in working for is the right one for you?

Workers entering a new company have many questions. What are the defining tasks of the job? How do people advance in this role? Who will I work with directly? What is the company culture? What are the benefits, such as health insurance, retirement plans, and parental leave?

One factor to examine is racial diversity. The US Bureau of Labor Statistics reported that in 2019, of the 983,000 workers employed in the design field, 54 percent were women and 82.2 percent were White. Only 5.7 percent of designers were Black or of African descent, 9 percent of Asian descent, and 11.1 percent Hispanic or Latino. (The total exceeds 100 percent because some people check multiple boxes.)

In 2020, after the murders of George Floyd, Tony McDade, Breonna Taylor, Ahmaud Arbery, and others, demands for police reform across the US forced corporations to examine systemic racism in their organizations. Employees and consumers challenged corporations to be accountable inside and out. For decades, many companies had toxic cultures and work practices, including unchecked abuses of power, covert racism, tolerance of sexual harassment, and a lack of diversity.

As companies move forward to reform and restructure their workplaces, what does this mean for new hires? While some managers may be transparent with you, it is hard to ask tough questions during a job interview. I conducted an informal survey through social media asking creatives if they would feel comfortable directly talking about diversity with a company's leadership. Most people expressed fear of jeopardizing their candidacy by bringing up controversial questions.

Consider reframing the question by asking about the company or organization's diversity initiatives—and do your own research. Look for reports or articles about the workplace culture. Seek out firsthand accounts from people who have worked there. If you have connections at the company, send an e-mail asking about it. Check websites like Glassdoor for honest opinions about salary ranges and worker satisfaction with the company's CEO, HR division, benefits, and workplace culture.

Some companies and studios post team photos on their websites, which can indicate whether there are people of color in senior leadership and what the overall staff looks like. Check LinkedIn to see who would be on your immediate team and in surrounding departments. Here, you can also learn about previous employees who have had held the position you are interested in and learn how long they held that position, whether they received promotions, what their prior job experience was, and where this position led them next.

Large organizations such as publishers, museums, universities, and tech companies will have a formal hiring process. Smaller studios and start-ups may be more informal in the way they conduct interviews and onboard new workers. Here's how the process might look at an established media company. After the first few interviews, and after you've met with your boss and other team members, someone from Human Resources will explain company policies and employment benefits. This is an opportunity to ask questions about retention rates within the company, how the company has changed structurally to diversify, and what anti-racism resources are provided.

Understanding diversity hiring initiatives

The company may have affinity groups or even a labor union. A union can inform you about specific protections and about legal actions for improving the workplace. Affinity groups for Black or queer employees offer ways to network with people who may share similar values and identities and can tell you about their experiences.

Many companies have launched diversity hiring initiatives, aiming to expand the number of racial and gender minority employees. Often, these programs are well intentioned but limited in scope. Many internships, fellowships, and apprenticeships are limited to a year; often, these positions pay a stipend or starting salary at minimum wage and fail to provide the same benefits as those received by permanent employees.

Some of these initiatives are little more than tokenism, the practice of hiring people from marginalized groups to improve the company's optics. When considering a position associated with a diversity initiative, ask the interviewer about the number of non-White employees that you would be working under. Were they hired specifically to manage this program? What kind of training have they received to lead this program? How is the company assessing the eligibility of candidates? What tangible goals will serve to measure the success of the program? Are there full-time positions that people can transition into once the internship or fellowship is over? What opportunities will exist to network and meet people in this field?

In her 1968 text "The Black Experience in Graphic Design," Dorothy Jackson described such obstacles as difficulty finding mentors, being relegated to low-profile assignments, or being mistaken for the delivery boy. Alas, these problems persist today. A program to increase diversity is not enough if managers are not working to improve a new hire's experience.

Employers looking to build these programs must consider many factors. Often, the criterion for hiring is to find "the perfect candidate who has talent," without considering the inequities that marginalized people face, such as reduced financial access, White supremacy, anti-Blackness, disenfranchisement, and lack of institutional support. The bar for entry is often set to a standard that is reachable by White students, and the definition of talent is a benchmark that was never equitable to begin with.

White saviorism occurs when a White person helps others for self-serving reasons, such as signaling their own virtue or raising their own consciousness. White students entering the workforce don't depend on special initiatives to break into their field because they already receive traditional entry-level jobs. Diversity initiatives exist to bridge the gap that corporations systemically create. Instead of giving marginalized hires a temporary test run, just hire them!

SOURCES US Bureau of Labor Statistics, "Labor Force Statistics from the Current Population Survey," Jan 22, 2020 →bls.gov/cps/cpsaat11.htm; Dorothy Jackson, "The Black Experience in Graphic Design (1968)," *Print* →printmag.com/post/the-black-experience-1968.

the hiring journey

land a job interview
Congratulations! You got an interview! If you feel comfortable asking about diversity, inclusion, and pay equity in this context, go for it! If not, seek information through other channels.

clean up your social media image Be aware of the information about you that is publicly available.

do your research
You can learn a lot about a company's culture by checking out its website and social media accounts.

reach out through your network
Someone you know will know someone who knows someone who works there.

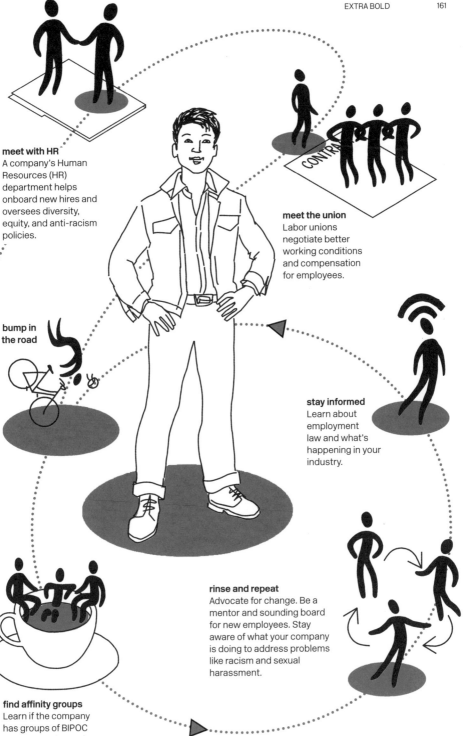

meet with HR
A company's Human Resources (HR) department helps onboard new hires and oversees diversity, equity, and anti-racism policies.

meet the union
Labor unions negotiate better working conditions and compensation for employees.

bump in the road

stay informed
Learn about employment law and what's happening in your industry.

rinse and repeat
Advocate for change. Be a mentor and sounding board for new employees. Stay aware of what your company is doing to address problems like racism and sexual harassment.

find affinity groups
Learn if the company has groups of BIPOC or queer workers who support and advocate for each other.

where are the black designers?

TEXT BY MAURICE CHERRY

Maurice Cherry is a designer, writer, podcaster, and digital creator in Atlanta, Georgia. He founded the podcast *Revision Path* and the website 28 Days of the Web to celebrate the work of Black designers. This essay is based on a presentation he delivered at the SXSW Interactive conference in 2015. Cherry's text explores the history of Black representation in the design profession and suggests concrete actions for moving forward.

Where are the Black designers? How many Black designers do you know? If you don't know many, that's perfectly understandable. We don't see them because they're not reflected in our design media, and they're not reflected on speaker panels, which have majority White speakers. We don't hear their voices in podcasts. We don't see them on blogs. We don't read about them in magazines. Unfortunately, that's just what the design industry looks like. The industry is a big monoculture, and Black designers have not been a highly visible part of it.

You might say, "Okay, Maurice, so Black designers aren't reflected in our media. What about top design and art schools? I went to an art school. There was a Black guy in my class. That means that there are black designers in the industry."

Well, yes and no. I looked at the percentage of Black students at some of the top design schools here in the United States.

Rhode Island School of Design, 2 percent. Pratt Institute, 4 percent. The New School/Parsons School of Design, 4 percent. Maryland Institute College of Art, 5 percent. Savannah College of Art and Design, 10 percent. This last number is higher because SCAD's campuses are here in the southeastern US, where a large majority of Black people live. There is an interesting parallel between these low percentages and what we see when tech companies talk about the diversity of their US workforces. They say they have a hard time finding Black employees. Art schools say the same thing. Why aren't there more Black students in these arts schools?

I want to introduce you to Cheryl D. Miller. In 1985, as a graduate student at Pratt Institute, this Black graphic designer wrote a searing eighty-nine-page thesis titled "Transcending the Problems of the Black Graphic Designer to Success in the Marketplace." Her thesis lays out several

The stories of Black designers and developers deserve to be shared and told.

MAURICE CHERRY

reasons why Black designers are starting behind in terms of their viability in the industry. There's a lack of family support. The cost of art school and tuition and fees is too expensive. There's not enough financial aid. There's a lack of mentorship. Miller wrote an article based on her thesis for *Print* magazine in 1987 called "Black Designers: Missing in Action."

The article in *Print* caught the eye of Michelle Vernon-Chesley, who wrote an *AIGA Journal* article in 1990, "Equal Opportunities? Minorities in Graphic Design." This article asserts that formal education in graphic design did not open up to minorities until desegregation, following the 1964 Civil Rights Act. Furthermore, companies are lazy in pursuing minority talent. The pipeline needs to start in high school because high school pushes young people toward college, which will push them out into the industry. Last, educators need to play a more active role by talking to minority students about careers in design.

AIGA published a report in 1991, "Why Is Graphic Design 93% White? Removing Barriers to Increase Opportunities in Graphic Design," written by Brenda Mitchell-Powell. AIGA also conducted a survey of 350 design firms, 235 design schools, and over 500 multicultural designers. The survey revealed a number of concerns that we're seeing to this day.

The first big concern is cultural exploitation. That's something we're seeing as brands say "bae" and try to be "on fleek." Then, there's stereotyping. For example, an ad for Nivea Men shows a black man hurling another black man's head with an Afro and a beard, with the phrases "Look like you give a damn" and "Re-civilize yourself." There are also corporate and societal assumptions about racial inferiority and a host of other issues. AIGA established various initiatives, including a mentor program for minority designers and the implementation of educational opportunities. AIGA has continued this work throughout the years, seen today in the Diversity & Inclusion Task Force. For AIGA, diversity means facilitating participation in multiculturalism at the chapter level and the national level.

But here is the gotcha. AIGA should not be the only organization having this conversation. As a trade group, being in front of this conversation is part of their purpose. However, they cannot be the only voice. The standard that you walk past is the standard you accept. Do you own a business? Do you hire employees? Do you have a design blog or podcast that has an active community of readers or listeners?

Through their effort, talent and innovation, Blacks affect the nation's economic bottom line every day.

CHERYL D. MILLER

Do you host a meetup? Do you organize a conference? Do you attend meetups regularly and talk with other designers?

If you answered yes to any of these questions, then you have a responsibility as a working practitioner in this glorious industry to help improve diversity. Granted, we are talking about Black designers here, and diversity is a large spectrum. This issue doesn't have to do just with race. It includes ethnicity, gender, sexual orientation, nationality, and ability. As a designer in this industry, you have an obligation and a responsibility to help improve diversity across the board.

From schools to educators to working practitioners, we all have to do our part if we are serious about sustaining the livelihood of our industry. You have more power and more privilege than you think you do to start to make change.

Let's talk about some solutions. First, mentorship is still sorely needed in this industry as it relates to Black designers. Mentorship is crucial, to let them know about the tools they need to use and the knowledge they need to have. Programs like the Inneract Project, founded by Maurice Woods in the Bay Area, provide free design classes for inner-city students. How can you get involved? Local high schools and middle schools could provide opportunities for mentorship. Talented students love to draw and love to design but may not know how to turn a hobby into a profession. If you don't like kids and you just want to talk to other adults, start your own group. Join your local AIGA chapter and get involved in the Diversity & Inclusion Task Force. As a member, you can influence change, you can talk to board members, and you can talk to other members.

If you organize a conference or a meetup, take actions to have more diverse attendees and more diverse speakers. If you own a design firm or a design agency or you're in a position of management at a design firm or agency, you can do things to bring in more Black designers. First, you will want to state a clear value proposition. From there, you will want to establish the facts, look at the root causes. Why do we not have more Black designers? From there, create targets. If your annual plan says, "We want to staff X number of Black designers," establish a target initiative to make that happen. Next, define governance. Who in your company is going to own this task? Who in your company is going to see this through to make sure it gets done?

Finally, you need to build inclusion. It's not enough to just hire Black designers. Does your corporate culture really make sure that you're including them, or are they just there as a token? If they're just there as a token, you're probably going to lose them sooner rather than later. Don't pigeonhole these designers. Don't just give them Black or African things to do. Don't exploit them for profit. Don't just bring in your Black employee and then make them do the inclusion work for you.

This work is not easy. This is going to be hard. It's going to take a sustained effort from a coalition of organizations, agencies, design firms, conferences, design media, and educational institutions. It's not the responsibility of Black designers or designers of color to fix this alone. We have our own shit to deal with. It shouldn't be up to us to fix a problem that we didn't create.

What are the real-world benefits of diversity for the design industry? First, you are creating design solutions that benefit people from different backgrounds. You escape the trap of homogeneity, where you only have people of a certain type in your company making decisions. Having a diverse group at the table ensures that you have a wider array of input so you can then make solutions that benefit a wider range of people. Second, it solves the infamous talent shortage problem because guess what? You're looking now in more places to find qualified people. Third, it prevents you from making stupid cultural gaffes that are born from homogeneity. It's good for business. A 2009 study in the *American Sociological Review* showed a positive correlation between racial and gender diversity and increased sales revenue, higher profits, more customers, and higher market share. So how much money are you leaving on the table by not trying to bring in a more diverse workforce?

Where do you find Black designers? My podcast, "Revision Path," features weekly interviews with Black designers, developers, and creatives. 28 Days of the Web features a different designer or developer for every day in the month of February. To date, we have highlighted hundreds of designers on these two sites. Facebook has several groups, including Black Designers United, and LinkedIn has groups like ADCOLOR, Black Creatives, and Urban Creative Network. Many of those groups are closed, so you can't just enter as an interloper. You need to add value, such as sharing information about job openings or calls for proposals. Another source for finding talent are HBCUs (Historically Black Colleges and Universities), including my own alma mater, Morehouse College, as well as Spelman College, Howard University, Hampton University, Florida A&M University, Jackson State University, and dozens more.

You can also look at your own network. Because, you know, everyone's got a Black friend, right? Ask your network who they know. Last, you have to look at yourself.

Look at your organization, your meetup, your firm, your agency, your corporate culture, the college where you teach, and ask yourself this: What are we doing that might be turning Black designers away? What are your core beliefs? What are you not being clear about as it relates to your corporate culture? Are the perks listed on your career page filtering people out on purpose? If diversity is one of your core values, you have to look within and ask, "What do I need to do to change the culture and make this something that designers that do not fall into the mainstream would be interested in?" Change is a process, not an event. This process will make you feel guilty, but that's okay. Guilt encourages you to have empathy for other people, to make corrective actions, and to improve.

People like Cheryl D. Miller did the research and laid out the groundwork for this issue nearly thirty years ago. AIGA has been doing their part with their symposiums, journal articles, and the Diversity & Inclusion Task Force. But it can't just be up to one person. It can't just be up to one organization. If we as an industry are serious about diversity, it's going to take a concerted effort to make sure this happens. It's time to stop making excuses and start making change.

SOURCES Cheryl D. Holmes-Miller, "Black Designers: Missing in Action," *Print*, Sep/Oct 1987 →printmag.com/post/blacks-in-design-1987; Michele Vernon-Chesley, "Equal Opportunities: Minorities in Graphic Design," *AIGA Journal* 8 no 1: 1990; Brenda Mitchell-Powell, "Why Is Graphic Design 93% White?" *AIGA Journal* 8, no. 1 (1990); →aiga.org/why-is-graphic-design-93-percent-white-diversity; Cedric Herring, "Does Diversity Pay?: Race, Gender, and the Business Case for Diversity," *American Sociological Review* 74, no. 2 (2009): 208–24 →academia.edu/6199683/Does_Diversity_Pay_Race_Gender_and_the_Business_Case_for_Diversity.

discrimination at work

TEXT BY JENNIFER TOBIAS

The US Civil Rights Act, passed in 1964, forbids workplace discrimination against people on account of their race, ethnicity, nationality, age, sex, disability, or genetics. Acts of discrimination against any protected group include getting fired, harassed, or denied opportunities to advance in a job. Discrimination need not be perpetrated by one bad actor—it can be systemic, baked into an organization's culture and pay structure. Discrimination on the basis of sex includes unwanted sexual advances, dehumanizing language about gender or sexuality, and pay or promotion penalties tied to pregnancy or parenthood. For over fifty years, queer and transgender people were not protected under the category of sex discrimination, but a Supreme Court decision changed that in June 2020.

If you think you are being discriminated against, speaking up is important. If you feel safe doing so, communicate directly with the person discriminating against you. If that's not feasible, ask your supervisor or HR to handle your complaint or to conduct a mediated conversation.

To take legal action, you will have to provide evidence, such as showing that sustained and repeated behaviors have been tolerated in your workplace. Keep a record of incidents and report those incidents. To understand local and national laws, read up online or talk to an employment lawyer. Many lawyers will offer a brief phone consultation for free. Brace yourself: litigation is a fraught process with no guaranteed outcome.

Legal action is not your only option if you have experienced discrimination. Your issue at work could be resolved after your bring it to light. You can help educate coworkers and create a more humane workplace for everyone.

A hostile work environment enables repeated, unchecked, and uninvestigated behavior, resulting in a severe negative impact on an employee's performance and/or well-being. Hostile behavior can be committed by coworkers, clients, independent contractors, or vendors, as well as by your supervisor. Examples include:

→ unwanted pinching, touching, hugging, kissing, etc.

→ exposure to offensive media, such as videos, GIFs, photographs, or drawings

→ persistent jokes and comments about your protected group

→ demeaning nicknames, such as "old-timer," "twink," or "bimbo"

→ creepy stares

→ exposure to your colleagues being harassed in these or other ways

→ getting assigned many more or many fewer hours than your colleagues

→ being denied opportunities to advance, such as attending client meetings, compared to your colleagues

SOURCE US Equal Employment Opportunity Commission, →eeoc.gov/employees-job-applicants.

when is it discrimination?

In the US, employers are permitted to enforce their own standards for dress, makeup, body modifications, and grooming, but religious practices are protected, and several states prohibit discrimination based on Black hair texture or style. This visual guide gives a sense of what types of expression or states of being are protected by US anti-discrimination laws and which ones aren't. This illustration isn't legal advice, just a quick take on some possible scenarios.

Employees have the right to wear garments required by their religion (such as a yarmulke, hijab, or turban).

Employers may enforce grooming standards (such as "no beards").

It is illegal to discriminate against neurodiversity that doesn't interfere with job duties.

Employers may forbid political expression in the workplace.

Employers may limit religious expression (not required by that religion) in the workplace.

It is illegal to discriminate against a person on account of their
→age
→race
→military status
→gender identity
→sexual orientation.

Employers may impose a dress code (such as "no shorts, bare bellies, or flip flops").

It is illegal to discriminate against people for being parents or becoming pregnant.

Employers may enforce a no-pets policy at work.

Service animals must be permitted at work.

It is illegal to discriminate against a person with a disability.

ILLUSTRATION BY JENNIFER TOBIAS

parents at work

TEXT BY ELLEN LUPTON

It turns out that the cradle of civilization is…that's right, a cradle. Societies grow and thrive in part because people have kids and raise them. In many families, parents who are women take primary responsibility for childrearing. These parents are also the main breadwinners in countless families—often the only breadwinners.

US labor statistics show that men often get pay raises after becoming fathers. Dads are rewarded for taking on this big responsibility; they are considered mature and dependable employees. The same is not true for mothers, who may be overlooked for a promotion or have a hard time switching jobs. Moms are seen as less committed to their careers and more likely to miss work or avoid late nights.

Paid parental leave is not typical for designers in the US. In 2018, 17 percent of civilian workers had access to paid parental leave; companies with more than 500 employees were more likely to provide this benefit. According to the AIGA Design Census 2019, only 7 percent of graphic designers were offered paid parental leave.

The rights of pregnant workers are protected under Title VII of the 1964 Civil Rights Act, which forbids discrimination on account of sex. The US national Family and Medical Leave Act guarantees that people can take unpaid time off to care for a child or sick relative. While the law requires the employer to reserve a job for the worker, they are not required to offer the same job. A person returning from family leave could end up in a new situation with fewer opportunities. When no paid leave is available, some new parents accumulate sick days and vacation in order to spend time with an infant. Such time should not be confused with paid leave. Those saved-up days or weeks have been earned on the job just like any other employee's vacation or sick pay. Asking a pregnant person if

they are looking forward to their "vacation" or "time off" perpetrates the myth that new parents have access to luxurious benefits.

Many new parents decide that one partner will stop working outside the home for an extended period. One parent staying home can make it easier for a second parent to excel at work. For the parent leaving the workforce, this decision can damage future earnings. Returning parents may be perceived as out of touch with developments in their field. The COVID-19 crisis forced many working parents to leave their jobs; the careers of parents who are women sustained high levels of damage.

The rights of parents and pregnant people vary from region to region. It's important to know your rights and advocate for them, as well as to advocate for the rights of people around you.

SOURCES Robin J. Ely, et al., "Rethink What You 'Know' About High-Achieving Women," *Harvard Business Review*, Dec 2014 →hbr.org/2014/12/rethink-what-you-know-about-high-achieving-women; US Bureau of Labor Statistics, "Access to paid and unpaid family leave in 2018," Feb 27, 2019 →bls.gov/opub/ted/2019/access-to-paid-and-unpaid-family-leave-in-2018.htm; "Family and Medical Leave (FMLA)" →dol.gov/general/topic/benefits-leave/fmla; New York State, "Pregnancy Rights for Employees in the Workplace" →ny.gov/working-while-pregnant-know-your-rights/pregnancy-rights-employees-workplace; A. Hoffkling, J. Obedin-Maliver, and J. Sevelius, "From erasure to opportunity: a qualitative study of the experiences of transgender men around pregnancy and recommendations for providers," *BMC Pregnancy and Childbirth* 17, no. 332 (2017) →doi.org/10.1186/s12884-017-1491-5.

pregnant bodies Supervisors or coworkers often worry that a pregnant person will become less engaged with their work following the birth of their child. Some people hide their pregnancy for as long as possible to avoid negative reactions. Many transgender men retain their uterus, and some desire to get pregnant and give birth. These expectant fathers overcome negative attitudes and barriers regarding pregnancy in the workplace as well as in health-care settings and the broader social arena.

ILLUSTRATION BY JENNIFER TOBIAS

coming out at work

TEXT BY LESLIE XIA

The process of coming out is a deeply personal experience that often takes multiple steps as you come out to different people in your life, starting with yourself, and then to your friends, your family, and your colleagues. Introducing your pronouns can be another step in this process of becoming normalized within your relationships with others.

There is no proper way to introduce your pronouns. Institutional spaces are often heteropatriarchal and do not have systems in place that allow for a formal process to acknowledge queer, trans, nonbinary, intersex, and other marginalized bodies.

In the US, the fight for LGBTQIA+ rights is still happening today. The historic Stonewall Uprising started on June 28, 1969, led by queer people of color, igniting the fight for gay rights. In 2003, same-sex relationships were deemed legal in the US Supreme Court case *Lawrence v. Texas*. In 2015, gay marriage was deemed legal in the US Supreme Court case *Obergefell v. Hodges*. In 2020, the US Supreme Court amended the US Civil Rights Act of 1964 to include work protections for LGBTIA+ folk, who can no longer be reprimanded or fired based on their sexual orientation or gender identity.

In some areas of the US and in many parts of the world, coming out in the workplace isn't taken lightly, and you will have to think carefully before deciding to out yourself. Often, LGBTQIA+ people default to the gender they "present" as and do not mention their sexual orientation or gender identity for their own safety and to avoid criticism and questions from colleagues.

Once you feel that your workplace is a safe space, there are several ways to begin introducing your pronouns. These suggestions are not a blueprint. Use your judgment to find what works for you!

Pensacola · Tallahassee · Jacksonville

rural, conservative areas

Orlando · Cape Canaveral

Tampa · St. Petersburg · Sarasota

major urban areas

Palm Beach · Coral Springs · Miami · Key Largo · Key West

historically gay community

safety first Coming out is a personal decision. Even within a single region such as the state of Florida, communities vary in terms of tolerance.

ILLUSTRATION BY JENNIFER TOBIAS

feeling safe about coming out at work

→ What city/town and state are you working in? Does your region lean more right or left? Are there state- or city-level job protections for LGBTQIA+ laborers in your area?

→ Is there a local LGBTQIA+ civil rights group who can help assess job protections in your city and state?

→ Does your company's employee handbook explicitly state job protections for LGBTQIA+ folks? Do you feel comfortable asking your Human Resources department about job protections or LGBTQIA+ affinity groups at your workplace?

→ Are your coworkers more right- or left-leaning? Have you gauged from conversations their experiences with LGBTQIA+ issues and their knowledge of preferred pronoun use?

→ Does your workplace celebrate or acknowledge Pride month?

→ Are there other openly LGBTQIA+ employees at your workplace? Are you comfortable reaching out to them for advice?

tips for coming out at work

→ Each time you introduce yourself, include your pronouns and ask others for theirs, too.

→ Send an e-mail to your colleagues introducing yourself with your pronouns and explaining preferred pronouns. Add your pronouns to your e-mail signature and invite your colleagues to do the same.

→ Add your pronouns to your social media accounts if you feel safe sharing your pronouns with the public. Use your best judgment because the internet can be a dangerous space where folks may attack, doxx, or spread information about you.

→ Ask your Human Resources department if preferred pronoun use can be added to the employee handbook and if pronoun introductions can become standard practice.

→ If your company has a queer affinity group or union, ask them to help standardize pronoun introductions.

→ Reach out to an LGBTQIA+ civil rights group for advice.

TYPFACE | ZANGEZI SANS | BY DARIA PETROVA

The template at right is based on a real e-mail I've sent to introduce my pronouns to folks where I work. I also send a copy (cc) to Human Resources, in case I receive any hostile responses from colleagues who may not understand, and also as a way to hold Human Resources accountable for facilitating these conversations.

Expect warm messages and exclamations of thanks for sharing from colleagues. If some folks don't fully understand and want to learn more, you can send them a link to an article explaining it or direct them to Human Resources (if you have notified them) to discuss further. If you receive hostile remarks, do not engage; forward these messages to Human Resources.

After sharing your pronouns at work, expect there to be slipups! The first few days may be tricky for some people, and some colleagues might not feel comfortable using your pronouns at all. Don't take this personally! One thing that I like to remember is that everyone possesses their own truth, and everyone is on their own learning journey. Although it is a bummer when people do not acknowledge your identity, you are making a big leap when you take the first steps to come out in your workplace. Good luck!

Hello colleagues!

I've been at [Your Workplace] for a bit now, and I wanted to send out an e-mail to sort of come out and voice that I identify with they/them pronouns and would like to be referred to with they/them pronouns.

[Your Workplace], like most companies, doesn't make it standard practice for people to share their pronouns when you first meet them. People-centric corporations have a duty to make it standard and mandatory to provide a safe outlet for every employee to communicate their pronouns, for all queer, trans, gender-neutral, gender-nonconforming, nonbinary, and gender-variant folks.

A good way to start is by including your pronouns in Slack descriptions, Twitter bios, and e-mail signatures. It should be standard practice for everyone to share their pronouns when introducing themselves. If every employee at [Your Workplace] began sharing their pronouns, we would all be helping create a comfortable and safe space for queer and trans folks.

I've seen this successfully done at colleges that actively discuss topics of race, gender, and gender identity. Many colleges have made it standard for every faculty member to voice their pronouns when they first introduce themselves and to include their pronouns wherever they have their titles, like in their e-mail signatures. Faculty set the standard for their students to follow, and it's become commonplace for students to share their pronouns when meeting for the first time.

I hope that everyone at [Your Workplace] can work together to make this something we are all comfortable with!

> Sincerely yours,
> Leslie
>
> ---
>
> LESLIE XIA
> Pronouns: they/them

salary transparency

TEXT BY JENNIFER TOBIAS

Making an image transparent is easy; pay transparency is harder to achieve. AIGA confirms, "Most places of employment work hard to keep pay opaque, and studios, agencies, institutions, and companies are increasingly savvy when it comes to omitting wage information from job boards." Why do companies hide their salary data? Managers can't always justify differences in pay, which could reflect biased hiring practices.

This information asymmetry on compensation puts all negotiating power in the hands of the employer. "Disclosing your salary to a colleague can be more than just uncomfortable—it may be viewed as a subversive act," notes AIGA. Discussing pay and benefits with colleagues is legal, however, and most US workers are protected by law. That doesn't mean, however, that you're required to reveal your previous earnings to a potential employer. Several US states bar job interviewers from asking applicants about their salary history

The annual AIGA salary survey breaks out pay by region and job type across the US. Salary aggregators help job seekers suss out salary information, while government salary data in the US are required to be accessible. Labor unions rely on shared knowledge to negotiate contracts. In the arts sector, check out grassroots surveys such as the 2019 Art/Museum Salary Transparency spreadsheet and the POWarts salary survey.

Your personal network is another tool for moving the transparency slider. Avoid comparing specific people—discuss job titles instead of the individuals who hold them. Explaining to colleagues that transparency benefits everyone helps to counter the common fear of a zero-sum game—that a higher salary for some means a lower salary for others.

Once you are armed with good information, it's time to speak your salary truth to management power. Promoting the overall benefit to your organization can be more effective (and less likely to result in personal backlash) than pursuing a raise just for yourself. Refer to facts and research. According to recent studies, salary transparency can increase productivity and make workers more likely to collaborate. Transparency also forces companies to rationalize positions that may have developed haphazardly over time—with bias toward White men and strong negotiators. Patterns of bias leave organizations open to discrimination lawsuits. In an opaque power structure, even those high on the food chain are likely to be in the dark and similarly insecure for themselves, if not their team.

Economic transparency isn't just for worker bees. Some independent creatives share information about their income as a way to educate others about how to survive as an artist. Be Oakley, founder of the publishing platform GenderFail, says, "As a working-class artist without a regular paycheck, I cherish every dollar I make from my work with GenderFail. Every time I get an order or sell an object I feel truly grateful and do not take it for granted. I want to make money off my work, and I want other artists I work with to make money from the books I publish with them. I want people to be paid for their labor in the arts."

Nudging the transparency slider to 100 percent takes more than a mouse click, but these strategic moves can help sharpen the career picture for yourself and others.

SOURCES "It's Time for Graphic Design to Embrace the Radical Potential of Salary Transparency," *AIGA Eye on Design*, Dec 9, 2019 →eyeondesign.aiga.org/its-time-for -graphic-design-to-embrace-the-radical-potential-of -salary-transparency; Art/Museum Salary Transparency Survey, 2019 →rebrand.ly/salaryspreadsheet; POWarts Salary Survey, 2019 →powarts.org/salarysurvey; Jessica Bennett, "I'll Share My Salary Information if You Share Yours," *New York Times*, Jan 9, 2020 →nyti.ms/2RcHBRp;

Kristin Wong, "Want to Close the Pay Gap? Pay Transparency Will Help," *New York Times*, Jan 20, 2019 →nyti.ms/2S0d4bJ; Emiliano Huet-Vaughn, "Striving for Status: A Field Experiment on Relative Earnings and Labor Supply," UC Berkeley Job Market Paper, Nov 2013 →econgrads.berkeley.edu/ emilianohuet-vaughn/files/2012/11/JMP_e.pdf; Be Oakley, "Small Publishing and Finding Ways to Live," *GenderFail Reader 2*, 2020.

ILLUSTRATIONS BY JENNIFER TOBIAS

exit strategies

TEXT BY JENNIFER TOBIAS

"Enough of these long hours and low pay!" you cry, leaping on to the desk you share with five other designers in the open-office cubicle farm. "I've been overextended and undersupported long enough!"

Shaking your fist at the nearest authority figure, you unleash an impassioned "Kern this!" as you bound off the table, swiping heaps of paper to the floor on your way to the elevator (where you are forced to wait for ninety awkward seconds).

Do not do this. Dramatic exits sound exciting but will not enhance your career in the long run. You might imagine that quitting your job will leave everyone weeping tears of remorse, but in reality, the place will probably survive just fine without you. Only quit if it serves your own best interests (if, for example, you have lined up a better job or you have decided to go to grad school, start your own business, or evacuate to Mars). If you are fantasizing about quitting out of anger, think about whether you could negotiate a change in your position instead. (More pay? Different projects? A desk by the window?) Rational thought won't win you an Academy Award, but it may help you keep your life in order.

Why is it important to leave your job in a calm and collected manner? For one thing, being a jerk adds toxic energy to the world. For another thing, your next job might not last forever, either, and future employers will check your references and find out how people feel about you. Trash-talking your boss or causing a Twitter storm on your way out will tarnish your own brand as much as your company's.

The same truths hold if you are fired. Although getting fired feels like a grave act of violence against your person, individuals are laid off for many reasons, and your employer may empathize with your situation and wish you a bright future. Make your departure as friendly and dignified as you can manage.

Approximately 7 percent of graphic designers envision quitting their jobs, according to the 2019 AIGA Design Census, and even the 50 percent of designers who are happy at work wish for better circumstances. Mobility is a characteristic of the design profession, where career arcs are likely to include internships, heavy labor as a junior designer, a climb to senior designer, and moves between different companies and institutions. In-house and agency designers, including permalancers, average four years with one company, while freelancers, solo, and small-studio owners tend to stay in place for a decade or more.

If, like most people in capitalist society, your life is structured around working for money, the process of moving between jobs can cause big changes to your pace, your social life, and your sense of self. One strategy for adapting: reimagine that dramatic exit as an equally compelling first day at an exciting new job.

how to quit

→ Find a new job first. You're more likely to be hired if you are employed, according to at least one published study and gallons of water-cooler wisdom.

→ Check your contract or company policy regarding minimum notice. Two weeks' notice is often required.

→ Notify, in order and in writing, your supervisor, HR, colleagues, and clients. Include your end date and contact information. Avoid drama: no snarky comments or hidden daggers. Keep it professional.

→ Check into transferring benefits such as a pension or 401(k) and cashing out any unused leave.

→ If you have health-care benefits, maximize coverage by ending your employment on the first day of a month. Get medical checkups and screenings before you leave.

→ Find out if you are eligible for unemployment benefits. In the US, resigning from your job (rather than being fired or laid off) usually disqualifies you for unemployment pay.

→ Build your network. Line up references. Collect names, as well as exact titles, addresses, and contact information.

→ Clean up and organize your work files to make it easy for others to carry on your duties. Transfer ownership of shared data. Delete browser histories.

→ Ask your employer if your e-mail can stay active for a reasonable period, to include a forwarding message that you will write.

how to get fired

If you get fired (or think you might get fired soon), all of the advice above applies. Plus:

→ Negotiate severance pay. Employers are not required to provide this, but it's a common enough practice to be worth requesting.

→ Find out how your organization responds to outside inquiries from new potential employers about your time on the job. Many companies will confirm only title and dates, but some will comment on your work performance.

→ Is it legal? If you are leaving your job because you believe you have been unlawfully discriminated against, do your homework. See more in our chapter "Discrimination at Work," on page 166.

applied arts

→ Refresh your brand by spiffing up your résumé and website. Post an easy-access pdf to your site. Give it a searchable name like lastname_resume.pdf.

→ Learn new skills. Take an online course. Go to grad school. Better yet, teach a class at a local art school or community college. Teaching forces you to polish and refine what you know.

→ Prepare for the big data demands of online job applications. Many employment sites require a detailed work and educational history down to month and year, including addresses and phone numbers for all employers and references.

→ Control your own narrative. To help people make sense of your situation, have a one-sentence story. Examples: making a change, repositioning, reskilling, or seeking challenge/flexibllity/pay/location/work-life balance.

→ Use your time and talent for the greater good. Offer your services to organiza-tions. Embrace mutual aid. Activate your inner activist.

→ Care for yourself. Breathe. Take walks. Work out. Call your mom.

ILLUSTRATION BY JENNIFER TOBIAS

the entreprecariat

TEXT BY ELLEN LUPTON

With the growth of the so-called gig economy and other shifts in business practice, many designers work as freelancers rather than permanent employees, either by choice or by necessity. This trend is global. In Italy, Silvio Lorusso writes about the "entreprecariat" as a struggling creative class balanced between entrepreneurship and precarity. AI-driven logo generators and online design platforms selling à la carte logos replace in-depth design consultation with cheap, fast solutions. Like dating apps, such services connect clients to designers with minimal cost and friction—no meetings, no lengthy proposals, no market research.

For someone selling custom cupcakes or operating a dry-cleaning shop, online design platforms offer easy access to design services that might otherwise be out of reach. Alas, such services also undercut the value of creative work.

Design contests are a form of "spec" (speculative) work, in which a designer produces creative material for a client with no guarantee of payment. Many designers consider spec work unethical because it downgrades the value of the profession as a whole and creates the expectation that designers should be willing to work to free. When creatives make work on spec, they imply that a logo is just a logo, rather than the result of in-depth research and thoughtful conversations between consultant and client.

Online design platforms drain work from traditional design agencies. At the same time, they offer new points of entry for designers. Global freelance platforms allow designers from anywhere in the world to connect with potential clients in a hassle-free, low-risk way. Emerging designers can find clients and build a portfolio. But those opportunities come at a cost. By working for low pay, gig designers lower the value of their own service along with everyone else's. It's hard to rebuild the value of a product that's been sold cheaply.

Around the world, independent designers operate more-traditional design firms on a freelance basis. Working as sole proprietors, designers can build personal relationships with their clients and provide high-quality work, often developing long-lasting business ties. Many freelancers value their independence. Freelance unions help these workers purchase health insurance and other products that are typically provided by larger employers. In the age of the gig economy, platforms like Fiverr make it easy for freelancers to hire other freelancers for everything from bookkeeping to social media management.

Lorusso, seeking to protect the entreprecariat against financial collapse, believes design schools should become think tanks that develop not just visual skills but new definitions of work itself. Concepts such as universal basic income could change the way society values creative workers.

SOURCE Silvio Lorusso, "Entreprecariat: What Design Can't Do—Graphic Design between Automation, Relativism, Élite and Cognitariat," Institute of Network Cultures, Feb 27, 2017 →networkcultures. org/entreprecariat/what-design-cant-do/.

diving into the gig economy

We plunged into the gig economy and explored it from the client side. First, we created a fictional product in need of a logo: a cryptocurrency called $h*tcoin. Then, we scouted for online design services. Companies like Logoglo ask clients to pay in advance, sign a contract, and answer questions to create a design brief. Fiverr connects clients with a network of freelancers and gathers information about the client's personal taste and business objectives with an AI-driven form. 99designs hosts design contests, inviting numerous creatives to compete against one another to win a fixed commission. The logos we ended up with vary widely in quality. Regardless of quality, however, it felt wrong to pay so little for graphic design.

$55

Logoglo was founded by Gary Robinson, who studied graphic design at City College Manchester, UK. He founded Logoglo after moving to the US. He says, "I was tired of seeing the people who I worked for charge ridiculous amounts of money for their graphic design services." From a client's perspective, Logoglo's design process was fast and friendly, yielding a logo as blunt and sturdy as a billy club.

$100

$H*TCOIN

The Fiverr platform connects freelancers with clients. Although some of Fiverr's designers really will design a logo for five bucks, we posted our job for $100. We received many responses from designers working outside the US; we picked sarahgraphix, a computer science student in Pakistan. She provided a very basic logo and was eager to build out a full identity package.

$299

99designs hosts design contests on behalf of clients. We paid $299 for a basic "bronze" package. Our contest attracted more than seventy-five entries, many of them multiple submissions by single designers. The winner we picked is Alejandro Batres, a designer starting his career in northern New Jersey. His rather brilliant design successfully combines the shape of an S with the curves of a turd.

confidence equity

TEXT BY ELLEN LUPTON

Confidence is a sense of certainty and optimism about carrying out a task. Who owns this magical feeling? Are we born with confidence, or do we earn it? If we don't have it, how can we get it? Confidence is something we feel about ourselves. It's also a feeling about other people. ("I have confidence in her abilities.") Confidence is not a fixed personality trait. It is a behavior expressed through actions, speech, and body language.

Confidence is not just personal. It's social. Belief in your own abilities derives from your proven successes (that single soccer goal you made in third grade), as well as from support received from others (your parents showed up and cheered at the game, and you got a participation trophy even though your team lost). People who are expected to succeed are more likely to do so than people who are expected to fail. Your personal confidence is boosted by numerous forces throughout our lives—by parents, teachers, and soccer coaches and by the norms and narratives of the culture we live in. People who grow up being told that running the world is their right and privilege are more likely to feel confident than those who are marginalized and whose success is downplayed.

If you are seeking to become more self-assured, it's helpful to view confidence as a social performance rather than an innate talent. Problems with confidence are yet another aspect of social inequality. Recognizing this can be a first step in enhancing belief in one's own abilities. You can also begin to help others who are being held back and pushed to stay quiet.

The term *confidence gap* refers to the doubt and insecurity that women and members of marginalized groups often feel in professional contexts. Social scientists in the US have tracked statistical differences between the confidence displayed by men and women. For example, men are more likely to initiate salary negotiations and to ask for more money when doing so.

The confidence gap is self-perpetuating. A person who says "Yes, I'll do it!" is more likely to be trusted with challenging tasks than a person who constantly doubts and downplays their abilities. The person who is positive and upbeat about their skills may not really be more talented or competent, but they build up their expertise each time they give it a shot. Believing you can do something may precede being able to actually do it. Confidence is a form of courage. Although courage can drive foolish behaviors (bungee jumping? karaoke?), it can yield serious dividends in personal growth and trust from others.

Too much confidence is a problem, too. Overconfident people suck up social oxygen. A designer with excessive confidence might avoid researching a problem or might refuse to try multiple solutions. Journalist Nathalie Olah points out that many world leaders were born into social elites. Their confidence comes from a place of privilege. Big corporations and entire nations have been destroyed by leaders who put too much trust in their own instincts.

Willingness to examine your assumptions, double-check your work, and prepare vigorously for important events shows respect for others and curiosity about yourself. By learning to be a patient listener as well as an active participant, you can help build confidence equity!

THE SOCIAL DYNAMICS OF CONFIDENCE

CONFIDENCE IS BOTH HOW WE FEEL ABOUT OURSELVES AND HOW OTHER PEOPLE FEEL ABOUT US.

INCOMING SIGNALS: "SHE'S GOT THIS."

OUTGOING SIGNALS: "I'VE GOT THIS."

OTHER PEOPLE INVEST CONFIDENCE IN AN INDIVIDUAL BASED ON BIAS AS WELL AS ON THE PERSON'S ACTIONS AND ABILITIES.

AN INDIVIDUAL EXPRESSES SELF-CONFIDENCE THROUGH THEIR VOICE, ACTIONS, AND DEMEANOR.

CONFIDENCE IS A FEELING OF TRUST PLACED IN ANOTHER PERSON.

A PERSON'S TONE OF VOICE AND CHOICE OF WORDS CONVEY BELIEF IN THEIR OWN ABILITIES.

IF YOU HAVEN'T SEEN AIRPLANE PILOTS WHO ARE WOMEN, YOU MAY DOUBT THEIR ABILITIES WHEN YOU DO ENCOUNTER THEM.

IN THE EVENT OF A SUDDEN LOSS OF CONFIDENCE, ASSIST OTHERS IN RESTORING MUTUAL TRUST AND RESPECT.

BADGES, BLAZERS, TROUSERS, TIES, AND MILITARY INSIGNIA SIGNIFY STATUS AND AUTHORITY.

BODY LANGUAGE COMMUNICATES POWER.

ILLUSTRATION BY JENNIFER TOBIAS

The term *imposter syndrome* refers to the feelings of doubt and inadequacy many people suffer even after achieving an impressive goal, such as landing a great job or publishing a respected book. Rather than believing we earned our new position, we fear being exposed as phonies, frauds, or wannabes. Njoki Gitahi, a designer from Kenya, is a senior design lead at IDEO, one of the world's most respected consultancies. Despite her success, she experiences doubt: "I wish I had the confidence of a straight White male, who might be thinking, 'Everything's going to go my way. I'm going to do this. I deserve this.' I marvel at that kind of confidence."

Although such feelings of self-doubt are, in Gitahi's words, "bullshit," they are nonetheless common, especially among people subjected to racism and/or sexism. The term *imposter syndrome* labels this feeling as an illness or delusion rather than a social problem. If we just tried harder to love ourselves, we wouldn't feel this encroaching sense of failure.

In fact, imposter syndrome is triggered by external social forces, not just inner anxieties. Perhaps we doubt our own achievements because the people around us are, in fact, doubting us. Marginalized people are pushed to prove themselves more strenuously than those with presumed dominance. People subjected to sexism and/or racism are often harshly judged when displaying strength. Stereotypes such as "ballbuster" or "angry Black woman" demean those who speak up and question the status quo.

Members of an underrepresented group may feel isolated at work. Joining an affinity group, seeking out a mentor with a common background, and writing down your professional accomplishments can be helpful techniques. Kevin Cokley, professor of educational psychology at the University of Texas, Austin, explains that a work diary can not only help you take pride in your abilities, it can also be used as evidence if you file a discrimination claim.

"Is she just a diversity hire?"

"Did he have a Tiger Mom?"

HELLO
MY NAME IS
Imposter

"Did he benefit from affirmative action?"

"Can a lady really fly an airplane?"

"Is she only on this panel because they needed a woman?"

the woman card

People are sometimes accused of "playing the woman card" when they mention their gender identity during discussions of power. The accusation implies that the woman in question could not succeed in the given situation on her own merits but only as a member of a victimized class. During the 2016 US presidential election, Donald Trump accused his opponent, Hillary Clinton, of using her identity as a woman to gain traction with voters. She replied, "If fighting for women's health-care and paid family leave and equal pay is playing the woman card, then deal me in." Clinton refused to accept the implication that gender is neutral.

the race card

Like the "woman card," the "race card" is a verbal tool for undermining people of color when they point out racist behavior. Accusing someone of "playing the race card" is a defensive move designed to deflect attention away from one's own racist actions or beliefs. The term is also used against politicians who seek solidarity with particular racial or ethnic groups and play to their interests.

READ MORE Katty Kay and Claire Shipman, "The Confidence Gap," *Atlantic*, May 2014 →theatlantic.com/magazine/archive/2014/05/the-confidence-gap/359815/; Stephanie Thomson, "A Lack of Confidence Isn't What's Holding Back Working Women," *Atlantic*, Sep 2018 →theatlantic.com/family/archive/2018/09/women-workplace-confidence-gap/570772/; Kristin Wong, "Dealing With Impostor Syndrome When You're Treated as an Impostor," *New York Times*, Jun 12, 2018 →nytimes.com/2018/06/12/smarter-living/dealing-with-impostor-syndrome-when-youre-treated-as-an-impostor.html; Richard Thompson Ford, *The Race Card: How Bluffing About Bias Makes Race Relations Worse* (New York: Farrar, Straus and Giroux, 2009).

ILLUSTRATIONs BY JENNIFER TOBIAS

In many college classrooms, women students outnumber men. International students and people of color are growing populations in design programs. Today, the White male design student may find himself in the minority rather than the majority. Nonetheless, White men often are among the most vocal students in the room and may be treated with special respect by faculty. Perhaps an outspoken young man grew up around teachers, parents, and coaches who praised him for sharing his views. However, others in the room should also have a chance to cultivate their talent for communication. Even someone who seeks to be a leader should share space and allow others to speak.

→ Be patient. After asking for comments from the group, give people a chance to think about their response.

→ Take turns. Instead of asking people to raise their hands to speak, go around the room in a sequence.

→ Use objects. Give everyone a card, straw, or other token. A person can't contribute again until everyone has used their token.

→ Invite participants to write down comments before asking for volunteers to speak. A shy person may feel bolder after noting their thoughts in writing.

→ Don't be a jerk. If you've been talking a lot, it's time to shut up and listen.

ILLUSTRATION BY JENNIFER TOBIAS

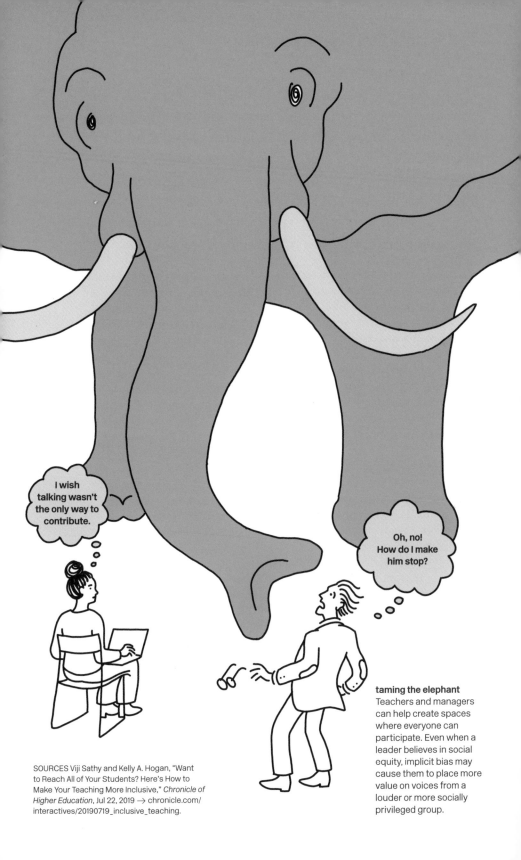

I wish talking wasn't the only way to contribute.

Oh, no! How do I make him stop?

taming the elephant
Teachers and managers can help create spaces where everyone can participate. Even when a leader believes in social equity, implicit bias may cause them to place more value on voices from a louder or more socially privileged group.

SOURCES Viji Sathy and Kelly A. Hogan, "Want to Reach All of Your Students? Here's How to Make Your Teaching More Inclusive," *Chronicle of Higher Education*, Jul 22, 2019 → chronicle.com/interactives/20190719_inclusive_teaching.

emotional housekeeping

TEXT BY JENNIFER TOBIAS

Office support tasks such as taking notes, soothing bruised egos, and organizing birthday parties often fall to women and members of minority groups. Although you might feel like an energetic team player when doing this work, you could be undermining your own power.

Pay equity advisor Katie Donovan of Equal Pay Negotiations says, "This stuff isn't helping us move up the corporate ladder." Becoming the office housekeeper or emotional camp counselor hinders the careers of people who may have a salary disadvantage from the outset.

According to researchers Linda Babcock and Lise Vesterlund, office housework is "non-promotable" labor—tasks that keep the company running but are invisible in performance evaluations. Leading a branding team could get you promoted; herding files or scheduling meetings won't. People marginalized by racism and/or sexism are likely to take on more non-promotable tasks and get less acknowledgment.

Racial stereotypes also play a part, exploiting associations of some groups with servitude, passivity, and the desire for social harmony. Ruchika Tulshyan observes that African American women tend to be assigned to the kind of administrative and low-stakes projects that are less likely to result in promotions.

Resisting these subtle but pervasive patterns could have negative consequences. People targeted by racism and/or sexism often get pushback in the workplace for displaying competence, confidence, or assertiveness, while those in dominant groups face few consequences for rejecting routine tasks.

Emotional labor describes warm-and-fuzzy work duties. Sociologist Arlie Hochschild, who first introduced the term, defines emotional labor as "the work, for which you're paid, which centrally involves trying to feel the right feeling for the job." A design firm's office manager may be expected to be cheerful and empathetic, for example, while the accountant is hired to be hard-driving and objective.

Librarian Anastasia Collins created a fictional invoice showing how marginalized people are expected to absorb racial tension and be helpful (but not angry) educators about systemic oppression. Her invoice enumerates the emotional labor required to tolerate microaggressions while also educating White people about racism, oppression, and other topics they should be researching on their own.

Placing the burden of change on emotional laborers produces more of the same problem. Still, workers have some power to make emotional labor visible. This work requires organizing, communication, and persistence. A prime goal: mobilizing managers to take action and become aware of how emotional labor is assigned and rewarded.

As your career progresses and you accumulate power, use it for good. Consider reframing emotional labor as a leadership tool. According to writer Gemma Hartley, women who are skilled in empathy and caring "make really great leaders, especially in grassroots activism. It [emotional labor] will help men in the workplace to connect with their peers. I don't think that there is a downside to men taking on emotional labor in the workplace at all."

EMOTIONAL LABOR
INVOICE

Marginalized Folks, Inc.

TO Potential Ally
Privileged Folks, Ltd.

SERVICE PROVIDER	**SPECIALIZATION**
Marginalized Person You know	Existing in Oppression

DESCRIPTION	PRICE
Helped you understand your racism/sexism/transphobia/ableism/etc.	$100
Endured your microaggression(s)	$200
Taught you about microaggressions and structural oppression	$300
Explained something about oppression that you could've Googled	$125
Clarified that you are not entitled to my time	$250
Clarified that you are not entitled to my pain	$350
Softened my reaction to spare your feelings	$500
Made you feel like a "good" ally	$600
Listened to "not all..." and similar derailments/fragility	$750
Smiled when you apologized for not speaking up at the meeting	$1000
AMOUNT DUE (with marginalization tax adjustment)	**$1500**

ANASTASIA COLLINS This invoice for emotional labor addresses
the burden placed on "marginalized folks" in the workplace,
who are often asked to do things like speak on behalf of an
entire social group, pose for diversity portraits, and keep
the peace by refraining from pointing out microaggressions
or offensive jokes. © Anastasia Collins, licensed under a
Creative Commons Attribution-NonCommercial-ShareAlike 4.0
International License

Pro tips for achieving a more equitable distribution of housekeeping at work

Reduce office housework. For example, instead of expecting one person to take multiple lunch orders and haul them back to the conference room, ask staff to set up individual delivery accounts.

Set up a shared rotation of tasks. Make a job list. (Wipe down the whiteboard. Clear the sink. Clean the fridge. Restock coffee.) Maintaining and complying with the system should be noted in performance evaluations. Once in place, this rotation should be tracked by an appropriate staff person, such as the office manager.

Conduct social experiments. Find opportunities to bring up housekeeping equity. Consider a test: agree with your allies to hold off volunteering to take notes at the next staff meeting and see what happens.

Don't start a race to the bottom of the sink. Instead of competing with other workers to see who's best at cleaning up, channel your energy back into your professional expertise. You are more likely to be noticed and rewarded for your design skills and organizational savvy than for keeping the countertops gleaming.

Be prepared for backlash and denial. "But I don't use the fridge." "Junior staff's job is to support senior designers." Don't let questionable assumptions and straight-up defensiveness block the effort to make everyone help maintain a clean, safe, and equitable workplace.

Beware toothless task forces. They tend to involve lots of effort for little result. Stick to the essential demand: workplace equality.

Avoid clever signs. Tempting as it is to post cute graphics nudging others to do their part, don't do it. No one reads signs.

gift flowers requiring immediate care and attention

coffee rings of hell

lip service

Wait, didn't you have a birthday last year? The task of organizing birthday parties and baby showers at work often falls to women. (In fairness, it may be women's idea to have these celebrations in the first place.) Party duties include everything from collecting money and choosing gifts to cooking, decorating, and cleaning up. Are these gatherings worth it? Could parties be combined for greater effect?

archaeology of the sink

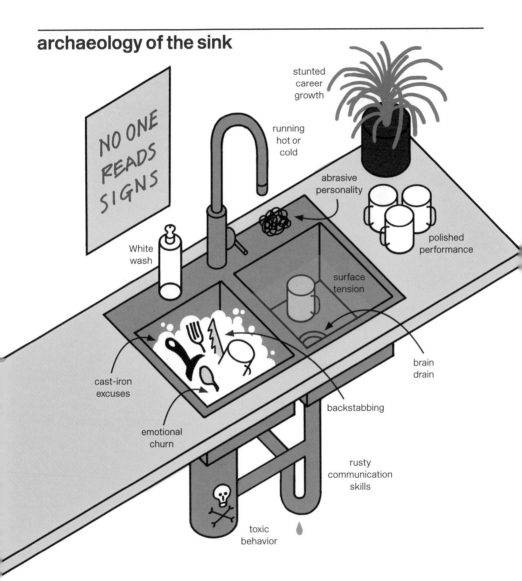

stunted career growth

running hot or cold

abrasive personality

NO ONE READS SIGNS

White wash

polished performance

surface tension

cast-iron excuses

brain drain

backstabbing

emotional churn

rusty communication skills

toxic behavior

SOURCES Julie Beck, "The Concept Creep of Emotional Labor," *Atlantic*, Nov 26, 2018, → theatlantic.com/family/archive/2018/11/arlie-hochschild-housework-isnt-emotional-labor/576637/; Linda Babcock , Maria P. Recalde, and Lise Vesterlund, "Why Women Volunteer for Tasks That Don't Lead to Promotions," *Harvard Business Review*, Jul 16, 2018 →hbr.org/2018/07/why-women-volunteer-for-tasks-that-dont-lead-to-promotions; Rachel Feintzeig, "Don't Ask Me to Do Office Housework!" *Wall Street Journal*, Oct 13, 2019 → wsj.com/articles/dont-ask-me-to-do-office-housework-11570959002; Gemma Hartley, *Fed Up:*

Emotional Labor, Women, and the Way Forward (New York: Harper, 2018); Arlie Hochschild, *The Managed Heart: Commercialization of Human Feeling* (Berkeley: University of California, 2012); Anisa Purbasari Horton, "Men, emotional labor is your problem, too," *Fast Company*, Nov 18, 2019. → fastcompany.com/90268277/men-emotional-labor-is-your-problem-too; Ruchika Tulshyan, "Women of Color Get Asked to Do More 'Office Housework': Here's How They Can Say No," *Harvard Business Review*, Apr 6, 2018 → hbr.org/2018/04/women-of-color-get-asked-to-do-more-office-housework-heres-how-they-can-say-no.

ILLUSTRATION BY JENNIFER TOBIAS

psychological safety

TEXT BY ELLEN LUPTON

Design is a team sport—whether it's played in a boutique studio or in a monster tech company. Some teams are driven by strong leaders (such as art directors or creative directors), while others are run by project managers (who facilitate the business end of the creative process). Egalitarian teams may have no hierarchy at all. Regardless of its structure, a team can function as a joyfully productive social organism or as a toxic stew of fear and inertia. What makes teams flourish or fail?

Psychologists have studied this problem for decades. It turns out that the success of a team doesn't depend on the sum total of its talent or on the sameness or difference of its members so much as on how people work together. Assembling a team consisting entirely of best friends, distant cousins, graduates of the same college—or representing a perfect rainbow of diversity—won't yield great results if bad behaviors govern the group. Each team supports specific social habits, yielding its own intelligence.

Amy C. Edmondson coined the term *psychological safety* in 1999 to describe a positive social climate that enables workplace teams to collaborate successfully. Edmondson is a professor at the Harvard Business School. In addition to holding degrees in psychology from Harvard, she studied design and engineering and worked as an engineer for the legendary architect and inventor Buckminster Fuller.

Edmondson observed teams at work in hospitals and corporations and discovered that every group is governed by rules of engagement that can have positive or negative effects on creativity and effectiveness. These norms aren't written down in a company handbook or printed on motivational posters. Rather, they evolve from the social habits of the group itself. A large company that has many different teams may have some teams the produce great results and strong job satisfaction and others that sputter with discontent.

The team leader often enforces the group's norms. For example, if a creative director talks over her colleagues, her behavior will encourage others on her team to speak without listening. Members of a good team share the floor with others. They don't focus on pushing their own point of view or proving their expertise. They are attentive to the moods and movements of the group. When expressing an idea or opinion, they know their contribution won't be ridiculed or pushed aside. In a psychologically safe environment, people experience laughter, patience, affirmation, and a willingness to share personal stories.

Psychological safety gives people the freedom to speak their minds, even when the subject is awkward or difficult. It takes courage to tell a teammate that their computer code has a major bug or that a careless typo caused a big problem for the client. When people don't feel psychologically safe, they shy away from hazardous conversations—it can be easier to ignore problems than to point them out and fix them. If the team leader throws tantrums when challenged or if members of the group resist making changes to their work, others will hesitate to ask questions or offer feedback. According to Edmondson, "Psychological safety is not about being nice." In a safe environment, blunt

Psychological safety is about candor, about making it possible for productive disagreement.

AMY C. EDMONDSON

comments and tough assessments are accepted because the group has built up intimacy and trust over time.

Members of strong teams know they won't be ignored or disregarded in meetings because of their gender, race, age, seniority, or appearance. Psychological safety doesn't exist unless everyone can feel it. A company that holds celebrations in a strip club or allows routine banter about gender, race, or body weight excludes some members of the group, denying them access to friendly camaraderie.

Even workplaces that are outwardly committed to inclusion can have cultures with subtle hierarchies that shut some people out. One such workplace was the White House of President Barack Obama. Although Obama's staff achieved groundbreaking racial and gender diversity, some women on the team still struggled to be heard during meetings with the president and other staffers. Their ideas could be overlooked or even picked up and claimed by the men who were dominating the room. Women staffers developed a strategy called amplification, in which one person adds value to the message of another person by mentioning that person's name and idea later in the conversation.

Amplification has been widely discussed and adopted since the practice was reported in the *Washington Post* in 2016. Although amplification originated as a way for women to support other women, the practice doesn't need to be gendered. Amplification can raise the visibility of anyone on a team. It enables individuals to show solidarity with their peers and to use their own power within the group to increase the power of another person, who might be on the sidelines.

Nearly every designer has participated in brainstorming sessions organized around gamelike rules of egalitarian engagement. Icebreakers! All ideas accepted! Yes, and! Such events are almost a parody of the psychologically safe workplace. The duration is finite and the stakes are low (two hours and three hundred sticky notes). Maintaining a safe, inclusive team culture for the long term is not as easy. Understanding what a high-functioning group climate looks like—and learning to recognize problematic behaviors, including one's own—are steps in the right direction.

SOURCES Amy C. Edmondson, *The Fearless Organization: Creating Psychological Safety in the Workplace for Learning, Innovation, and Growth* (Hoboken, NJ: Wiley, 2018); Geoff Colvin, "The Science Behind Team Intelligence," *Fast Company*, Aug 7, 2018 →fastcompany.com/3049524/the-science-behind-team-intelligence; Charles Duhigg, "What Google Learned From Its Quest to Build the Perfect Team," *New York Times*, Feb 25, 2016 →nytimes.com/2016/02/28/magazine/what-google-learned-from-its-quest-to-build-the-perfect-team.html; Juliet Eilperin, "White House Women Want to Be in the Room Where It Happens," *Washington Post*, Sep 13, 2016 →washingtonpost.com/news/powerpost/wp/2016/09/13/white-house-women-are-now-in-the-room-where-it-happens/.

low psychological safety

XYZ StartUp is creating Naptop, a wearable device designed to encourage competitive napping at work. The team's poor behavior includes taking credit for one another's work and behaving defensively.

hijacking

Maya presents her concept for Nodcast, a Naptop plug-in that would soak the minds of nappers with useful information while they sleep.

Bob talks over Maya and hijacks her idea. He says that he goes to sleep every night listening to reruns of Science Friday. He wakes up smarter in the morning.

defensive behavior

Maya wonders if a wearable device is the right delivery mechanism for the Naptop service. She thus questions the validity of their current prototype.

Luis shuts down this dangerous line of questioning.

high psychological safety

The team learns to build a safe environment for collaboration. They use amplification to avoid hijacking one another's ideas and to help everyone be heard. The team can accept challenging ideas.

amplifying others

Maya has another idea—Chillennial, a community forum for competitive nappers.

Charmayne and Elia amplify Maya's idea and mention each other's names.

accepting feedback

Maya questions the value of competitive napping—and the legitimacy of their entire platform. It's a tough message to hear, but Elia encourages everyone to listen. The team ends up creating a totally new product—an alertness tool called Slap.

giving and taking credit

TEXT BY ELLEN LUPTON

Why do we create? Designers are artists, makers, and thinkers who enjoy sharing content and solving problems with other people. The late Middle English word *create* means "to form out of nothing." Yet creativity never comes from nothing. We borrow materials from Mother Earth or purchase them at the art store. We collaborate with users, clients, developers, and content producers, and we soak up a flood of fonts, images, sounds, songs, tropes, trends, customs, and clichés. We tap into languages and traditions that have been stewing for centuries in the primordial soup of culture, and we use software that predetermines countless steps in the design process. Creativity is a group endeavor. How and when can a designer claim to have authored a project, and how should we acknowledge our cocreators?

Emerging design students sometimes feel that it's okay to use images found on the internet in a mockup for a magazine or a website because they aren't selling their work to clients. Yet students have many opportunities to share their work—on social media, on public portfolio sites, and in competitions. It's a good habit to give credit for a photograph, illustration, or song that comes from another source. Many museums, online archives, and photo collectives offer free material for reuse. Some sites allow creators to collect a fee based on what the user wants to pay. Creative Commons copyright licenses allow content creators to make it easy for other artists to build on what they have done without commercially exploiting them.

It's not always possible to contact a creator. When you find a quirky line drawing or vintage photo in an old book or magazine, the original maker may be dead or unknown. However, crediting the source (*Rand-McNally World Geographic Atlas*, 1972) is a way to say thanks to history and build a culture of gratitude. Giving credit is generous. It's an act of respect for the value of the creative process.

Taking credit for your own work can be as important as sharing credit with others. Designers need to build up a body of work in order to grow their careers. In a collaborative setting, individual designers are often restricted about what they can say about their work. Some workers sign NDAs (nondisclosure agreements) that forbid them from discussing their work outside the company. In the tech industry, the design process is embedded in a layered process of product development and engineering, making it difficult to pinpoint individual contributions. Designer and educator Rachel Berger, working in the San Francisco Bay Area, noticed that traditional design portfolios have started to disappear. She asked around and found that many designers in the tech industry aren't interested in showing their work publicly, since interface design often aims to disappear into the user's experience. However, some of these designers enjoy creating zines and indie publications on the side—these more personal media are designed for sharing.

What if you are working in a studio that creates brand identities, publications, and

misappropriation?

stereotypography Cultural appropriation occurs when a dominant group copies ideas from a culture that has been historically oppressed and marginalized. This is considered exploitative or degrading when the borrower hasn't conducted meaningful research or collaborated with or honored that group. We purchased this illustration from a stock image service. The word *Zumba* refers to an exercise program invented by a Colombian, which in turn references a Spanish dance called "rhumba." Several tags describing the alphabet allow potential buyers to find it, including "African Tribal Font," "Folk Scandinavian Script," and "Ethnic Alphabet." These marketing tags enforce stereotypes about cultures that are marginalized as "tribal," "folk," or "ethnic."

TYPEFACE | ZUMBA | BY EKATERINA BURTSEVA

campaigns for clients? Always ask your supervisor before sharing this work on your own portfolio site. Sometimes, the client may not want the work to be shown publicly or the studio may have guidelines for how to share (or not share) credit. In a packaging project, for example, a design firm might develop many different directions; a client may not want every one of those ideas circulating on the internet.

If you are an art director with the privilege of commissioning outside talent, consider how you want to credit your collaborators, from interns to illustrators. Why not err on the side of generosity? Naming your people shines light on your enterprise. When you have the opportunity to commission creative work, seek out illustrators, photographers, writers, musicians, and others from underrepresented groups and commission content that celebrates the diversity of human experience in an authentic way.

SOURCES Eric Schrijver, *Copy This Book: An Artist's Guide to Copyright* (Eindhoven, NL: Onomatopee, 2019); Anoushka Khandwala, "What Does It Mean to Decolonize Design? Dismantling Design History 101," *AIGA Eye on Design*, Jun 5, 2019 →eyeondesign.aiga.org/what-does-it-mean-to-decolonize-design/; Rachel Berger, "The Death of Design Portfolios," *Modus*, Aug 26, 2019 →modus.medium.com/the-death-of-design-portfolios-218bcbc11080.

mentoring

TEXT BY ELLEN LUPTON AND LESLIE XIA

Typically, we think of a mentor as an older person helping out a younger person. Your mentor could be a boss, a teacher, a school-appointed career counselor, a respected person in the community, or a relative with knowledge of your field. Guidance from your instructor or supervisor may be part of their job description, but most mentorships are more informal, flowering when both parties find a natural fit.

Mentoring doesn't require a top-down power imbalance to be worthwhile. Two people close in age and experience can be great mentors for each other. Peers may have distinct skills and knowledge to trade—or just have the time and patience to listen. An older person with an open mind can learn a whole lot from a younger one.

The most productive mentorships are valuable to both parties. Meeting with a professional who is higher up on the food chain can yield useful advice and vital networking contacts. However, top-down relationships are often tough to maintain over time. Talking with peers can be more rewarding and sustainable in the long run.

Once upon a time...

Imagine Yajing, a junior designer at Mid Co., a midsize design studio in a midsize city. Her one-year contract is coming to an end, and she wants help planning her next career move.

Yajing reaches out to Fernanda, a well-known creative director at a big agency. They meet for coffee. Fernanda tells Yajing to cut some weaker projects from her portfolio and to create more digital work. She suggests some companies that could be a good fit for Yajing. The conversation is friendly but formal. Two weeks later, Yajing wants to ask Fernanda to look at her portfolio again but decides not to. It feels like too much to ask.

Meanwhile, Yajing enjoys working with Frankie, a UX designer at Mid Co. They get coffee. Frankie has a permanent position and thus has more job stability than Yajing but is frustrated about always creating wire frames for websites without getting a chance to explore visual design. Yajing and Frankie decide to collaborate on an outside gig—a freelance website for a local theater group. The project helps Frankie build their visual skills while boosting Yajing's digital confidence. A few months later, Yajing lands a new job (thanks to a tip from Fernanda), and Frankie gets a promotion. Yajing and Frankie continue being friends and peer mentors.

Yajing finds her mentors.

less power

YAJING is a young designer looking to change jobs. She asks Fernanda for advice about what to do next.

more power

FERNANDA is a senior designer and a leader in the local design scene. She has helpful suggestions for Yajing, but their unbalanced relationship is limited.

equal power

YAJING loves her current job, but she has a temporary, one-year contract. She enjoys working with Frankie.

FRANKIE is frustrated about not being offered creative assignments. Frankie and Yajing collaborate on a project outside of work.

TYPEFACE | MAGASIN | BY LAURA MESEGUER

ILLUSTRATIONS BY JENNIFER TOBIAS

meeting your mentor

Take notes.

Reach out. Send a succinct e-mail or message. Explain why you are seeking their advice. If appropriate, mention that you have a mutual friend, went to the same school, or have a shared identity or background. Don't ask for a huge favor, such as "Read my thousand-page rough draft" or "Let me camp in your office for a week."

Prepare. Before you meet, write down questions. Research your new mentor to find specific touch points and connections. What is their expertise? Did they work on a project or give a talk that has influenced you?

Take notes. When meeting in person, use a pad or notebook to write down suggestions. Taking notes may feel like a burden, especially if you are feeling nervous. Don't overestimate, however, your ability to recall the conversation. If your mentor suggests a book to read or a studio to check out, you will need to write these comments down in order to act on them. Taking notes shows your mentor that you take the meeting seriously. If writing is difficult for you, ask permission to record the conversation.

Watch the time. If your mentor has offered to meet for half an hour (either in person or online), start wrapping up the session a few minutes before. Just because the conversation is flowing nicely doesn't mean that your mentor has more time than you agreed upon.

Offer to pay. If you are meeting in person in a café or restaurant, it is polite to offer to pick up the tab. However, it is likely that an older mentor will prefer to pay. If so, accept their generosity graciously.

Say thank you. Follow up with a note. (E-mail is fine.) Mention a specific comment that was helpful to you. (Aren't you glad you took notes?) We recently received a detailed thank-you note for advice given ten years ago. What a thrill!

Be realistic This meeting with your new mentor could be a one-time shot. It will be up to you to test the waters and see if future meetings are viable. That's more likely if your relationship has mutual benefits. How can you be helpful to your mentor? (Translate a text? Assist with coding? Introduce them to a copywriter or illustrator?)

becoming a mentor

The best advice is welcome advice.

red flags

Tread lightly. Just because you are older than another person or have more experience than they do doesn't mean you understand their current situation. Avoid pushing advice they haven't requested. (This can quickly devolve into 'splaining. See page 34.)

Listen. A colleague or acquaintance may just need someone to talk with. They don't necessarily want you to tell them to quit their job, kill their boss, or subscribe to your podcast. If you do offer advice, don't be offended if they don't take it.

Offer specific help. Perhaps there are concrete ways to assist someone in their career, such as writing a letter of recommendation or making an introduction. If you do offer a specific favor, be sure to actually do it.

Find a mentorship program. Many high schools and colleges offer ways for professionals to guide young people, from mentoring programs to portfolio reviews and job shadowing. Such programs are accessible to students who wouldn't reach out to you on their own.

Watch out for behaviors that indicate the abuse of power. If any mentor, supervisor, teacher, or other person in a position of power is engaging in manipulative behaviors, speak out. This is harassment.

→ Sharing intimate details about their personal life, or asking you for details about yours

→ Pressuring you not to take jobs or pursue interests that "interfere" with your working relationship

→ Continually breaking personal boundaries that you have set

→ Pressuring you to "work" in uncomfortable ways, such as shooting photographs in the nude

→ Repeatedly asking you to work late so they can drive you home

→ Pressuring you to commit behaviors that could impair your judgment, like drinking

→ Pressuring you into having dinner, drinking at a bar, or going to a party

→ Trying to pursue a physical relationship while promising you more opportunities in the future

This list is not exhaustive; there are other nonconsensual behaviors that could fall into a gray area, but if you are not comfortable, it is best to remove yourself from a situation and reassess your relationship to this person.

cover letters

TEXT BY ELLEN LUPTON

No one likes writing cover letters, and no one likes reading them, either. That's why yours should be short, passionate, and well researched. In the age of automated job boards, you may wonder if cover letters are obsolete. They aren't—yet. When reaching out to someone through a personal referral, introduce yourself with a cover letter in the body of your e-mail. Job application sites sometimes do—and sometimes don't—request cover letters, submitted as plain text or an attachment.

No typos. Don't ignore spell-check and grammar-check features. Those squiggly lines are usually right. These tools are good! Not using them is bad! Many potential employers will reject any application containing typos.

No lies. Don't be tempted to say you have a graduate degree if you never finished your thesis or that you were a product lead at Google if you were actually a summer intern. If you get an interview, these facts will be checked. Even if you do slip by on a lie now, a falsified résumé could get you fired later or could discredit you if you have reason to file a complaint.

Who do you know? If you have a personal connection at a company, state this up front. How can you build these ties? Use your college alumni network to meet people who are a few years ahead of you in their careers. (Find them on LinkedIn.) Big tech companies may reward their employees with cash bonuses when they bring in new talent. Firms place a high value on personal contacts. Here's the downside: an individual's network often favors people from their own gender or racial or class background. If you belong to an underrepresented group, build your network by joining an affinity organization or reaching out to other people like you working in a particular company or field.

No spilled secrets. Don't reveal the names of former clients unless you have permission to do so. Many companies have confidentiality agreements with their clients, and you could be breaking that agreement by naming those clients in your cover letter or résumé. This gaffe of indiscretion is a red flag for hiring managers.

Research the company. Instead of sending generic letters to dozens of leads, slow down and do some research. If the company makes widgets, don't gush about their gadgets. Explain why you love their work. Reference a specific project, their social values, or a conference presentation.

Beware the search for a perfect match. Women are more likely than men to avoid applying for jobs for which they are not fully qualified. Why? Researcher Tara Sophia Mohr suggests that because girls are socialized to follow the rules, they are less likely to apply for jobs that exceed their skills or experience. However, many unqualified people who do apply for these jobs get hired anyway. A job description isn't necessarily iron-clad—your skill or passion in one area may compensate for your lack of exposure in another. A candidate with a strong portfolio, an exciting personality, enthusiasm for the work environment, and connections to the company has a decent chance of breaking through.

anatomy of a terrible cover letter

Find the name of a real person.

D'oh! You just wasted time asking for forgiveness. Typos will not be tolerated.

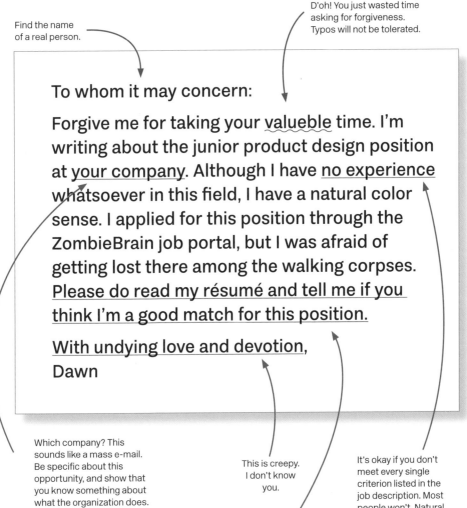

To whom it may concern:

Forgive me for taking your valueble time. I'm writing about the junior product design position at your company. Although I have no experience whatsoever in this field, I have a natural color sense. I applied for this position through the ZombieBrain job portal, but I was afraid of getting lost there among the walking corpses. Please do read my résumé and tell me if you think I'm a good match for this position.

With undying love and devotion,
Dawn

Which company? This sounds like a mass e-mail. Be specific about this opportunity, and show that you know something about what the organization does.

This is creepy. I don't know you.

It's okay if you don't meet every single criterion listed in the job description. Most people won't. Natural talent, however, is an unacceptable substitute for concrete skills, achievements, or projects.

A hiring manager is not a job counselor. Save this question for a mentor or friend who has already broken into the field. Your cover letter should convey confidence in your abilities.

SOURCES Tara Sophia Mohr, "Why Women Don't Apply for Jobs Unless They're 100% Qualified," *Harvard Business Review*, Aug 25, 2014 →hbr. org/2014/08/why-women-dont-apply-for-jobs-unless-theyre-100-qualified; Holly Ojalvo, "How You Should Actually Write Your Résumé and Cover Letter," *Quartz*, Apr 30, 2020 →qz.com/work/1849010/how-you-should-actually-write-your-resume-and-cover-letter/.

presentations

TEXT BY ELLEN LUPTON

A few years back, we saw a talk delivered with way too much confidence. The speaker paced around the stage with loads of swagger, but he tripped over his own jokes and had no idea what his next slide was going to be. His talk was too self-promotional, and he rambled as he struggled to remember what to say. He delivered a canned presentation but hadn't sufficiently reviewed it in advance. Shivers! It was bad!

Even a shy or introverted person can deliver engaging presentations. Whether presenting online or in person, you don't have to give a car to everyone listening to produce a strong performance. Be sincere, plan ahead, respect the audience—and be heard.

Prepare. Practice your presentation or pitch and adjust your material for the specific venue. Are you speaking to clients or design professionals? Students or the general public? Is this a deep dive or a lightning talk? Run-throughs are especially important if you are presenting with a team. To prep for a high-stakes online talk or presentation, record your practice session and watch it with your team. Don't wing it! Overconfidence can make you look unprepared.

Don't read from notes. It's well known that audiences feel more engaged when the speaker is not reading from notes. Unless you're a professionally trained actor, reading a script will sound flat, lacking the natural intonations that guide living conversations. Furthermore, complex sentences written for the page can be hard to follow in real time. Although speaking without notes may yield a few extra *ums* and *ers*, it will help your audience understand your content.

Or, read from notes. Sometimes, it's better to stick to a script. Short remarks conveying specific information—such as introducing a speaker or thanking spon- sors—should be read verbatim, so that you don't botch someone's bio or forget an important supporter. In any formal situation— such as a eulogy or graduation speech— reading a prepared text is appropriate, but it's still appropriate to deliver an occasional spontaneous aside.

Producing a video that will be edited and shared online may also go more smoothly if you read a script. However, a live webinar or any other live presentation will likely be dull if you are reading aloud.

Newcomers to public speaking may also choose to read from notes, knowing their confidence will grow with practice.

Be heard. When planning an online pitch, presentation, or webinar, make sure you have good audio. Consider using a headset or a professional microphone. (Test what works with a colleague.)

When speaking in an auditorium, use a microphone if available. Some people think they will appear more likable and modest if they decline to use the mike. Many women and girls feel are brought up to be quiet and demure, whereas people with deep voices may assume their voices are always audible. However, using a microphone will help most people in the audience feel immersed

in your presentation. Microphones are especially helpful if your voice has a higher pitch. Such voices can be tough to pick up for people who are hard of hearing. Using the mike will make your talk more inclusive and accessible.

Be seen. When presenting on a stage, don't hide behind the podium. Body language helps you communicate. Dressing up for the occasion can make you more aware of your body language. Nice clothes also send a signal to the audience (and to yourself) that this event is important. When presenting from a computer, standing up can give you more energy. Use a standing desk or elevate your laptop with boxes.

Stay on time. Short talks (six to twenty minutes) are popular, especially for online presentations. Events featuring several short talks are fun and inclusive, with more voices and less rambling. Speaking too long disrespects your hosts, the audience, and your fellow presenters. Talks

by a single presenter should be no longer than forty-five minutes when presented in person in an auditorium or classroom, while online talks should be thirty or less. If you are the moderator, lay out the ground rules in advance. Let the speaker know when their time is nearly up and politely interrupt if they go significantly over. If you are in the middle of a presentation and you realize you have too much content, just skip a section and wrap it up.

Know your public. Who is attending your event? Experts or laypeople? Students or professionals? Do you speak the same language or do you come from different cultures? If possible, read the room as you go. If people seem checked out, skip ahead to a livelier section of your talk.

Interact. When appropriate, pause and ask for feedback, especially when using online conferencing software. Digital environments make it hard to know how the audience is responding. Stop and ask them.

beginning, middle, end

Movie scripts are often organized into three acts. If your talk seems to have too many ideas, try sorting them into three main topics. Cut what doesn't fit.

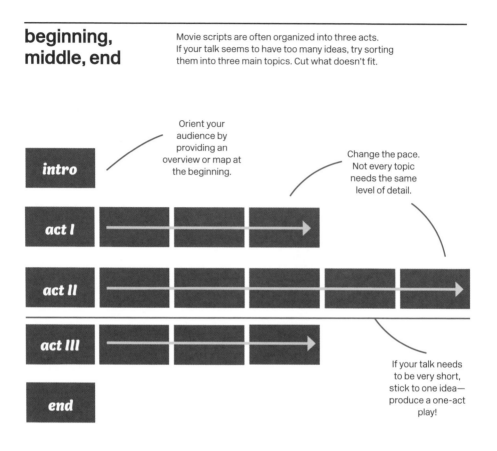

Orient your audience by providing an overview or map at the beginning.

Change the pace. Not every topic needs the same level of detail.

intro

act I

act II

act III

end

If your talk needs to be very short, stick to one idea—produce a one-act play!

ask questions

What does your audience want to learn from your talk? Create suspense by posing a question and then delivering the answer over time.

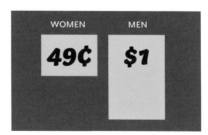

what's the real gender wage gap?

WOMEN   MEN

49¢   **$1**

TYPEFACE | CAPUCINE | BY ALICE SAVOIE

tell less

The statement "Show, don't tell" appears on inspirational posters in writing classrooms around the world. Like many clichés, this one is quite useful. Although it's important to state the facts and explain ideas ("tell"), abstract statements can be dull and hard to follow. Be purposeful about using text. A short phrase may be a prompt for delivering your next point; a longer text could help the audience follow your argument. Since many viewers watch online presentations from their phones, keep your text big and concise.

show more

Reveal your ideas with active stories and vivid examples ("show") in order to create an enjoyable experience that is easy to grasp. Demonstrate a product in use or illustrate how a process unfolds. Tell stories about how a design solution will help people or where an idea came from. Stories about people can make your subject more relatable. These stories can be about users, historical figures, people you admire—or about you. Keep your stories short. Is your audience sitting in an auditorium or watching from a laptop or phone? Optimize your visual design!

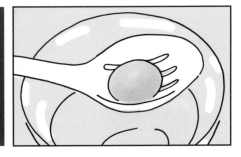

Separating Eggs with a Slotted Spoon

1 *Choose a spoon with small slots.*

2 *Hold the spoon over a bowl.*

3 *Crack an egg over the spoon.*

4 *Let the egg whites slip through the slots.*

vary the intensity

Don't spend your whole talk yelling at your audience. Pause to let them think about a point or consider their own answer to your driving question. Mix humor and brief anecdotes with hard-hitting facts and big ideas.

kill the monotony

No matter how punchy your tone or how gut-wrenching your stories, your voice will get boring after a while. Online presentations suffer from a lack of audience feedback. When listeners are in mute mode, presenters can't tell if they are making a connection (or just bombing). This feedback vacuum diminishes the sense of presence for listeners as well as speakers. People are more likely to laugh at a joke or voice their approval when they are sharing physical space with other warm bodies.

To break up the monotony of an online talk, consider hosting a conversation between two people in place of a soliloquy. The second speaker can function as an interviewer or an equal player. Ask for audience feedback in the chat window or Q&A panel. Keep the main presentation short, saving more time for Q&As or a group brainstorm. Appoint a moderator to field questions from the audience. Create breakout rooms where attendees can meet each other.

social media

TEXT BY LESLIE XIA

Building an online presence allows you to reach out to employers, art directors, and peers in your field. Many templated website services have affordable student plans and free trials that allow for users to try out their platform. Some schools also have partnerships with these websites that offer free subscriptions to students. These websites allow you to build your own portfolio site, experiment with digital design, showcase client work, and use html to customize the site experience. Some services include e-commerce tools for building online stores for selling design work, merchandise, and other goods. Websites are also a great way for designers to stay connected with people who follow their work by sharing events they will be involved in or posting blog updates.

LinkedIn is a tool for building your professional network. Here, you can list your résumé, awards, volunteer work, memberships, and other factoids about your career. Your peers, coworkers, teachers, or previous supervisors can write endorsements and recommendations that appear with your profile. Users can also search for and apply for jobs directly within LinkedIn. LinkedIn is also a great place to reach out to recruiters, and a place for recruiters to find you—but make sure to keep your profile engaging and updated!

The LinkedIn Learning platform allows users to find out how to manage their time, edit their writing, rock an interview, make a short film, and develop many other professional skills. LinkedIn Learning also offers courses about combatting racism, recognizing implicit bias, and fostering a diverse and inclusive workplace.

Portfolio platforms, such as Behance, Dribbble, ArtStation, and Ello, offer a cross between a traditional website and a professional network. These platforms are built specifically to post and share work. Employers, creative directors, journalists, and curators often look here to find new talent. These websites often publish highlights and roundups to generate interest and visibility. Some platforms enable members to livestream themselves working on projects, so audiences can watch how they create and learn new techniques.

Many other platforms, from Instagram to TikTok, enable artists and designers to connect with a global community. When presenting one's life online, however, be aware of the border between personal and professional. Some creatives maintain two accounts on platforms such as Twitter or Instagram. While it can be fun and stimulating to be transparent about your life, the comments you make or the images you post can affect your professional career. A media account that you consider personal could end up being shared more broadly, with damaging consequences.

If you want to use your platform to speak out about a political issue, consider getting a second opinion from someone you trust. If you are worried that a post may be offensive or problematic, then it is probably not a good idea to post it.

how to avoid making offensive posts on social media

Consider this quick checklist of questions before you post content that is combative, sensitive, or potentially offensive.

Who is your post centering?

Does your post include humor or criticism at a larger group's expense?

Have you done your research on this subject?

What purpose does your post serve? What will others get from this post?

If this post is directed toward an individual, might you address them in a private message instead?

If you have already researched the issue, what else are you trying to learn by engaging with this person?

If you are feeling upset, angry, or activated, create a draft before posting and reassess the next day.

What are you trying to say in this post?

Should you ask someone you trust (who may be more knowledgeable about this subject) to assess the post?

publishing

TEXT BY JENNIFER TOBIAS

Got something to say that's NSFW (not safe for work, web, or whatever)? Are you processing a memorable or traumatic experience? Imagining Mr. Spock beaming into Hogwarts? Longing to connect and collaborate with your tribe? One of the best ways to satisfy that urge for self-expression is to get out your laptop (or scissors and glue stick) and make a zine or other indie publication.

Mashing up your design skills with something you really want to say puts you in a lively tradition of self-publishing that includes pamphlets, manifestos, little magazines, samizdat, mail art, and artists' books. Wherever there is publishing, there is someone taking advantage of it after hours.

Self-publishing is a tool for building community, stretching your visual vocabulary, flexing your content muscle—and for just having fun. People with a message—not just professional designers and writers— have long used easy-access tools to spread ideas and enjoy being creative. Zines are a particular form of underground publishing with a fascinating history.

In the 1930s, science fiction fans started circulating ideas and stories among themselves. These pop-culture enthusiasts mobilized typewriters, mimeograph machines, and low-end letterpress printing to spread the word and spin off their own versions of famous storylines—creating the first zines. By the 1960s, office photocopiers were being "liberated" for small print runs. Inexpensive printing and cheap postage spawned self-published content about everything from sexual liberation to survivalism to riot grrrl adventures. The relative anonymity of small-scale printing and distribution has also empowered free speech and underground culture-building within conditions of censorship.

This capacity of independent print publishing to surface personal, experimental, and radical ideas continues to thrive— and you can join in. Tools for today's self-publishers range from laser printers and Risograph machines to letterpress and silk screen. Typewriters are back, along with open-source software and commercial layout tools. Indie publications are still passed around from person to person; they also are distributed online, in bookstores, and at book fairs. Whether it's your grandma's couscous recipe or an advice column for fellow immigrants, there's an office printer and a book fair out there just waiting for you.

zine city

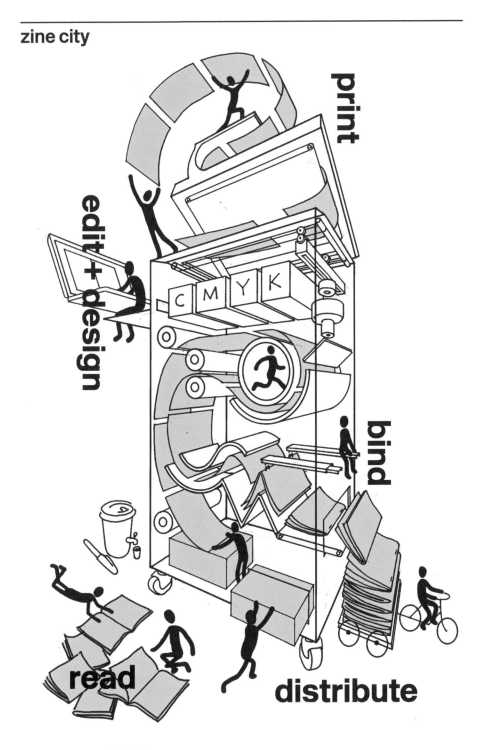

ILLUSTRATIONS BY JENNIFER TOBIAS

activism

TEXT BY LESLIE XIA

For many marginalized people, the very act of existing is political. When living in a society that is patriarchal, xenophobic, ableist, and homophobic, marginalized people are often confronted with rhetoric that feels like a direct attack on their humanity. Historically and globally, political unrest and assaults on unalienable rights have led to protests and politically charged art. Graphic design has the power to create passionate, action-oriented imagery to engage with communities and to influence, empower, and spark change through visual messaging.

There are many questions to ask yourself when creating an activist practice. Does your workplace have a policy limiting expression of political views publicly? Do you live in a city or nation that protects your freedom of speech? Do you feel safe voicing your political opinions within your community? Are you prepared to have your views scrutinized in public and private spaces, online and offline? Furthermore, what are your own intentions for creating this messaging? Have you taken the time to decolonize your mind and your own practice? If you do not identify with the community you are creating this work for, how are you benefiting from this work?

In her essay "Black Lives Matter Is Not a Design Challenge," Schessa Garbutt criticizes non-Black creatives for jumping into the conversation around Black Lives Matter. Too many designers are creating political posters, illustrations, and fonts without critically scrutinizing their position within the movement. Garnering likes, comments, and exposure on design blogs can become a form of virtue signaling, the act of expressing opinions or sentiments to demonstrate one's moral goodness without actually helping the communities facing oppression and trauma.

Activist design is often open source. Margaret Cubbage of the Design Museum in London says, "Professional designers see themselves as [relinquishing] ownership or releasing the copyright as they realize the greater impact they can have if they let their work spread—not just through technology, but through protest." The internet makes it easy to share and quickly distribute posters, zines, fliers, and other activist materials.

Organizers are also using social media to connect graphic designers with communities. Design to Combat COVID-19, founded by Rachel Smith, has connected more than 1,500 volunteers with community groups, clinics, displaced workers, and small businesses damaged by the pandemic.

In the words of adrienne maree brown, "We have to design structures; we have to design relationships; we have to design justice." Creatives have the power to shape the world we live in. How are we using our skills and resources for the better? Imagine an equitable and just future. How are you creating design for change?

SOURCES Schessa Garbutt, "Black Lives Matter Is Not a Design Challenge," Design Toast, Jun 2, 2020 →medium.com/design-toast/black-lives-matter-is-not-a-design-challenge-f6e452ff7821; Alice Bucknell, "Design As Protest," *Harvard University Graduate School of Design News*, Jun 22, 2020 →gsd.harvard.edu/2020/06/design-as-protest-how-can-designers-stand-for-fight-for-and-build-an-anti-racist-future/; Emily Gosling, "Nope to Hope: The Power and of Graphics in Politics + Protest," AIGA Eye on Design, Mar 29, 2018 →eyeondesign.aiga.org/nope-to-hope-the-power-of-graphics-in-politics-protest/; "adrienne maree brown on Creating the Future," interview with Alice Grandoit, Deem, Jul 2020 →deemjournal.com/stories/amb.

saytheirna.me

PROJECT BY LESLIE XIA

STICKER DESIGNED BY
SEAN-KIERRE LYONS

STICKER DESIGNED BY MOREL DOUCET

STICKER DESIGNED BY HEATHER ABBOTT

STICKER DESIGNED BY
N'DEYE DIAKHATE

This sticker project invited BIPOC illustrators and designers to create beautifully lettered stickers of the names of Black people lost to police brutality. Using the Kickstarter platform, Saytheirna.me raised funds that were donated directly to Black, trans, and queer people and organizations.

starting up

funding Services such as Kickstarter, Patreon, GoFundMe, or direct payment platforms like Venmo or Cash App can be used to raise funds. When running projects involving donations, maintain honesty, transparency, and communication among everyone involved.

budget Factor in costs for production, time, labor, materials, packaging, shipping, and handling of the design product. Explore whether the project can sustainably and realistically raise enough money to achieve the stated goals.

image rights If the project can be openly shared, reproduced, or altered, include a clear reproduction rights statement, which can be easily generated with Creative Commons templates.

personal safety

doxxing To avoid getting doxxed (the malicious act of publishing private information about an individual), consider working anonymously or using a pen name to protect your identity.

alternate address Sign up with "burner" e-mails and contact information to limit your paper trail. Use encryption services to share sensitive files and messages.

the mud test In her book *Dragnet Nation*, journalist Julia Angwin describes testing the cybersecurity of an online service with a "mud test." She writes, "Imagine you drop your device in a mud puddle, slip in the mud, and crack your head so that you forget your password to access your data. Now, can you get your data back from the service you were using? If the answer is yes, then you have left a data trail. If [your service] lets you recover your lost password, then the service has access to your data."

advice for new designers

While researching this book, the authors asked people we met to offer advice for designers starting their careers. What would they want to tell their younger selves, looking back now at what they have learned? The ideas presented here overflow with love and kindness.

Carly Ayres Trust yourself and your gut instinct. Part of that comes with confidence, so surround yourself with people who care about you and want to support you. If something isn't fulfilling you or sustaining you, don't do it. Invest in people and projects that serve your goals and ambitions. Be critical of how you spend your time and energy. I spent too much time in my career making excuses for people who made me uncomfortable and, conversely, in trying to make other people feel comfortable, to the detriment to my own well-being.

Elaine Lopez Bring your culture and your whole self and your identity into design. Design is a set of skills. It's a set of software. Those things can be really powerful for telling stories or for educating other people or for bringing in content that isn't found in the mainstream narrative. As a designer, you have the power to tell your own story or to tell a story about your family, wherever they came from, or even to research those stories and then bring them into your work. It's similar to what an artist might do, but you can now use design to make things that other people from your culture or your identity can connect to. You can self-publish. You can make a website. You can have an Instagram feed.

One of my favorite educational Instagram feeds is @knowyourcaribbean by artist, filmmaker, and historian Fiona Compton. This platform provides me with a broader understanding of the Caribbean, which helps to contextualize my Cuban heritage.

This is a crucial time to be a designer. It's also a tough time to be a designer, because we are tackling difficult topics and it's hard emotionally and mentally. Confronting structural oppression and racism are difficult tasks that can weigh you down. It is important to find community and practice self-care and healing.

Irene Pereyra If you are learning to be a designer and you're just starting out, focus on that. Spend the ten thousand hours you need to really become a designer. At the beginning, our capabilities don't yet match our taste. Spend the first five years as a designer bridging the gap between your taste and your ability so that you can execute exactly what you want.

Your next job is to help other designers to get to that point as well. Open the door for them and spread the karma around. I think we're all overly focused on ourselves. The biggest power comes from enabling other people to do their best work.

As a woman, I think it's important to do that for other women. Women still make up a small percentage of people who create in this field. That's why you still have ridiculous beer commercials and sexist shit—because it's just a bunch of dudes in a room making decisions. If women were in the room making decisions, there wouldn't be commercials like that.

Jiminie Ha Try to read stuff outside of Wikipedia. Know your references. People expect quick answers because information is so widely available, but it is worthwhile to dig deeper and conduct more research on any kind of project. Try to learn all the basic, rudimentary tools in design before creating new forms and breaking rules. Don't start just messing with design without actually understanding typography, image-making, basic color, and composition.

When my designers present a concept to me, I ask, "Why did you choose this color? Why this typeface?" Learn how to substantiate design decisions. Bigger clients demand rational reasons as to why you are making choices that cost them hundreds of thousands of dollars.

Natasha Jen Really, really work as hard as you can—meaning you really have to put the hours into your work. You really have to put in the effort. Maintain a high level of curiosity so that you to continue to learn regardless of any situation or job you are in. Be curious, be open-minded, and be aware of your environment, meaning the people who are around you and the organization you are in. Try to absorb as many of the good things coming out of your environment as you can.

Njoki Gitahi My advice is to always ask. The worst someone can say is no. Ask for advice, ask for mentorship, ask for opportunities. This is one place where either my gender or identity or race has colored my experience. At times I have not been as ambitious as I could be because I tell myself, "Maybe I'm lucky to be here in the first place, so I shouldn't press my luck. I shouldn't ask for things because I shouldn't even be here." But that's bullshit.

If someone doesn't want to help you, then move on. If you ask ten times, you'll probably get two or three nos. You can take solace in a no because it just means that you will find another path. More often than not, I found people are so open and so willing to share what they know—connecting you with a friend, pointing you in another direction. You also put yourself in a position where you can help others. If you asked for something and moved up or found an opportunity, you can help the next person.

Paula Scher Learn to express and defend your work. Know how to understand, analyze, and explain what you're doing and why you're doing it. And also understand that you may be wrong and that you just might learn something from somebody else. As a designer, you make a visual thing. It's not you that is being discussed; it is a thing on a piece of paper or on a screen. Get out of yourself as a person and into the thing that you have made and defend it and talk about it. If you can't talk about the work, it's going to be difficult to succeed.

Sabrina Hall Find a way to balance work and play whenever you can. Burnout is very real, and setting time aside to renew yourself is so important. I do this by making art and taking breaks. There will always be more work to do. Also, take the time to learn more about the history of anything you are working on. There is so much more context to take into account. Take a moment to examine the past, whether it's a font or how a design could impact people.

Shira Inbar Don't wait for things to happen to you. No one's going to ask you to design a cool magazine just because you graduated from an interesting school. You need to get things started by yourself and exercise your skills to make the work you want to make. Choose a cause you care about, connect with friends and collaborate, make something you enjoy. I have a friend who said that New York is a city where people make work for themselves outside of work. That's true, but it's not work for the sake of work. It's for the sake of finding a voice and having agency over how and when you use your skills.

We often need to navigate a complicated system to make space for ourselves. Participate in the conversation, or create it, and publish your work and ideas. Keep making—that can be hard, especially if you work full-time. It's not easy. But once you start, you can't stop.

Another important thing is not to be too precious about making something perfect. Publish things, share things, show your process, engage with others. Look for ways to participate in things around you. For example, if you have a friend who is a musician, ask them if you can make a poster for their show, or projections, or something completely new that inspires both of you. Find ways to collaborate and seek opportunities independently.

Last, don't underestimate mentorship. I don't think I was aware of how important mentorship is. In hindsight, I could have connected more with my creative directors and learned from their experience. I could have kept in touch more. I could have revealed more of myself and developed a more meaningful relationship with them. This advice is also for students. Many of your teachers are not that much older than you. They're also still learning all the time. You are memorable! Don't think you're invisible. Friends are important, too, so keep in touch. Your friends are your best mentors.

Valentina Vergara I was clueless when I first started, but every experience has made me more sure of the kind of work I want to be a part of. Write down your goals—both creative goals and general life goals. Work on a mission and set priorities. Collaborate as much as you can and uplift and empower marginalized creatives! Success comes more easily if your head is clear, so take care of yourself first.

JENNIFER TOBIAS New York City, Summer 2020

index

PAGE NUMBERS IN BOLD REFER TO GRAPHIC ELEMENTS OR THEIR CAPTIONS.

217

PUBLISHED BY
Princeton Architectural Press
202 Warren Street
Hudson, New York 12534

www.papress.com

LIBRARY OF CONGRESS CATALOGING-IN-
PUBLICATION DATA

Names: Lupton, Ellen.

Title: Extra bold : a feminist inclusive antiracist nonbinary field guide for graphic
designers / authors Ellen Lupton, Farah
Kafei, Jennifer Tobias, Josh A. Halstead,
Kaleena Sales, Leslie Xia, Valentina Vergara.

Description: New York : Princeton
Architectural Press, [2020] | Includes index. |
Summary: "Critical essays link theories
about feminism, racism, inclusion, and
binary thinking to design principles and
practices. Type specimens, biographies, and
interviews showcase the work and ideas of
people marginalized by sexism, racism, and/
or ableism"—Provided by publisher.

Identifiers: LCCN 2020036740 | ISBN
9781616899189 (paperback) | ISBN
9781648960222 (ebook)

Subjects: LCSH: Design—Human factors. |
Design—Social aspects.

Classification: LCC NK1520 .E98 2021 | DDC
745.4—dc23

LC record available at https://lccn.loc.
gov/2020036740

PRODUCER | Ellen Lupton
LEAD ILLUSTRATOR | Jennifer Tobias
EDITOR | Sara Stemen
EDITORIAL CONSULTANT | DIVERSITY,
    EQUITY, AND INCLUSION | Nirmala Nataraj
BOOK DESIGN | Ellen Lupton
COVER DESIGN | Shivani Parasnis

PRIMARY TYPEFACE | NEW RAIL ALPHABET
    Margaret Calvert & A2-Type

FEATURED TYPEFACES
AMPERSANDIST | Lynne Yun
BAYARD | Tré Seals
CAPUCINE | Alice Savoie
CONFITERIA | Julieta Ulanovsky
CHARVET | Kevin Karanja
CHOLLA | Sibylle Hagmann
ERNESTINE ECKSTEIN | Nat Pyper
ESCALATOR | Jesse Ragan
FILOSOFIA | Zuzana Licko
G.B. JONES | Nat Pyper
GILBERT | Justin Au
GLYPH WORLD | Leah Maldonado
HALYARD DISPLAY | Joshua Darden
INJURIAL | Sandrine Nugue
KARBID | Verena Gerlach
KOPIUS | Sibylle Hagmann
LACA | Joana Correia
MAGASIN | Laura Meseguer
MANDEVILLA | Laura Worthington
MARTIN WONG | Nat Pyper
ODILE | Sibylle Hagmann
PASSENGER SANS | Sabina Kipară & Diana Ovezea
PIROUETTE | Shivani Parasnis
QUAT | Ani Dimitrova
ROBERT FORD | Nat Pyper
STONEWALL 50 | Bobby Tannam & Feeld
TRADE GOTHIC DISPLAY | Lynne Yun
WOMEN'S CAR REPAIR COLLECTIVE | Nat Pyper
ZANGEZI SANS | Daria Petrova
ZUMBA | Ekaterina Burtseva